LOOK BACK ON ENGLAND

LOOK BACK ON ENGLAND

JOHN BURKE

WITH PHOTOGRAPHS BY IAN PLEETH

ORBIS PUBLISHING · LONDON

Above: Liverpool waterfront. The road running parallel to
this was called the Goree after an island off Senegal where
slave ships assembled to collect their cargoes.
Title page: Bamburgh Castle, Northumberland. Built above a
150-foot cliff formed by the Whin Sill, it was the principal
fortress of the kings of Northumbria.

First published in Great Britain by
Orbis Publishing Limited, London 1980
Text © John Burke 1980
Photographs by Ian Pleeth
Orbis Publishing Limited 1980

Printed in Great Britain by
Hazell Watson and Viney Limited
ISBN: 0 85613 065 6

CONTENTS

INTRODUCTION

A PLOUGH JARS against some unyielding object in the earth, to reveal a hoard of ancient silver treasure. A farmer driving posts for a fence disturbs a long-buried mosaic floor, and a game-keeper trying to dig out a ferret opens the way into a spacious villa. More purposefully, archaeologists investigating a mound which has long tantalized them discover a funeral ship containing jewellery as beautiful as the day it was made and as beautiful as anything made today. The thin layer camouflaging the past is abruptly removed. Past and present are one.

Even when it has not been sheltered under-ground, a great deal of England's past is still visible all around us. It lives, and not merely as an academic study. The rocks came before the geo-logical text-books; man-made communities before the sociologists; and colourful reality before the history lecturers. At no point in time did life suddenly freeze into 'history', any more than the present can be seen to meet the future at some clear-cut dividing line. History is as much the story of what is happening now as of something which once happened, ceased to happen, and has now become fossilized. For that matter, even a fossil is not really dead: it continues to tell us about itself and its environment, and so re-creates another aspect of our living, breathing world.

What is that obelisk on the skyline; who fired the cannon-balls embedded in this church tower; why have certain cryptic folk songs and dances come down to us through the centuries, and what was their original meaning?

In this book I have tried to pick out salient features of different English regions and fit them into a coherent pattern, shaped not from doc-uments and old chronicles but from what can still be seen or heard. A country is the sum not only of its royal families and statesmen but of its soil, climate, buildings, music and industry. One's interest may be provoked, according to the loca-lity, by a freakish rock formation, a relic of old railway line, or the mere name of a street. To pick out just one old building in an old city and trace it back to its creation is to bring back to life a succession of events which may be more vivid than what goes on in the neighbourhood here and now. A tale from local legend can prove to be of more than local significance and have its echoes right across the country.

I do not believe that history can ever be made real by the study of a straightforward chronology of dates and names. Everyday life for even the humblest individual is rarely, when looked back on over one year or even one week, a tidy sequence so much as an accumulation of apparent-ly random experiences, some happy, some dismal. Appetites and interests vary from day to day. Even when we speak of a pattern, it is not a geometrical one. Each county, each hamlet – like each person – has its own special character; but at the same time shares with neighbours and often with remoter cousins some mutual need, some family accent, some related skills. The conflicts, politics, topography, arts and crafts and customs of a nation form a multitude of jagged shapes which may nevertheless, with loving care, be slotted together into a jigsaw. The picture will be complete only when the last piece is in place.

In this book I do not claim such completeness. Each time I have bridged a gap I have been conscious of further yawning chasms beyond.

The Marylebone Memorial by C. L. Hartwell outside Nuffield Lodge in St John's Wood, London, commemorates those who died in the First War.

But even with these faults running through it the pattern does, I hope, in the end begin to make sense. I have tried to follow England's progress through centuries of physical and political change while at the same time bringing out specific regional contributions. Within each chapter there are inevitable digressions into other periods and other topics. The discussion of place names in Chapter 2 obviously does not mean that only Saxon names are of any interest. Though Chapter 4 deals specifically with surviving castles, this does not rule out mention of other fortifications in other chapters. In many cases, amplification of a subject or digressions into other regions can be found in illustrations which complement rather than merely echo the text.

Readers may wish to choose other related themes for themselves: other threads, other emphases. But for all of us I hope the final product will be a pattern rather than a patchwork.

FOUNDATIONS

AT MILLOOK HAVEN IN CORNWALL, alternating layers of sandstone and shale form a zigzag pattern in the cliff face because of ancient crumpling and faulting under enormous pressure. The cliffs of Alum Bay on the Isle of Wight blaze with a dozen different sandy hues. At Beachy Head the chalk of the South Downs is sliced through and brightly exposed above the sea. The millstone grit of Brimham Rocks rears in grotesque dark shapes against a picturesque backdrop of the Vale of York. We think of these and our other favourite spots as 'scenery' – and especially pleasant scenery in its solidity, firm before our eyes and beneath our feet since time immemorial.

The stones

In fact the very contrast of these rock formations shows that they have been far from immutable. Their ancient turmoils have conditioned the complexion of our countryside and prompted every ridge, furrow, scowl or smile. Their variety is the cause of such variety in our villages and towns, gardens and woodlands. Certain vetches and orchids are found only on the chalk uplands. Samphire flourishes on the mud of coastal salt marshes. Only the hardiest of trees grow in what was once the Breckland wilderness, while not so many miles away are the richest farmlands in England. The experienced geologist will know from each flower or grass what lies beneath.

At the same time an architectural student will find himself inevitably becoming something of a geologist. Old cottages, built from local materials before road and rail transport made the distribution of stone, brick, concrete and timber easier and so blurred the dividing lines, grew out of

Above: *The millstone grit of Brimham Rocks has been sculptured into weird shapes by continuous erosion on exposed moors above Nidderdale in Yorkshire.* Left: *Folded culm measures at Millock Haven, Cornwall.*

9

*Pre-Cambrian outcrops and 'bomb rocks' of Charnwood
Forest are among the oldest rocks in England, formed
from hardened volcanic ash and debris.*

their own landscape as naturally and appropriately
as the fruits and vegetables of the region. Even
larger mansions, whose owners could afford to
mix the textures of stones from remoter quarries,
or churches and castles for which monarchs and
nobles imported favourite materials, have a tale to
tell from that very complexity.

'Our soul', said Jeremy Taylor, 'is, above half
of it, earth and stone in its affections and dis-
tempers.' The earth and stone beneath our feet
are as much our heritage as are the birthplace of a
famous soldier, the palace of a bedizened ruler,
the cottage museum in memory of a revered poet.
Innumerable turns and twists took place during
the thousands of millions of years before man first
appeared in Britain. Titanic upthrusts brought
alternating sheets of solidified sediment to the
earth's surface, split them with the expectoration
of igneous rock, and left the whole chaotic residue
for us to study and relate to the shallow scratches
we have ourselves made in soil and rock during

our brief existence on this planet.

The study of radioactive materials in the
earth's crust has established that the oldest rocks
in Britain must date back more than 4000 million
years, to an era known as the pre-Cambrian.
There was no life as we know it, and all we can
deduce from surviving formations is that for
millions of years there was ferocious heat and
compression deep within our turbulent globe.
Those formations are now most clearly visible to
us as mountain ranges forced up by cataclysmic
forces, remaining tough enough to withstand or
adapt to later volcanic action, floods, sedimenta-
tion, and earth tremors. Witnesses to that distant
period are the Malvern hills, formed from hard
metamorphic rocks which were given an additional upthrust much later in time, along with the
Pennines.

By 600 million years ago, at the beginning of
the Cambrian era, an ocean basin had formed
between Scandinavia and what is now Ireland, in
which huge deposits of mud accumulated. Continuous additions of sediment, including the ash
and lava of volcanoes, compressed the muddy
carpet. Then subterranean upheavals thrust these

masses to the surface and began to sketch a notional coastline of Europe and our islands.

In the formation and deformation of such seas the earliest recognizable forms of life appeared. Fishes gradually evolved. Fossils confirm much of the story of these developments, and are the main source for dating and classifying different rocks. The oldest fossil so far identified in Britain is *Charnia masoni*, named after a Leicester schoolboy, Roger Mason, who in 1957 found this relic of some primitive animal organism in the ancient rocks of the Charnwood Forest region, which more than 500 million years ago emerged from a sea-bed covered with volcanic sediment.

Later marine deposits created the rocks of what is now Devon, from which the period has been named the Devonian. At the same time mountains to the north were subjected to folding, compression and constant erosion, their dust creating a red desert over much of the country. In time this hardened into the Old Red Sandstone which forms the basis of, for example, Exmoor and the Brecon Beacons – contemporary with the Devonian rocks but utterly different in appearance. Fishes continued to evolve in warm inland lakes.

In the Carboniferous period, beginning about 345 million years ago, the land sank and the sea came flooding back. Layers of limestone formed, to be covered by silt from huge rivers and deltas. Forests grew in extensive swamps, but when the land sank further, the trees rotted and were compressed eventually into coal. A further spell of buckling and folding left us with the Pennine backbone firmly established, and with veins of iron ore conveniently close to the coal seams.

The limestone swathe from the Dorset coast to the moors of north Yorkshire, taking in the Cotswolds on its way, has had a marked influence on man's contribution to the appearance of the land. All four main types of limestone are in fact to be found among our commonest building stones: Carboniferous, Magnesian, Oolitic and Liassic, and Cretaceous chalk. The chalk is both the purest and the softest. Impurities in the others are responsible for some of their more attractive qualities. One of the most appealing is the oolitic, named from the Greek words for egg and stone because of the small granules which give it the appearance of fish roe: indeed, it is also known as roestone. In several varieties, minute fragments of shell and fossilized animals provide patterns in which it is even possible to trace the

The eroded granite pile of Hay Tor on Dartmoor.

wave markings of currents which once scoured the stone.

Two types of freshwater limestone from the Isle of Wight have been used in a number of historic buildings. Romans and Normans employed Quarr stone for Portchester, and it can be seen in Winchester cathedral and several southern abbeys. Binstead stone, darkened by its iron content, contributed to Chichester cathedral and Winchester College.

Hard limestone from the Isle of Portland could not be readily used until the development of improved cutting tools in the seventeenth century, but it then became a favourite among the most ambitious builders. It is related that a visitor, looking down into the vastest of the Portland quarries, once said: 'You could put St Paul's cathedral in there.' To which the truthful response was: 'St Paul's cathedral came *out* of there.' Nearby Purbeck produces a darker limestone rich in fossils, much used for monuments. In Lincolnshire a more easily worked oolite from Ancaster appears in many local churches and

many in Norwich, including St Peter Mancroft. Barnack rag provides the main fabric of both Peterborough and Ely cathedrals; the subtly differing shades from Clipsham, Colly Weston and Weldon quarries are to be found all about the Rutland area and as far away as Buckingham Palace and the House of Commons; and of course there is the incomparable mellow stone which gives Cotswold towns and villages such a warm, creamy appearance, and whose porosity accounts for the steep pitch of their roofs, designed to throw off rain or snow before it can seep through.

The onset of the Tertiary era, 65 million years ago, brought a new outbreak of volcanic activity and another inrush of the sea over south-east England and the lowlands. Folds of chalk reared up, to be cut into by rivers which laid new sediments in the valleys and on retreating left the fertile Weald between the North and South Downs.

Finally, in what by geological standards might almost be called our own time, there came the Ice Age, which might more accurately be referred to as three main glaciations, between which tundras, forests and finally deciduous woodlands struggled to establish themselves. The ice sheet, gouging out mountainsides and carrying earth and rock with it, had by about a quarter of a million years ago clamped down on most of the land north of the Thames valley. The U-shaped valleys of the Lake District show the power of the glaciers, and owe the smoothness of their contours to the wearing away of unevenness and projections by the ice. Lakes formed easily in the hollows of glacial valleys and basins when the ice melted.

The last melting caused a rise in sea level which, among other things, about 5000 B.C. broke the land bridge joining Britain to the Continent and left these islands shaped very much as they are now.

During the movements of the ice sheets, many new hills and undulations were formed. Also, vast quantities of miscellaneous debris and scattered stones were carried far from their place of origin. Some of these glacial erratics, so obviously not native to their present setting, were used by primitive man in his religious monuments and circles. Others, heaped up by the glaciers or grotesquely eroded from much older pillars of

Durdle Door is one of the last fragments of a hard Purbeck limestone barrier through which the sea has eaten to scour bays out of the softer rocks behind.

Long Meg and her 59 'daughters' in a ring of 350 feet across are the survivors of a Bronze Age place of worship in the Eden valley, Cumbria.

igneous rock forced up through the fissured earth, sometimes look so much like prehistoric man's dolmens and cromlechs that it can be difficult to distinguish one from the other. Perhaps those first builders, imagining the lineaments of fearsome deities in their legacy of warped stone, set out deliberately to copy the conformations which had been there before they ever set foot on these shores.

The stone workers

Near Keswick in the Lake District stand 39 stones in a circle, with traces of some other stone structure at the centre. Also in Cumbria, near Little Salkeld, is a menhir – a single standing stone, the name deriving from the Welsh *maen*, a stone, and *hir*, long – surrounded by a ring of 59 attendants, the whole family known as Long Meg and her Daughters. On Stanton Moor in Derbyshire a menhir called the King's Stone is encircled by Nine Ladies. (One wonders whether another

stone erection on the moor's edge will last as long, to interest future generations – a monument raised in celebration of the 1832 Reform Bill and dedicated to Earl Grey.) At Arbor Low in the same county, a circle of stones within a bank and ditch must once have been a religious sanctuary of great importance, judging from the wealth of burial mounds in the near neighbourhood.

The greatest congregation of burials, however, in long barrows and bowl, bell and disc barrows, is around one of the most ambitious of all ancient stone circles. Interpretations of the meaning of Stonehenge, which has presented a number of different appearances during the 4000 years of its existence, have been as varied as those successive patterns. There have been religious, mathematical and astronomical explanations; and conflicting theories about the origin of the massive stones themselves. One favoured story concerning the huge bluestones has them being transported from a holy site in the Prescelly mountains of South Wales by rafts along the Bristol Channel and the Avon, and then being manhandled on tree-trunk rollers overland to their Wiltshire setting. Yet it is surely just as plausible to suppose they were torn from their Welsh home by an advancing ice sheet which dumped them here when it receded, like so many glacial erratics. The sarsen stones, also dubbed 'grey wethers' because of their resemblance to sheep when seen from a distance, were local blocks of hard sandstone. Yet even to call these local is misleading: not only did they have to be dragged 20 miles or so from the Marlborough Downs, where they had lain as alien sandstone lumps on a countryside of chalk, but the word sarsen itself derives from 'Saracen', meaning foreign.

But whatever the origin of its components, and whatever puzzles it may forever leave unsolved, Stonehenge does stand as a memorial to the beliefs and techniques of some of the earliest skilled immigrants into England.

The first men to set foot here would have been Old Stone Age hunters crossing the land bridge from the European mainland. Some may have stayed on in the few tracts left unconquered by the ice sheets, while others went back to less hostile climes; but scattered relics of stone axes and primitive tools in eastern England testify to their having spent some time here, living off animals they could catch and such plants as existed near their hunting grounds.

After the final inundation of the linking causeway, explorers of these islands came in dug-out canoes, and the nomadic hunters began to give way to men seeking fertile settlements. About 3000 B.C. came New Stone Age (Neolithic) people who knew how to sow and reap, and how to rear animals in more stable rural communities.

These immigrants favoured the chalklands. They pastured sheep on the Downs, and tilled the light upland soil because their primitive ploughs did not have the strength to break the heavier clays below. And in the chalk they found materials for their most important tools and weapons – flint. Veins of this tough stone had formed in the chalk after it had been upfolded from the sea.

Although fragments occur near the surface in such quantities that Sussex ploughmen ruefully assert to this day that flints 'grow' like malignant crops from the ground, to reach sizeable deposits the Neolithic settlers had to drive mine shafts to depths as great as 50 feet. They carved their way down with picks made of deer antlers; and brought up stone to be trimmed for tougher uses. The cutting and trimming of flint, known as knapping, is a craft now lost along the South Downs, but survives into this century at Brandon in Suffolk, not far from the Neolithic flint mines of Grime's Graves, Norfolk, where over 300 shafts and tunnels have been discovered.

The simplest everyday implements would undoubtedly have been fashioned by each man to suit his own immediate needs. But as communities grew more sophisticated, there came the earliest specialists – men with a flair for the making of axes and picks not only for their own use but for trade and barter with others. Many a museum, including the local Breckland museum in Thetford, Norfolk, has displays of painstakingly wrought arrowheads which, found on a heathland or forest track – as they may still occasionally be found in Breckland – might be mistaken for delicately marked, finely serrated leaves.

Stone implements survive. Homesteads and clothing of the downland settlers do not. Faint traces discernible in a number of excavations suggest that, although the men farmed the uplands, their primitive villages of wooden huts were generally set lower down. Access to a regular water supply made this essential. In addition, however, they built large camps on the ridges, partly for sheltering sheep and cattle and partly to provide the community with a fortress in time of attack from rival groups or fresh invaders from the Continent. These causewayed camps, so called because of the pathways which break through the earthen ramparts and across the protective ditches at intervals, presumably for the entrance and exit of the herdsmen and their flocks, may also have had a religious significance: it has been suggested that some were tribal meeting-places occupied for only brief spells during special annual gatherings or rituals.

One of the best preserved of such camps is that on Windmill Hill in Wiltshire, which has given its name to the whole local culture. Within three concentric circles of earthworks have been found pottery, combs made from antlers, the bones of sheep and cattle and even those of a domestic dog. Many of these finds are displayed in the museum at nearby Avebury.

While few of their living quarters have survived in any recognizable form, burial chambers of Stone Age peoples are, in spite of weather, farming, urban development and vandalism, to be found in plenty throughout the British Isles. The megalithic quoits, dolmens and cairns are in fact often more clearly identifiable than when they were constructed. The basic technique, whether for the burial of individual dignitaries or for communal interments, was to build a chamber of large stone slabs, roofed with a capstone, and pack the gaps with smaller stones and rubble before covering the whole with an earth mound. Over the centuries this outer soil has been washed away to expose the stones; and in most cases all human remains, too, have decomposed.

An outstanding example of a large communal burial chamber is the West Kennet long barrow, another of the ancient sites in the Avebury region. Within this 350-foot long chalk mound, dug out of two parallel ditches, were stone burial chambers housing the bodies of about 20 adults and a dozen children. These inhumations appear to have taken place over a protracted period until it was decided to seal the interior off with large stone slabs and drystone walling.

Of the smaller surviving tombs, Kit's Coty House in Kent may well have been a section of a long barrow, set up by people detached from the more populous western and south-western tribes. The greatest concentration of quoits and dolmens is in the west, especially in the granite country of Cornwall. Here it was easy to assemble stones of all shapes and sizes from the open moorland: so much so that these granite slabs were long known as moorstones. As well as providing burial chambers, the granite was used in drystone walls of such enduring quality that boundaries of many primitive fields remained much the same throughout succeeding centuries.

Although successors of Neolithic men not only continued to use local rock in graves and religious monuments, by about 2000 B.C. what we define as the Stone Age proper was giving way to something new – one of the first industrial revolutions, brought about by something more malleable and more useful in a score of everyday tasks.

The metal workers

The Bronze Age was heralded in Britain by the arrival of tribes from the Continent known as the Beaker Folk because of their custom of burying a particular style of pottery beaker with their dead. Flint was still used for a number of mundane purposes, and at first these newcomers seem to have been importers rather than creators of implements and weapons from the recently discovered alloy of tin and copper; but as time went on their warriors used more and more bronze weapons, and their chieftains were buried with an accompanying wealth of bronze goods and even, occasionally, gold personal ornaments.

The Beaker Folk lived in more corporate societies than their predecessors, developing not just local farming facilities and communal crafts but also a trade in the metal goods from their smithies. They brought in wheeled carts and a more advanced plough. And it was they who, with a mighty communal effort, established the final forms of Avebury and Stonehenge.

Avebury, like Stonehenge, was largely made up of natural sarsen blocks from the adjacent downs. A hundred of these were set up in a wide circle within a ditch and earthwork, with four entrances through the rampart. An inner concentric circle was added, and there are indications of smaller groupings within that. It must have served as a meeting place for the devout from far and wide for some seasonal festivity, and there is more than a hint of fertility symbolism: the Kennet Avenue to the south, stretching more than a mile to an enclosure known as the Sanctuary, once had a full complement of 100 pairs of stones, one high phallic pillar beside a plump short one, of obvious male and female significance.

Beside some of the avenue stones, and in some profusion within the Sanctuary itself, are burial chambers of the Beaker Folk. Strangely, despite their closely knit communities which might almost be described as pioneer-urban, they did not have collective interments: their characteristic grave holds only one person, crouched by the inevitable pot.

What was in effect a straggling cemetery between Avebury and Stonehenge displays nearly every kind of funerary barrow, established over a great stretch of time. We have the Neolithic long barrows, the bowl-shaped barrows of the Beaker Folk, and the less common bell barrows of the Wessex culture which followed soon after the arrival of the Beaker Folk. These consist of sizeable hummocks on a flat footing, surrounded by a ditch and usually containing men and their most valuable possessions. Women were more frequently buried in disc barrows, little more than a shallow circle with a ditch and a diminutive knoll at the hub.

Another collection of burial chambers can be found in a very different setting, in the woods of Bow Hill near Chichester. On the crest of a ridge are four round barrows known as the Devil's Humps, from the early Bronze Age. There are also a couple of bell barrows, traces of an ancient flint mine, and signs of later occupation by the Celts.

The Celts flowed in between 1000 and 500 B.C., bringing with them iron tools and iron weapons which soon established their supremacy. They attacked some existing settlements and collaborated with others. Their craftsmen sought local supplies of iron ore, and set up workshops. Iron was dug out of the thick Sussex forests and the Forest of Dean to make tips for their ploughshares, iron hoops for their chariot wheels, and iron sickles.

Large farmsteads and well defined villages came into existence. At Chysauster in Cornwall, a sturdy hamlet of granite rubble houses has been excavated in the heart of an efficiently planned field system.

The small fields which predominated from this period until close to Roman times have come to be described, rather loosely, as Celtic fields or lynchets. Strictly speaking, the lynchet refers to the bank or drystone wall enclosing tidy square or rectangular fields. It was usual to form these boundaries as clearance of the land proceeded: stones removed from the soil would be piled at the ends and sides, and regular ploughing pushed a certain amount of earth against the resulting

Oval houses with thick stone walls, paved floors and terraced back gardens open off the central lane of Chysauster, near late Iron Age tin mines.

walls, especially if the field was on a slope. Characteristic formations can still be seen in parts of Dorset and Wiltshire, including Smacam Down with its earthen banks, and the far west of Cornwall with its granite-walled fields around Zennor.

No traces remain of wooden homesteads, but the open-air museum at Avoncroft, Worcestershire, offers an interesting conjectural reconstruction of a community from about 200 B.C., including a number of stone and wattle-and-daub huts.

In the first century B.C. much fiercer and more determined immigrants began to take over the country. The Belgae were a blend of Celtic and Germanic tribes dominating the part of Gaul farthest from Roman influence. When under threat from warlike neighbours and ultimately from the ever-advancing legions, large numbers of them turned towards the comparative safety of Britain. Some settled in Kent, and have left their traces in cemeteries different from those we have

Chalk ramparts of Maiden Castle in Dorset were elaborated by successive Celtic tribes until breached in A.D. 45 by the Roman Second Legion.

so far noted: they practised cremation and buried the ashes of their dead in gracefully fashioned urns. We also have samples of their coins and stylish pottery. They had already transformed agriculture in their homelands with their heavy ploughs, employing a longer and broader share than the earlier Celts had known, with the addition of a coulter (a vertical iron cutting blade) to slice into the soil ahead of the share. Now larger expanses of land could be opened up: lynchet embankments were too restrictive. Within a short time of establishing themselves, the Belgae were not only feeding their own people from British fields but producing a surplus for export back across the Channel.

They also exported things which Julius Caesar disliked intensely – encouragement to their rebellious cousins on the Continent to resist Roman domination, and iron weapons to help them in the struggle. Caesar felt there would be no peace in Gaul until he could silence these offshore dissi-

dents, and decided to invade barbaric Britain.

The first two Roman visits in 55 and 54 B.C. were not among Caesar's major triumphs. On his second attempt he did penetrate inland far enough to defeat Cassivellaunus, the Belgic chieftain whose earthworks can still be traced near Wheathampstead in Hertfordshire, and won a promise of regular tribute to Rome and a cessation of internal strife between the aggressive Belgae and more peaceable indigenous tribes; but from then on he was too preoccupied with wars closer to home to be able to ensure any continuing observance of his terms in Britain.

It was not until A.D. 43 that Belgic harassment, which had grown so savage as to drive many lesser chieftains to Rome to ask for imperial assistance, provoked Claudius into ordering a full-scale invasion. An army landed at Richborough, established a fort and supply base whose massive walls stand to this day, and set about subduing the warlords of Camulodunum (Colchester) and southern Britain.

There are no dramatic records of these campaigns to match those of Caesar's Gallic Wars, but the inexorable progress of the legions can be deduced from a number of relics and scattered details. It is reasonably clear that, when pitched battles with the highly trained invaders were found to be inadvisable, many folk left their farms and villages and took to the old hill forts. The downland enclosures may once have been religious centres; now they offered sanctuary of a more immediately worldly nature.

What had once been a fairly simple bank and ditch fortification on Hod Hill, near Blandford in Dorset, was hastily amplified as the Romans approached. The inner settlement must have been quite a substantial one, as the footings of circular huts can still be identified. But the Romans seized the fort, and built their own fort within the defences to accommodate a garrison for quite some time after the conquest.

Most impressive of all the ancient strongholds is Maiden Castle, so called from the Celtic *mai-dun*, a large hill. The four lines of ramparts certainly are large; but they are late additions to what was always a well guarded site. Originally there was a Stone Age causewayed camp into which later occupiers dug ditches in connection with some ritual enclosure of their own. When the Celts arrived they added further banks to make a small inner fort, later expanding these to encompass most of the hill. Then, when other tribes fled into the region from the Roman threat on the Continent, the great stage of building truly massive ramparts began, and thousands of stones from Chesil Bank near Portland were carried in as ammunition for the defenders' slings.

When an all-out attack came at last, the slingers proved inadequate. Under the generalship of Vespasian, later to become emperor, the Romans stormed the fortress and subjugated the entire region. Remains of two men long dead recall some of Maiden Castle's story. Buried in the earlier ritual site was a corpse whose arms and legs had been dismembered and the skull split open, apparently so that the brain could be removed; and among a mass burial of slain defenders in the last days of resistance to the Romans has been found a man with the bolt from a Roman ballista in his backbone.

The defeat was so final that the Romans do not seem to have bothered to establish a fort here as they did at Hod Hill and elsewhere. But one incongruous feature was later added to the original fort. In the twilight of the Roman occupation a shrine was erected here – perhaps by Romanized Britons experiencing the collapse of the Empire and turning away from official Christianity to older gods in a setting of ancient sanctity.

Few tribal chieftains fought on to the bitter end. The Iceni in East Anglia hastened to make their peace. Cartimandua, queen of the Brigantes around York and the Pennines, ingratiatingly handed over the doggedly defiant Caratacus when he sought refuge with her. And the Regni of what is now West Sussex seem not merely to have collaborated with the Romans when they got here but actively to have encouraged their invasion.

The local tribal capital had for some time been in a hill fort surviving near the western edge of Goodwood racecourse, known as The Trundle from the Old English word *trendel*, a hoop or circle. There is in fact more than one circle: an outer Iron Age wall, and an older one inside. During excavations a female skeleton from about 2000 B.C. was unearthed from the junction of a Neolithic ditch and the Celtic rampart. There seems to have been a consistently large population throughout many centuries and regimes, until the Belgae drove out the inhabitants and a new capital and trading centre was established near the coast at Noviomagus Regnensium, modern Chichester.

It was from here that a king of the Regni, under threat from the contentious sons of Cunobelinus (Shakespeare's Cymbeline), is known to have made a direct appeal to Rome – an appeal answered not merely by an invasion but by the bestowal of great riches on the king's successor.

WESSEX AND THE SOUTH-EAST

IN THE FRONTAGE OF Chichester's Council House and Assembly Room is set a stone dug up during excavations of a street corner in the eighteenth century. The Latin inscription dedicates a temple to Neptune and Minerva with the authority of one Tiberius Claudius Cogidubnus as *Rex et Legatus Augusti in Britannia*. This indication of Roman favour goes beyond any title previously bestowed on a local chieftain. Verica, his predecessor, had been recognized as *Rex* by allies in distant Rome, but without the strength to assert this over quarrelling rivals. As pressures on his kingdom grew worse, Verica was among those who fled to Rome to plead for direct intervention. He may well have returned to Noviomagus with the Romans, who for three or four years after the invasion used a harbour near his capital as a military supply base for their western operations. But by the time Vespasian had moved on and the installations were handed over to civilian collaborators, it seems that Verica had been succeeded by Cogidubnus, with all the prestige and opportunities of a 'client king'.

City and villa
Since the temple stone is undated it is impossible to tell whether this promotion came swiftly or, as some scholars suggest, was accorded for support of his old ally Vespasian's cause after Nero's death. What is certain is that near the harbour of what is now Fishbourne someone possessed the wealth and power to create for himself a magnifi-

The polygonal Roman lighthouse in Dover castle, 40 feet high, from the top of which beacon flames guided the seafarer into harbour.

cent palace. It was the home not of a purely Roman administrator but of a favoured local ruler; and everything points to its founder as being that Romano-British King and Imperial Legate who had sycophantically prefixed his own name of Cogidubnus with those of his benefactor.

Several sections of this palace have been brought back to light in recent decades. There had been occasional finds of mosaic fragments and even remains of a bath-house in the early nineteenth century, but it was not until 1960 that really substantial discoveries were made. The driver of an excavator cutting a trench for a water-main came up against a mass of ancient building rubble which, when examined by representatives of the local archaeological committee, proved to contain broken roof tiles, pieces of mosaic pavement and other relics of a building larger than one would have expected from its presumed date.

Continued excavation revealed walls, a hypocaust to provide bath water, steam rooms and central heating, a number of tessellated corridors and extensive mosaic floors. A few floors have been salvaged almost complete, including one with an elaborate design of a cupid riding a dolphin in a surround of fabulous sea creatures, and one purely geometric one. Later extensions to the original buildings included a huge reception hall, audience chamber, and guest rooms, with colonnaded walks, a courtyard, and gardens whose original bedding trenches have been exposed, together with the channels of ceramic water mains to supply fountains and marble basins.

The palace of Cogidubnus has been opened up, but little of his city can be traced in modern

Chichester. A forum and basilica are known to lie beneath the cathedral; and parts of an amphitheatre were identified in 1935, only to be built over again. The grid pattern of the inner streets, however, testifies to their Roman or Romano-British origin, the medieval walls stand on Roman foundations, and from time to time new building developments unearth unexpected treasures such as the Eastgate bastion, located in 1972, guarding the end of Stane Street, the Roman road to London.

Near many such roads out of their major cities the Romano-British built smaller versions of the grandiose Fishbourne palace, for more practical use. These villas were not, as modern application of the word might suggest, holiday homes or country cottages for the well-to-do. To the Romans a villa connoted a farm, and although some may have been the property of urban dignitaries who visited their estates only from time to time, leaving a *vilicus* or bailiff to handle the day-to-day running, there was no question of tax-loss farming or amateur dabbling. In the Roman Empire everything had to contribute to the imperial, social and economic organization, and especially to the upkeep of the legions.

The earliest sign of Roman influence taking over from the circular British huts with primitive wattle-and-daub or drystone walls was the sort of single-storey rectangular cottage with two or three small interconnecting rooms which was discovered at Park Street near St Albans (Verulamium). Internal corridors were later introduced to link individual rooms, or there might be an external veranda, and then wings were added. Sometimes the children of a household would live in one wing, sometimes the farm bailiff and his family; or the bailiff might be accommodated in a separate aisled barn, referred to as a basilican villa, combining living quarters with storerooms and stables.

More ambitious developments can be traced in the winged corridor house at Folkestone, Kent, which expanded into a spacious courtyard villa with bath-house, tessellated pavements and mosaics. Perhaps the most luxurious we so far know, and certainly the one in the loveliest setting, is that at Chedworth in Gloucestershire, with its private inner garden surrounded by a terraced walk. The remains of the Chedworth hypocaust confirm that this was the home of a man who demanded a high standard of comfort in his everyday life.

At intervals along Stane Street from Chichester traces of posting stations and bridges, and close to the highway a number of villas, including those at Pulborough and Wiggonholt, have been found. Farms needed ready access to main roads for the transport of their produce. The best preserved, now attractively sheltered within thatched flint huts, are the remains at Bignor. This farmhouse began as a small timber-framed erection which was burnt down and refashioned in stone. As the farm grew into a virtual ranch, with great flocks of sheep pastured on the Downs, the house also grew until it must have had some 50 or 60 rooms and a wide courtyard. Its heating system was fed through trenches from a stream to the north of the house; the walls were adorned with coloured plaster; and there were fine mosaic floors, one of which drew attention to the existence of the villa when in 1811 a ploughman drove into the Ganymede mosaic. Other floor designs include a vase of flowers framed in geometric patterns, a brooding head of Winter, and a far lovelier head, that of Venus, made of much smaller stone cubes than the usual mosaic and so producing a much more delicate effect.

Another concentration of villas occurred along the line of Watling Street, a Roman highway following the route of an ancient British track. In the Darent valley lies one of the most lavish of these estates, at Lullingstone. It was found some 200 years ago when posts for a fence were driven into a mosaic floor, causing considerable damage, but expert excavation did not start until after the Second World War. As well as its mosaic floors and unique second-century marble busts, Lullingstone offers one especially interesting feature. Beside a room whose wall paintings imply the usual worship of a local well or spring nymph is a Christian chapel.

Although the Romans not only tolerated the worship of different gods by their subject races but often amalgamated certain aspects of those tribal deities with their own, it took them a long time to look benevolently on Christianity. Yet this proscribed religion managed to penetrate even the Britannic outposts. Clandestine groups communicated with one another by means of secret signs and cryptograms. A surprising discovery in 1978 was that of a second-century wine jar fragment from the Roman fort at Manchester, bearing an anagrammatic palindrome which can be resolved into the word 'paternoster' twice, plus Alpha and Omega, the Beginning and the End.

When Constantine the Great, who proclaimed himself Emperor at York in A.D. 306, was converted to Christianity, he urged it upon the Empire and adopted as his emblem the *Chi-rho* monogram, the two initial letters of the Greek word for Christ. This symbol began to appear on walls, pottery and pewter vessels, and was often superimposed on older pagan inscriptions. At Chedworth it can be found on the stone rim of the well once dedicated to a water nymph. Distorted heads of some otherwise shapely mosaics could owe their appearance to last-minute efforts by the masons to convert faces of pagan deities into those of the newly fashionable Christ or various evangelists. But, as we can see at Lullingstone, there were those who, while professing obedience to the new religion, were cautious enough to keep a place for the old gods and not too brusquely dismiss them.

Of all our cities with Roman lineaments, the old legionary centre of York (Eboracum) is perhaps the most rewarding, despite its frequent sufferings at the hands first of the Danes and then of William the Conqueror, plus the usual twentieth-century depredations. As at Chichester, the lines of the Roman walls provided the basis for those of the Middle Ages. One public house considerately floors a section of the bar with glass so that customers can look down into its Roman cellars. The Multangular Tower is one of the most impressive authentic relics of the days when Eboracum was the base for soldiers always on call to fend off the Brigantes from the central British mountain range, or march against the barbarians further north. The museum owning the site on which the tower stands has a touching display of domestic relics: a woman's lock of hair from a coffin disinterred from beneath York railway station, pins and rings and brooches, and a number of tombstones.

In spite of their iron weapons and iron rule, the Romans still worked largely in stone. In England we can deduce more from their milestone, tombstone and statue inscriptions than from the scanty writings of Romanized bureaucrats producing officially approved propaganda.

There was stone, too, on their roads. Stane Street is buried now, though for much of the route the main road from Chichester to its original termination at London Bridge follows the Roman agger – an embankment constructed from the earth dug out of ditches flanking the road, compacted with large stones and chippings. Some roads in Kent and Sussex were metalled with slag from iron furnaces which the Romans continued to develop in the Wealden forest. Many a straight road in England can be traced back to those times: Stone Street from Lympne (Portus Lemanis) to Canterbury (Durovernum); Watling Street marching through Canterbury and on towards London; the line of Peddar's Way from Holme-next-the-Sea on the north Norfolk coast to Chelmsford (Caesaromagus); or the clear marking of an abandoned road across the Lincolnshire and Cambridgeshire border near Barnack. But to tread an unspoilt, unmodernized Roman road one must climb to Blackstone Edge in Yorkshire and, looking down that sloping cobbled thoroughfare with its central trough, imagine the dismay of those legionaries from warmer lands who trudged into the biting moorland winds; or pursue the stretch of road through the Forest of Dean.

Attempts were made to grow vines in England, to save the cost and inconvenience of shipping wine from the Continent. It is doubtful whether the vignerons achieved any great success, though grape pips thought to be left over from local wine pressings have been found at Silchester (Calleva Atrebatum). It is said that The Vyne, a sixteenth- and seventeenth-century house administered by the National Trust near Basingstoke, is so called in memory of a Roman wineshop or vineyard by the Roman road, or perhaps in honour of the Emperor Probus who in the third century gave his approval to the development of viniculture in Britain.

If British vineyards were too far from Latin climes to flourish, the British themselves were also too far from the central authority to be protected when danger threatened. As Rome itself shuddered before the impact of northern European barbarians, more legions were gradually recalled to guard the home frontiers. Around the end of the third century, ripples from these conflicts began to beat more insistently on British shores. Saxon pirates, taking advantage of the weakening of Roman dominance, turned their attention to the rich pickings of south-eastern England. A Belgic seaman in imperial service, Carausius, was given the task of clearing the North Sea and the Channel of these predators, but played off one faction against another and, sharing out booty with those he was supposed to harry, managed to amass a fortune large enough to buy over several British legions to his personal cause. Declaring himself Restorer of Britain, he made his priority the strengthening of the old fortresses on what had come for grimly obvious reasons to be known as the Saxon Shore, not merely against the barbarian raiders but against possible attempts to reassert Roman authority.

Invasion coast

The south-east, so close to the Continent and in many stretches so low-lying and lacking in natural defences, has always been the favourite landing-stage of invaders. Julius Caesar, Claudius's general Aulus Plautius, Saxons and Normans, all concentrated their forces here; and we know from Nazi documents studied after the Second World War that if Adolf Hitler's 'Operation Sea-Lion' had ever been launched, it would have been against this same shore.

The forts of the Saxon Shore retain traces of defences against many of these attacks or possible attacks. Portchester (Portus Adurni), overlooking Portsmouth Harbour, was a haven for the *Classis Britannica*, the fleet in which Carausius once served. Its walls, parapets and bastions are Roman; the great keep is Norman, the work of Henry II; and from here, invading rather than being invaded, Henry V sailed on his way to victory at Agincourt. Portchester housed Dutch prisoners in the seventeenth century, and some laborious carving on the stones recalls French prisoners during the Seven Years' War.

To the east, the old fortress of Pevensey (Anderida) once also commanded a port, but the waters have now receded. The curious shape of the original Roman building, again with massive bastions, follows the irregular contour of the ground. In the foundations can be detected grooves in which timber supports were once set. It is known that William the Conqueror landed close to this site, perhaps in what is now known as Norman's Bay, and speedily took possession of the castle before heading for Hastings and rushing up a motte-and-bailey castle there. Later a Norman keep rose inside Pevensey. Its subsequent career was stormy: frequently besieged, it held out against William Rufus for six weeks, was starved into submission by King Stephen in 1144, refused to submit to Simon de Montfort, and was once stoutly defended by a woman – the wife of Sir John de Pelham, constable of the castle, who was away supporting the cause of

Henry Bolingbroke, later Henry IV, against Richard II. Even in our own time the fabric remained strong enough to support a couple of machine-gun posts and a 'pill-box' disguised as part of the Roman structure.

Little remains of Lympne (Portus Lemanis) but a few stones which seem to have cascaded down the slope from the ridge on which now stands a castle restored from the eleventh and fifteenth centuries. Beyond it, Dover is surely one of the most complicated defence systems in the country. The old Roman fort of Dubris was built over, and was revealed again only briefly during road-building in recent years, but the Roman *pharos* or lighthouse still stands beside a Saxon church within a medieval courtyard. Henry II's Norman keep rises 90 feet from walls 22 feet thick at the base, and his successors continued to enlarge it. The imposing Constable's Tower is a replacement for an earlier gateway which almost succumbed to one of the many French assaults on this coastline. When Napoleon seemed poised to invade, further fortifications and dry moats were added, with tunnels riddling the hill – 'horrible holes and hiding-places', as William Cobbett described them in his *Rural Rides*, 'at an expense of millions upon millions.' Some of these horrible holes won greater appreciation from the citizens of Dover when they were subjected to bombardment and air attacks during the Second World War, which left many scars on the town.

Richborough (Rutupiae) was, as we have already seen, the reception area for the successful Roman invasion and its main supply base. The platform on which the victors raised a monument can still be identified, as can the line of earthen banks and ditches from the original fort. The usurping Carausius added stronger walls, as he also did at Reculver (Regulbium) on the north-east Kent coast, though in this latter case the sea claimed most of them. The most striking remnants of Reculver are its twelfth-century church towers, preserved as navigational landmarks when the rest of the building was pulled down at the beginning of the nineteenth century.

North of the Thames were three more strategic forts: Bradwell (Othona), now close to an atomic power station, Burgh (Gariannonum), and Brancaster (Branodunum) on the fringe of the Wash. Burgh is the most substantial of these.

In spite of all his ambitions and efforts, Carausius did not survive long. He was assassinated by one of his own ministers who aspired

At least six Saxon kings, including Athelstan in A.D. 925 and Ethelred 'the Unready' in A.D. 979, were anointed and crowned at the coronation stone in Kingston ('the king's farmstead') upon Thames.

to ape him, and in a short time Rome had reimposed its suzerainty. But the Empire was beset by enemies, and it was difficult to maintain fully trained and equipped garrisons against Picts and Scots from the north and Saxons from the east. In the fourth century responsibility for the coastal forts was handed to a new functionary, the Count of the Saxon Shore, and signal stations were installed to link the key points. But by A.D. 410 the Emperor Honorius found it necessary to inform his Britannic province that no further military backing could be offered and that the inhabitants must see to their own preservation.

At Ebbsfleet in Kent stands the *Hugin*, a replica of a longship with dragon prow, rowed and sailed from Denmark in 1949 to mark the fifteen hundredth anniversary of the landing of the Saxon chieftain Hengist and his brother Horsa. They and their men came at first not in open aggression but as mercenaries invited by Vortigern, king of a large tract of southern Britain, to help against the Picts. The newcomers soon quarrelled with their employer and overran his kingdom.

The Saxons were accustomed to living in huts and congregating in wooden halls. They did nothing to preserve the Romano-British urban way of life or even to take over the stone-built villas. Few genuine Saxon homesteads have therefore come down to us. It was not until the second half of the ninth century, by which time Christianity had returned to these shores, that Alfred the Great set about a campaign of church building and ordered that Romain remains should not be neglected but should be repaired and also studied as models for future architecture. Although the Saxons still did not house themselves within stone walls, they did apply themselves to offering God a worthy place of worship.

At Worth in Sussex stands the largest surviving Saxon church in England, clearly Romanesque in conception. Among the most attractive of other legacies are the once secularized church at Bradford-on-Avon, Wiltshire, and the fine Saxon tower of Earls Barton, Northamptonshire. There is also a seventh-century nave and apse – that is, a structure pre-dating Alfred by some two centuries – at Cockley Cley in Norfolk, which must be related to some of the earliest Christian missions easing their way back into paganized territories. In spite of Norman additions and long service in post-Reformation times as the parish parson's house, this little building almost unquestionably belongs to the period when St Augustine tried to establish Roman Christianity in a land torn between Celtic beliefs and resurgent paganism.

Certain additions to the little church at Cockley Cley show a Danish influence. So do many churches in the south-east. Although we associate the northern coasts of England with Danish invasions, their imprint is found – along with so many others – in the shores, creeks and townships of the south. At Bosham in Sussex the Saxon church tower was once a lookout post over the waterways along which Danish marauders might infiltrate. The restoration of the tower and the construction of the nave are probably owed to King Canute. For centuries there was a tradition, scoffed at by academics, that Canute's eight-year-old daughter was buried here; but in 1865, masons working on repairs found a stone coffin containing the remains of a female child about eight. Reinterred, it is now marked by a Royal Copenhagen porcelain plaque carrying Canute's emblem of the black raven. The meadow between church and creek has been said, in defiance of Southampton's claim, to be the stretch of land from which Canute ordered the sea to go back; but is certainly the shore from which Harold Godwinsson set out in 1064 on that ill-fated voyage which delivered him into the custody of William of Normandy and so led in due course to the Norman Conquest.

The Norman presence in England is solidly represented by their castle keeps, churches, early cathedrals and monasteries. William the Conqueror was a harsh but devout man, who had sworn that in the event of victory he would dedicate an abbey to St Martin on the site of this victory. King Harold was defeated on Senlac Hill, and the abbey was duly founded. Additions were made during the twelfth and thirteenth centuries, and in the fourteenth it was impressively fortified, incorporating a mighty gatehouse which still looks out over the main square of what is now the town of Battle. In the grounds a small monument has been set up by modern Normans to mark the spot where Harold fell, and in the museum across the street is a reproduction of the Bayeux Tapestry, telling the whole story of the invasion and conquest.

Quite apart from their stone buildings the Normans had a lasting influence on the social structure of the nation, and thus in due course over the landscape itself. Gone was the loosely knit Saxon way of life, in which a leader was chosen and to some extent controlled by his equals. The feudal system introduced by William I gave the king absolute power. His nobles were given generous grants of land on the understanding that they were only tenants-in-chief, owing complete allegiance to the ruler. Below them, their knights and men-at-arms and vassals were offered a home and security in return for their loyalty and for rigorously specified military and civilian duties. Few even among the wealthiest really owned their estates or anything on them; though after William's death his successors were faced with frequent rebellions from barons who had come to regard themselves as virtually local princelings. The so-called 'freeman' who might be allowed to acquire a plot of land not rigidly attached to the manorial demesne was often, despite certain privileges, worse off than the serf, finding himself forced to sell his labour and produce to a local lord under conditions less favourable than those the bondsman enjoyed.

The quintain at Offham Green, Kent. In jousting practice the pivoted target could swing round and jerk an unskilled tilter off his horse.

Norman forest law weighed heavily on the poor. It was said of William I that he 'loved the tall deer as if he had been their father'. He demonstrated this love by passionately hunting them through vast tracts of personally sequestered forest and open country. Saxon villages within game reserves were demolished. Peasants caught gathering kindling or snaring rabbits were hanged, blinded, or otherwise mutilated. Grazing rights on common land ceased to exist. There were no such things as traditional rights, and no such thing as common land: every square inch was royal land. Only for a two-month pannage season each year were pigs allowed to feed on woodland acorns – and then only because during that specified period the acorns were poisonous to the cherished deer.

William II, dubbed William Rufus because of his red hair, was by no means as devout as his father, and aroused widespread antagonism by raiding the coffers of the church. But he shared with his father the love of the chase. In the New Forest, the most extensive of the Conqueror's royal reservations, Rufus was killed by an arrow – some said by accident, some that his infuriated barons had chosen one of their number to murder him. In 1745 a stone was put up near Minstead to mark the spot where the king was believed to have met his end.

Fortifying not merely castles but religious buildings and private manors became a fashion through centuries of baronial and dynastic conflict. Knowing how ready so many of their supposed liegemen were to turn against them if there was profit in it, kings tried to limit the construction of too many private strongholds by insisting that only with a royal 'licence to crenellate' could nobles add battlements to their homes. Sometimes, on the other hand, a monarch in need of support might actively encourage private castle building. William I's division of Sussex into five administrative Rapes and his grant of these to five of his most trusted followers carried with it the responsibility of building and maintaining castles, or expanding existing castles, to guard the vulnerable ports and river entries – Hastings, Pevensey, Lewes on the Ouse, Bramber on the Adur, and Arundel on the Arun – backed up by subsidiary motte-and-bailey forts at strategic points. In the late fourteenth century Sir Edward Dalyngrudge had no difficulty in obtaining permission from Richard II to build himself a castle at Bodiam on the Rother estuary, near a part of the coast plagued by French raiders. Sir Edward himself, home from a career of plundering the French countryside and holding French widows and heiresses to ransom, might well have feared reprisals.

War with France was a recurrent disease propagated by the claims of English kings to French territories, and buttressed by English determination to keep a firm hold on Gascony and the prosperous Bordeaux wine trade. Quite apart from the intermittent land campaigns there was a perpetual Channel battle between English and French pirates, each taking it in turn to raid the other's coastal towns. On one occasion the French, having set fire to Rye, were pursued homewards and Boulogne sacked in retaliation. In 1377 the French returned to Rye, set fire to it again, and stole the church bells; these were recovered the following year during a large-scale operation all along the Normandy coast.

On such a battlefront, individual communities could not be expected to provide their own defence. To coordinate defences in this region an association known as the Cinque Ports was formed: the five ports of Dover, Hastings, Romney, Hythe and Sandwich, to which were soon added the Ancient Towns of Rye and Winchelsea. The date of the original founding is not certain, but the oldest surviving charter is dated 1278. Each port later acquired subordinate 'limbs' such as Pevensey, Seaford and Tenterden. Their combined forces formed the backbone of the royal fleet in the days before a full-time Royal Navy existed. In return the Portsmen were granted freedom from many tolls and taxes, and for several centuries they enjoyed special fishing rights which stretched as far north as Yarmouth in Norfolk, where they had jurisdiction over the annual herring fair.

A Lord Warden was appointed to administer the privileges of the confederation and represent it in any clash between Portsmen and the Crown. One of his personal perks was the right to all wrecks cast on shore between Seaford and Harwich. He presided over the Courts of Shepway, Brotherhood and Guestling, at which the Barons of the Cinque Ports met to settle differences and combine against any threat to their liberties. At one of the Shepway meeting places near Lympne, with a superb view across Romney Marsh, a twentieth-century Lord Warden, Lord Beauchamp, has set up a commemorative cross; and these and earlier convocations are echoed in the name of Guestling Green, a village a few miles from Hastings.

Hastings itself still carries some scars from the old days. St Clement's church was wrecked by French pirates in 1377, rebuilt in 1390, and then in the seventeenth century a cannonball was fired into its tower by some passing French or Dutch man-of-war. Instead of gouging it out, the parishioners inserted another one close by to even up the pattern.

There seems rarely to have been a period in English history when some threat was not to be feared from the coasts across the Channel. The Cinque Ports declined as the sea receded, leaving only Dover and Hastings of the original seven still actually on the water's edge; but they found themselves back in the front line in Tudor times. After excommunication by the Pope, Henry VIII feared an attack from both Spain and France, and added further fortifications to those of the Saxon Shore, several in the pattern of the Tudor rose.

27

Above: The relay tower on Telegraph Hill in Surrey once semaphored warnings from the coast to London, and Admiralty orders back to the Navy. Right: On each side of the belfry window of St Clement's, Hastings, is a seventeenth-century cannonball: one fired in spite, the other inserted for tidiness.

Ruins of one of these, Camber Castle, stand on the levels west of Rye. Another, Walmer, has for a long time been the official residence of the Lord Warden of the Cinque Ports, now only an honorary title. The largest is at Deal: a Tudor rose within a moat, not so much a castle in the old sense as a glorified gun-turret. It was not until the eighteenth century that residential quarters were added, and these suffered badly during an air-raid in the Second World War. The castle museum now displays a fine sequence of plans and drawings illustrating coastal defence through the ages.

The French were expected again during the days of Napoleon Bonaparte. Chains of semaphore stations were set up on hilltops to relay messages between London and Portsmouth, and London, Sheerness and Deal. One of the former chain still stands on Telegraph Hill near Cobham

in Surrey, and the advance warning station at Deal is to be found on the sea front, a few hundred yards east of the castle.

Fortifications from previous centuries were too few and far between to control the exposed stretches of coastline threatened by Napoleon's modern resources. William Pitt the Younger, then Prime Minister and Lord Warden of the Cinque Ports, ordered the construction of more than 70 minor forts between Seaford and the Suffolk coast, and some on the Channel Islands. Shaped like squat, truncated cones, they were based on a tower which, with only three cannon, had held out against a British naval assault in Mortella Bay, Corsica. It had to be attacked from the land, and before being destroyed was analysed and sketched. Copies of these diagrams are now on display in the Wish Tower, Eastbourne, a restored Martello tower – the name of its forerunner having been thus anglicized from Mortella to Martello.

Rightly suspecting that Napoleon planned his main attack across Romney Marsh, the military engineers devised a second line of defence which would narrow the front to a well-commanded 19 miles of canal. A parapet behind this, formed from earth dug out by the canal navvies, would shield the defenders from enemy fire, while artillery from the foothills behind could bombard the attackers making their way across the dyke-crazed marsh. The canal itself was built in long straight sections, stepped back a few yards at regular intervals so that guns could fire not only across but right down each length.

Plans were made for evacuating cattle from the marsh. All the carts and wagons in Appledore and neighbouring villages were listed and numbered, and a number of farmers were appointed as drovers.

At the time there were many who scoffed and accused the Government of squandering money on defences which would never be used. This proved true; but the same might have been said of the miles of tank traps and barbed wire along this same stretch during the Second World War, traces of which still appear on Romney Marsh and across fields in the foothills.

Whatever its other failings, the Royal Military Canal proved invaluable to the drainage system of the levels, and by helping to drain many noxious swamps it also helped to drive out the fevers of the 'marsh ague'. At one stage there was a regular barge service along the canal. The bank on the

parapet side was not finally disposed of by the military authorities until 1935, when an Appledore resident bought an attractive stretch between Appledore and Warehorne, which she promptly presented to the National Trust. The land was all requisitioned again when needed for refortification against possible Nazi invasion; and still sports a few of the concrete emplacements which provide the modern equivalent to Martello towers.

The naming

The annual accounts of the town of Rye no longer record frequent payments for repairs to woodwork and bell-rope of the warning device high on its hill, but the name of Watchbell Street tells us where it stood. Yew trees are no longer royally protected as the essential source of longbow staves, and young men are no longer compelled to do regular archery practice; but the gracious square of the Buttlands in Wells-next-the-Sea, Norfolk, recalls an era when it was set aside for that purpose. Do thorns still abound on their island of Thorney; is there still a swing gate at Lidgate?

Our own names, and the names of our fields and villages and streets, are as real and as much a part of the historical pattern as any mansion or bridge or battleship. From them we see more clearly than ever what a mixture of Celt, Roman, Saxon, Dane, Norman and Fleming we are.

The earliest tongue whose echoes we still hear in these islands was a Celtic type which survived throughout the Roman occupation in spite of some toadying to Latin. One can only hazard guesses as to how far some Latin phrases may have been introduced into or deformed into the native language, just as contemporary American speech has twisted English and even French and German into strange new formations.

One type of Celtic language was taken to Ireland, Scotland and the Isle of Man by those making way for successive invaders. Another survived for centuries in Cornwall. But although it had sturdily withstood the Roman influence, the Celtic tongue proved unable to compete with the Anglo-Saxon invasion within what was to become England, the land of the Angles.

Most genuine Celtic names to survive are those of rivers: Avon simply means a river, and is echoed in the Welsh 'afon'; Ouse basically means water, though the Sussex Ouse derives from an English word for mud; Derwent, Darent and

Above: *This Rye street once rang to invasion alarms.* Left: *The straight sections and regular bends in the Royal Military Canal were calculated to allow for covering gunfire angled along each main stretch.*

Dart all refer to the oak-tree vegetation on their banks; and the Dee had a holy Celtic significance which the Romans preserved in Deva, their name for Chester. Hill and field names are often Celtic in origin, and a few county or regional names may be so. But the blending of an old Celtic word with a Roman or English one can lead to confusion – often to a fascinating and provocative confusion. The Portus Lemanis which we have already seen as one of the forts of the Saxon Shore was, in effect, a Roman port of Celtic elms. Doncaster is the *ceaster* or *castra* (fortress) on the river Don. Lichfield was originally Letocetum, meaning a grey wood, but the Old English 'feld' – contradictorily meaning open land – was grafted on to it.

The coming of Angles and Saxons, with a tongue derived from Nordic, Germanic and early Flemish sources, led to the establishment of the majority of our existing place names. It is thought

Wrought initials of Sussex iron
in the garden gate of Bateman's, once a prosperous
ironmaster's house near Burwash, recall the days when
Rudyard Kipling lived here and was inspired by a local
hill and old legends to write Puck of Pook's Hill.

that the Saxons themselves owed their name to the *seax*, their dreaded single-edged short sword. They tended to call settlements after their chieftains or dominant families. When Aella's great force arrived in A.D. 477 one of his sons, Cissa, took possession of the derelict Noviomagus and so made it Cissan-ceaster, later resolving itself into Chichester; and it may well be that he also imposed his name on the old hill-fort which became Cissbury. During the earliest decades of Saxon settlement the suffix *ing* or *ings* spread widely. It meant simply 'son of' or, in the plural, 'descendants of' or 'dependants of'. Godalming was the residence of Godhelm and his people, Angmering of Angenmaer. Hastings was settled by the followers of a warrior leader, Haesta.

Our modern counties took some time to acquire settled boundaries, being at the mercy of local chieftains struggling for supremacy; but in general we can think of Essex as the region of the East Saxons, Middlesex of the Middle Saxons, and Sussex of the South Saxons. By an irony of history, the West Saxons who most successfully asserted themselves over their neighbours and provided most of the important Saxon kings have lost the name of Wessex.

As the old Romano-British towns and farmsteads fell into ruin, new villages and hamlets and steadings evolved, named after founders and functions. The suffix *tun* or *ton* speaks of an enclosure, *den* of a forest clearing, *ham* the home of a chief or tribe. We can almost trace the Saxon penetration of the tangled forest of Andredsweald – the Weald or Wild where nobody dwells – through the names of Newenden, Tenterden, Benenden, Horsmonden and Marden. As for the group settlements of those who hacked out swine pasture from the woods, there are indications not just of family names but of the local speciality: Egham was the home of Ecga, but Shipham denotes sheep-rearing area. Is Horsham a homestead of Horsa or of horses?

Things become a trifle more complicated when the 'home of' and 'descendants of' run on one from the other. *Ham* and the *ingas* are added to personal or tribal names to produce places like

Effingham, Warlingham, Mottingham, and Buckingham – the home of the followers of Bucc. And just to make things even more difficult, there are usages of *ham* which result from a compression of *hamm*, meaning a water-meadow, which makes it likely that the proper interpretation of the little river Tillingham in East Sussex should not be the home of Till's dependants but the water meadows from which they drew sustenance.

Pagan names introduced by north European invaders squashed lingering practices of Romano-British Christianity. Wednesbury and Wednesfield both offer allegiance to the Nordic god Woden or Wotan. Thursby and Thoresby add the Scandinavian *by*, a town, to the name of Thor.

Our Norman conquerors contributed less than one might have expected to the English language. They were, after all, Nordic rather than French: the name of Normandy was bestowed on Norsemen's territory when Vikings so unruly as to have been exiled by their own people settled in (or, rather, unsettled) a slice of the Continent unfortunately close to the shores of England. But such Latin-French as they had acquired seeped through here and there: Beaumont is obviously a fair hill; Egremont is Aigremont, a sharply pointed hill; and Beaulieu and Bewdley must presumably have been fine places in their time. Less obviously, Beachy Head is not a headland overlooking shingle, but a Norman-French corruption of 'Beau Chef'.

Many names have so many possible interpretations, misinterpretations and variations. All are worth pursuing if you wish to go beyond researching your own family tree and the reasons why you live in, say, a side street called Forge Grove. Was it perhaps a blacksmith's forge before your village became a suburb? Possibly: but it is worth pursuing the matter even further.

The luscious farmlands of the Kent and Sussex Weald were once the Black Country of England. Celts and Romans had already discovered iron ore in the forests. The Saxons stepped up extraction of the ore and the building of forges and foundries. Later generations fanned the blaze until the Weald became an industrial centre. In 1254 Henry III commanded the sheriff of Sussex to supply him with 30,000 horseshoes and 60,000 nails, and got them with little delay. Sheffield Park, now a beautifully landscaped garden and arboretum, and the terminus of the restored Bluebell Line steam railway, once employed over a score of iron workers. When Tudor England faced the naval might of its enemies, more and more trees of the ancient Wealden forests were thrown in to feed furnaces supplying cannon for the fleet – and from those same forests came the oak which made the ships themselves. A competing industry was that of the glassmakers around Chiddingfold, who also needed fuel for their furnaces. The ironmasters challenged the glaziers, and in time of national crisis won. Today all that is left of the defeated industry is to be found in St Mary's church, Chiddingfold, and in the model of an old glassworks in Haslemere museum.

Since we have been discussing names, may we suppose that Chiddingfold was the animal pound of Citta's people; and Haslemere perhaps the boundary (meer) or pool of a hazel plantation?

'Mad Jack' Fuller, himself an eighteenth-century ironmaster who used his profits to build some of the most enchanting follies in southern England, called the iron foundries of his native Sussex 'little tinkers' shops'; but they steadfastly carried on a tradition started in Roman times until the last Wealden furnace ceased to blow at Ashburnham in 1809. They have left their hammer ponds and small scattered deposits of slag. Above all they have left names to baffle the uninitiated. Who would expect to find Cinder Hill in the middle of sparse woodland? Furnace Lane seems inappropriate as a rural by-way; and what of Iron House Cottage, Ashburnham Forge and Beckley Furnace? But from the Weald came not just cannons but wheel hoops, iron firebacks and the iron tombstones of Wadhurst. We have seen that St Paul's cathedral came out of a Portland quarry: its railings came from a Lamberhurst foundry.

There are names to goad the imagination: Tanyard Farm, Poison Cross, Smoky House, Gibbet Lane, Highbuilding.

And moving on from the lands of the Saxons to those of the East Angles, we face further tantalizing derivations. Holland, in Lincolnshire, resembles the flat countryside of the Netherlands so much that we may think its meaning obvious. But it derives not from any Dutch source but from an Old English word for highland. Yet in that same region Holbeach is not a high beach but a hollow – as in Holbrook and Holborn.

We can learn from the rocks which existed before man ever came into being; and learn more from the names and attributes he bestowed on their conformations.

EAST ANGLIA

ON A CORNER OF RISBYGATE, one of the busier main roads out of Bury St Edmunds in Suffolk, the pavement is partially blocked by an octagonal mound of old masonry. Generations of school-children hurrying out of the side streets, passing it or stubbing toes against it, have known it as the Plague Stone; many have probably taken it so much for granted that they have never asked the questions which would lead them back into a remote yet vivid past. Which plague: and what was the stone's function?

A cross and a saint

It was in fact the focus of a gruesome seventeenth-century market when the Great Plague reached out from London into the provinces. The epidemic, beginning in May 1665, had been spread through the capital by rats and their fleas, killing nearly 70,000 people there alone. Towns and cities in regular contact with London were soon infected: it took only one pedlar, coachman or passing traveller to act as carrier. Families fleeing urban congestion took the infection with them into villages and hamlets. In the cities, fires were burned in the streets in an unavailing attempt to smoke out the plague. The only flames which did actually contribute to its defeat were those of the Great Fire of London, which in 1666 destroyed so many cramped and insanitary slums that the conditions most favourable to the spread of pesti-lence were alleviated.

Outside Bury St Edmunds, and other country markets, vinegar rather than fire was used. Farmers bringing produce to the outskirts of the stricken town would take payment from coins left to steep in a hole full of vinegar in the centre of

Above: *The plague stone, Bury St Edmunds.* Left: *Prehistoric Peddar's Way provides a walk avoiding most communities of any size, but has not escaped the modern adornment of an abandoned motor car.*

the stone, believing that this would cleanse them from infection.

But the hole in the Risbygate mound had not been scooped out expressly for this purpose. Further back in time it was the socket holding a cross to mark the western boundary of Bury St

Edmunds' abbey jurisdiction. There would have been such a cross at each of the four gateways into the town. Crosses and gates were demolished long ago when the population increased, religious houses were dissolved, agriculture prospered, and larger waggons needed a wider passage for their loads.

There remain other testimonies to the abbey and its power. After the seizure of the monastic foundation by Henry VIII, many of its stones were sold off for use in private houses and walls, where they can be readily identified to this day. The wall behind the Farmers' Club in Northgate, for example, is made entirely of abbey stones. The fine vaulting of the cellar grill-room in the famous Angel Hotel across the road from the present ruins makes it clear that this, too, was once part of the vast complex of monastic buildings; the similar stonework of Moyse's Hall in the Butter Market, now the town museum, suggests it may originally have been a guest house for pilgrims visiting the shrine.

Pilgrimages to Bury began late in the ninth century. Before then the settlement had been known as Beodericsworth ('the homestead of Beoderic'), and was of no great importance save for a small wooden church and monastery founded by a minor Anglian king, Sigebert.

When the great Danish host invaded and occupied large tracts of eastern and south-eastern England, one of their targets – all too literally, at the end – was the young Christian King Edmund of East Anglia. In 870 he and his men were defeated in a bloody battle near Thetford. Local tradition has it that a number of hummocks at Barnham are the burial mounds of the slain. The young man escaped, however, and fled to a place referred to in later chronicles as Heglisdune. There is still controversy about the exact identification of this. Some claim that it was Shottisham, not far from that other mound which in our own century has yielded up the great Anglian treasure of Sutton Hoo; but this seems a long way for him to have travelled with the Danes hard on his heels, and a more popular tradition associates Heglisdune with Hoxne, in the valley of the little river Dove. A bridge across the stream bears a plaque recording the king's capture. Hiding under the bank, Edmund was betrayed by the glint of his spurs to a wedding party who, crossing the bridge, either deliberately or unwittingly revealed his presence to his pursuers. When dragged out, the king laid a curse on the spot, and to this day

no bride will go to her wedding over what became known as the Bridge of the Golden Spurs and, later, Goldbrook Bridge.

Edmund refused to recant his Christian beliefs and serve the Danes, and so he was bound to an oak tree, used as a target for archery practice, and finally beheaded. When a Hoxne oak fell in 1848, a corroded Danish arrowhead was found embedded in its trunk, which then supplied some of the timber for the Victorian screen in the church; a marble memorial was set on the site.

Representations of the martydom are to be found throughout the region, and the fatal arrows are incorporated in the county arms of Suffolk and the arms of Bury St Edmunds. After his canonization the cult of Edmund King and Martyr spread far afield: the fine medieval wall painting in Pickering church, below the Yorkshire moors, is just one example of his influence. A modern interpretation is to be found in Whistler's engraved glass window in St Edmund's church, Southwold, in memory of the writer, Julian Tennyson, killed in the Second World War.

Another legend of the king's death has given rise to another familiar local symbol. It was related that when his grief-stricken followers came searching for his body they could not find the head until it was brought to them by a wolf who had guarded it while awaiting their arrival. The depiction of the animal with the saint's head in its mouth or between its forepaws appears on, for example, a fourteenth-century bench end in Hadleigh church, in stained glass windows and, again, in the arms of Bury St Edmunds.

Beodericsworth acquired its new name of St Edmundsbury when the martyr's remains were housed there in a wooden chapel. The relics had to be removed under threat of new Danish assault, but were brought back and interred in a richer tomb in 1013. Such shrines were of great value to the religious foundations of the time: reports of miracles brought pilgrims by the thousand, enriching the abbeys and their abbots, and enriching the townsfolk who housed and fed them. The modern Suffolk Hotel in Bury is based on an inn originally managed by the abbey. Such store was set on sources of income of this kind that when a spring at Elmswell, some eight miles away, was found to have curative properties for diseases of the eye, it was at once dedicated to Our Lady, and the powerful Abbot Samson travelled to Rome solely to ensure that revenue from pilgrims visiting the well should be paid into his

A fourteenth-century carved bench end in Hadleigh church, Suffolk, shows the head of the martyred St Edmund in the jaws of a guardian wolf.

abbey coffers. Quite apart from such devout offerings, farmlands and fishing villages had to pay their dues to this spiritual centre: as early as Domesday Book in 1086 it is recorded that a diminutive port like Southwold owed the abbey 25,000 herrings a year.

Magna Carta

The most solemn day in the calendar was the feast of St Edmund on 20th November. Then the faithful – lords and commoners alike – came from all over the country and from other Christian countries to Bury St Edmunds. In 1214, when the Archbishop of Canterbury wished to meet 25 of the most influential barons of England to make certain plans without attracting undue attention or arousing the suspicions of their despised King John, nowhere could have provided better camouflage than that holy spot on that holy day.

Since the Norman Conquest in 1066 the barons had swung between supporting and opposing their King. William I's lavish rewards to those who supported his invasion had, on the whole, commanded their loyalty. His successors were less fortunate – or less firm of purpose. Arrogance was no substitute for authority. Quarrels broke out not merely between one envious lord and another but between the lords and their monarch. In Suffolk the Bigod family were a constant menace; or perhaps, more appropriately, an inconstant menace. Granted 100 estates by the Conqueror, Roger Bigod built himself a castle at Framlingham. His son Hugh first supported the weak King Stephen, then opposed him. He was pardoned and created first Earl of Norfolk; but even before Stephen's death he was openly urging the cause of Henry II. Once Henry was on the throne, Hugh again turned traitor and supported the king's troublesome sons and their mercenaries. After one clash he fled to another of his castles, at Bungay in the Waveney valley, about whose strength he is said in an old rhyme to have boasted:

> Were I in my Castle of Bungaye
> Above the Water of Waveney,
> I would ne care for the King of Cockneye
> And all his meiny.

Any reader who protests that, according to the Oxford English Dictionary, the word 'Cockney' was first applied to citizens of London in 1600 can pass an interesting few hours tracing the original Old English derivation of the word, debating whether this was what Bigod meant rather than a direct reference to London itself, and then checking the date of the ballad. The only trouble with such pastimes is that they all too often open up a dozen more by-ways of inquiry.

Henry II was forced to build castles of his own, such as the one whose undulating earthworks and massive keep survive at Orford, which, though ostensibly designed to watch for pirates and foreign invaders from the sea, was equally a defence against his unreliable barons. These dissidents were at last, after the anarchy of Stephen's reign, brought to heel. Hugh Bigod saw his favourite strongholds dismantled; but both Bungay and Framlingham were later rebuilt, much in the form we see today. The surviving masonry of Bungay is so strong that when a late eighteenth-century purchaser tried to break it up and sell the stones for road-mending, he could

make no impression on it and had to abandon the exercise completely.

Henry's successor, Richard I, was a fanatical Crusader who spent little time in his own kingdom, which in due course fell into the hands of his avaricious brother, King John. Once again the barons grew restless, watching their sovereign lose most of England's French possessions, quarrel with the Pope, and try to recoup his losses by imposing crippling taxes on his own realm. They and Stephen Langton, the Lincolnshire scholar whose appointment by the Pope as Archbishop of Canterbury had for some years been resisted by John, decided that the king must be compelled to restore those liberties which Henry had conceded after setting the country in order. So on St Edmund's Day they met at the high altar of the abbey of St Edmundsbury and vowed to unite in the framing and imposition of a Great Charter – the Magna Carta to which John reluctantly affixed his seal at Runnymede the following year, laying down the fundamental principles of English law and the rights of the citizen.

Proudly the aforementioned Bury coat of arms bears the motto: *Sacrarium Regis, Cunabula Legis* – Shrine of a King, Cradle of the Law.

Where St Edmund's remains now lie, we have no way of telling, in spite of various theories. Some say that during the struggles between John and his barons the holy relics were carried to safety in France; others that this did not happen until the Reformation. Later a Duke of Norfolk brought them back to Arundel for his private devotions: a recent examination of the bones claims to have authenticated them. The story has something in common with that of Abbot Samson's priceless ivory cross, taken by devout monks to sanctuary in France and lost from sight until after the Second World War, when it found a new home in the Cloisters Collection of the Metropolitan Museum of Art, New York.

In 1960 work began on refashioning the church of St James the Greater into the cathedral of the diocese of St Edmundsbury and Ipswich. In 1970, the eleven hundredth anniversary of Edmund's martyrdom, there was a festival to celebrate its completion. Suffolk flint has been ornamentally combined with freestone in the characteristic regional patterns of chequered 'flushwork'; and high above the new choir gleam the armorial emblems of the barons, presented by the American society of the Dames of Magna Carta.

Another dazzling expanse of East Anglian

Above: *Flushwork, a Suffolk speciality involving the blend of knapped flint and freestone, provides ornamental chequerwork on Long Melford church.* Left: *The three-storeyed keep of Orford castle with multiangular faces and three square turrets, largely built from septaria, a local clayey limestone.*

chequerwork is to be found in Norfolk on the façade of King's Lynn Guildhall of Holy Trinity. It was not so many miles from here that King John, towards the end of his reign openly at war again with many of his barons and their French allies, set out to cross the quicksands of the Wash and lost much of his personal treasure on the way. Within the Guildhall are preserved 'King John's Sword' and the 'King John Cup' – the latter a beautiful piece of craftmanship, but almost certainly a century and a half too late to have been the king's. Whenever there is talk of damming the Wash to create a Dutch-style polder, many an eager treasure-hunter must dream of perhaps digging John's lost valuables out of the mud.

Baronial and religious dissensions have left

many another echo. Framlingham, which we saw earlier as a Bigod castle, came eventually into the hands of Henry VIII's son, Edward VI. He presented it to his older sister Mary, and it was here after his death in 1553 that she raised her standard when there was a threat of Lady Jane Grey's supporters seizing the throne, and, with the support of many East Anglian notables, marched on London. The fanatical Roman Catholicism of 'Bloody Mary' took more than 30 people to the stake in Suffolk alone. Among them was Rowland Taylor, to whom a memorial stands on Aldham Common where he was burnt to death.

Succeeding her sister, the Protestant Queen Elizabeth tilted the scales the other way by using Framlingham castle as a prison for recusant priests. Another of her prisoners was Mary, Queen of Scots, who whiled away her time with embroidery, many fine examples of which are now to be seen in Oxburgh Hall, the Norfolk home for more than four centuries of the Catholic Bedingfeld family.

The wool trade

In addition to the sumptuous St Edmundsbury abbey and the abbeys of Thetford and Castle Acre, East Anglia gave birth to some of the most impressive churches in the land. As the wool trade flourished and the wealthy weavers began to think it advisable to take out heavenly insurance as well as laying up treasures on earth, they raised the great towers of Lavenham, Stoke-by-Nayland, Kersey and Dedham. In Lavenham, Thomas Spring 'the Rich Clothier', who at one stage had to seek a royal pardon 'for all false deceptions and offences in making cloth, in stretching out the length, or the breadth of it, and all deception in the selling of woollen cloth', sought divine forgiveness also by helping to finance the construction of what has been declared the noblest example of Late Perpendicular architecture in the world. Near his tomb in the Spring Parclose of this church is a carving of St Blaise, patron saint of wool-combers because of the tradition that he was combed to death during the Emperor Diocletian's persecution of Christians. This saint appears in other local churches, a comb often forms one of the plaster reliefs on pargeted cottages of the region, and there are also many representations of the fleur-de-lys woolmark attesting the standard length and breadth of cloth for taxation purposes, often surmounted by Blaise's mitre. He is also to

be found, not unnaturally, in Yorkshire woollen areas – including appearances in pub names and local inn signs.

The rearing of sheep for their fleeces had been a profitable occupation for centuries, especially on Romney Marsh, the South Downs, and East Anglia. Once shorn, however, the wool was generally shipped abroad to be made into garments, fetching such high prices that there was a brisk trade in smuggling it out, despite successive royal ordinances forbidding it. Then Edward III, married to Philippa of Hainault in the Low Countries, made an offer to Flemish weavers that if they would come to England, 'bringing their mystery with them', he would guarantee them a regular diet of 'fat beef and mutton till nothing but their fulness should stint their stomachs'. Many came and settled; and many of the half-timbered or plastered cottages of Suffolk, like their counterparts in the Weald of Kent and Sussex, still retain rooms and windows designed for a well-lit cottage industry.

This custom of employing out-workers for weaving and fulling at home in their own 'loom places' continued until trade grew too big. Larger looms demanded larger premises. Individual cottages gave way to high-ceilinged 'hall houses' of the fifteenth and sixteenth centuries. Warehouses had to be built. Wages, prices and disputes were all settled in such imposing centres as Lavenham's Guildhall of Corpus Christi, which now houses exhibitions of weaving and, in the cellars that once housed the trade guild's wine butts, of the cooper's craft.

The Flemings also brought to this region, as to the Isle of Thanet in the south-east, characteristic architectural influences. Their brickwork graced many early manor houses, and there is hardly a village street which does not boast its 'Dutch gable'. Names, too: Shilling Street in Lavenham has nothing to do with coinage but is a version of Schylling, one of the immigrant craftsmen. It is generally accepted that Strangers' Hall in Norwich is so called because of the coming of a fresh wave of 'foreigners' or 'strangers' fleeing Spanish persecution in the Netherlands and, with the aid of the city corporation, opening up fresh markets with their 'new draperies'.

As trade prospered, certain villages gave their

Half-timbered Lavenham Guildhall, which after the decline of the wool industry served as town hall and gaol – with half-timbered car in foreground!

names to specific types of cloth. Lavenham blue cloth was much prized. Kersey – once Carseye, 'Car' being the old name for a stream such as that which runs across the road here, and 'Seye' meaning a ditch – wove a sturdy cloth known as kerseymere, while nearby Lindsey produced a lighter mixture of wool and flax called linsey-woolsey. From Worstead in Norfolk came closely twisted worsted yarn.

The invention of machines operated by running water instead of by foot for fulling – that is, cleansing and beating cloth – drove trade away to the more powerful streams of the west, where weavers' houses and halls grew up in Cotswold building materials; and then, ultimately, to the dark satanic mills of the north. Among old fulling mills preserved in idyllic settings are those at Alresford, Hampshire, and by the weir below Durham cathedral; and there is a forlorn wool-drying oven at Woodchester, Gloucestershire, whose lancet windows give it the appearance of an abandoned church tower.

The name of a public house at Stradbroke, 'The Hempsheaf', recalls attempts to provide substitute employment for Suffolk weavers in making sacking and sailcloth. And in Lavenham, horsehair weaving was carried on by individual outworkers in their own homes until the First World War.

If it is difficult to see these picturesque backwaters as the industrial centres of their day, or to imagine their vast churches with adequate congregations, it is surely even more difficult to see them in their own right as they are today. Imposed on us is the vision of a man who has somehow made his interpretation of these scenes more vivid than the reality. Standing below the church of Stoke-by-Nayland, riding like a huge ship along its commanding crest, or beside the river Stour with Dedham church framed between the trees of the vale, we have difficulty in seeing any of it without superimposing John Constable's version.

Constable country

In earlier times the valley of the Stour was impassable, choked by a thick forest which, with the aid of the Devil's Dyke and the treacherous marshes and fenlands of the west, kept Norfolk and Suffolk effectively shut off from their neighbours for many centuries. But by the time Golding Constable, a well-to-do miller, crossed the river from the Essex bank and settled at East Bergholt in Suffolk, the vale had long been a gentle expanse of rich pasture. His son John, whom the miller had hoped would follow him into the business, wanted to use the valley's riches in quite a different cause. 'Painting with me is another word for feeling, and I associate my careless boyhood with all that lies on the banks of the Stour; those scenes made me a painter.'

Many of the scenes have survived. His friend Willy Lott's cottage is still there; his father's Flatford Mill is still there, leased by the Field Studies Council; the village of East Bergholt is as charming as the artist's studies of it in the Victoria and Albert Museum. Locks and staunches along the river are as creaking and slimy as when he spoke rapturously of their dripping greenness and tried to capture them on canvas. One can still reach the vantage point above Stratford St Mary from which he painted his 1805 and 1828 studies of Dedham Vale (in the Victoria and Albert Museum and the National Gallery of Scotland respectively) and see the church and its setting not too hideously distorted by the ravages of time. Unfortunately the pretty little bridge in the foreground has now been engulfed by the dual carriageway of the A12.

During his early strivings for success, Constable fretted that he 'seemed to see the shadow of Gainsborough under every hedge and hollow tree'. His distinguished predecessor did indeed claim to have sketched by the age of 10 'every fine tree and picturesque cottage' in the locality, but his approach was less richly earthy, and he relied for his income on portraiture rather than great bravura landscapes.

Thomas Gainsborough was born in 1727 in the street now named after him in Sudbury – the corrupt 'Eatanswill' of Charles Dickens' *Pickwick Papers*. His birthplace originally had a Tudor frontage, but his father added the Georgian façade we see today. The house now contains mementoes of the painter, including the plaster model horse which he incorporated in many apparently naturalistic paintings when he was unwilling to cope with a real-life animal; but the building itself has a truly real-life, lived-in feeling which makes it something more than a mere museum.

After an early marriage, young Gainsborough set up first in Sudbury and then in Ipswich as a portrait painter, much as a local photographer would set up in business today to record weddings, babies and school groups. He first became fashionable, though, after moving to Bath in 1759, and was one of the founding members of the Royal Academy in 1768. His portraits made him famous, and in 1774 he settled in London in a house in Pall Mall, where he painted many of the great figures of his time, including Dr Johnson, Sheridan, and Mrs Siddons, whose replica for many years inclined gracefully to the audience at the beginning of a Gainsborough film, and may still occasionally be seen doing so on television.

The Royal Academy did not treat its founder member's greater successor with any marked enthusiasm. It was not until he was 53 that John Constable was grudgingly elected to full membership; and even then the President, Sir Thomas Lawrence, commented that he should count himself fortunate to have been chosen when there were so many other landscape artists of greater talent. The atmospheric fury of some of his paintings displeased suave academic critics, who sneered at the glowing truth of his colours, the simple accuracy of his view of a field or cottage, and above all the turmoil of his skies. But as a miller's son he knew how to interpret clouds: perhaps the best way to recognize what a true son of Suffolk he was is to stare up into the vast skies of East Anglia. If Constable saw Gainsborough under every tree, we see Constable in every scudding, racing, shining or lowering cloud.

In 1978, experts made the uncomfortable discovery that a great many paintings supposedly by John Constable, mainly in foreign galleries or in the hands of private collectors, were most probably the work of one of his sons. This caused a great stir in the art world, but one wonders if it matters too greatly. If the son's work was so talented that it has taken all this time for experts' suspicions to be aroused – and then largely on technicalities – one can only be grateful to the family for producing such creative artists. It is pleasant to think that there is a painting dynasty as gifted and prolific as the musical Bach family.

John Constable himself was buried in Hampstead, but his parents and his old friend Willy Lott lie in East Bergholt churchyard. Inside there are a memorial to his wife, Maria, and a memorial window to the painter himself, incorporating his sketch of the chancel and sanctuary, and Willy Lott's cottage.

For those with a taste for strange epitaphs, that in East Bergholt to John Mattison provokes any amount of speculation. Having, it is declared,

'profited and pleased, mixed business with pleasure, to his pupils a terror and a delight', he was 'eleven years the beloved schoolmaster of this Town, and then unfortunately shott'. It is not recorded whether this was an accident or the work of some vengeful pupil who managed to indulge in violence long before the advent of television.

Across the border in Norfolk there grew up another influential body of essentially local painters. The Norwich School included the older and younger Crome, and John Sell Cotman. It is instructive to compare Old Crome's view of Norwich from Mousehold Heath with that same vista today. Robert Kett and his rebels looked down from this vantage point in 1549 when they were massing to take over the city. Kett, a tanner and small landowner of Wymondham, had stirred up protests against the enclosures of common land by the greedy magnates of the time. With 20,000 supporters he succeeded in capturing Norwich, but was finally defeated by an army under the Earl of Warwick and hanged from the castle walls. That same castle, however, today has a plaque at the entrance commemorating Kett as a fighter for justice and freedom. Within are the art galleries containing the most representative collection of works of the Norwich School.

Lost shores and paths

Among the Roman forts listed as part of the Saxon Shore defences there is today no mention of one at Dunwich in Suffolk; yet there is every reason to suppose one existed. Unfortunately no stone of it can be identified, for since Roman times the coastline here has receded more than a mile.

Erosion of the unstable sandy cliffs has resulted in the destruction not only of a Roman fort but of one of the most important Saxon and medieval ports in Britain. In the days of Sigebert, Dunwich took precedence over all other East Anglian towns. By King John's time it was a walled town with a number of gateways, at least nine churches, and a number of monastic foundations. The number of king's galleys stationed here equalled those at London. When Henry III needed aid in 1242, Dunwich was still the major port on this coast and owned 80 ships.

One can see the process of erosion almost weekly – hourly, in times of the great east coast gales. All Saints' church, still on the clifftop at the end of the last century, has completely dis-

appeared now, though occasionally at night it is still possible from the sea to detect phosphorescent traces of bones in what is left of the graveyard. Despite what local fishermen may say, however, it is not possible to hear the bells of drowned churches ringing below the water!

Greyfriars Monastery had one wall some 30 feet from the edge of the cliff in 1978. At the present rate of erosion this is likely to disappear by 1990 at the latest; and one authority has calculated that the single remaining church of St James, set well back on the road entering the village, will have been inundated by 2300.

Between Southwold and Covehithe the rate of destruction is even more spectacular. In the late nineteenth century a loss of 130 feet was recorded in four years. The modern visitor, with a weekend cottage or returning each year for summer holidays, will find cliff paths crumbling, cottages which two years earlier were set back up a lane now in process of demolition before they crash down to the beach, and gun emplacements of the Second World War mingling their concrete fragments with the sand and pebbles.

But, in local parlance, while in some places and at some times the sea 'scours', at other times it 'makes'. Some of the material dragged away from Dunwich has helped increase the dimensions of the 11-mile shingle spit of Orford Ness. Great Yarmouth, once a scattering of fishing huts on unstable sandbanks, owes its present shape – still virtually an island – to the solidification of those banks into a long spit of firm land, sheltered by the secondary ridge of Scroby Sands building up to seaward.

As the tidal estuary narrowed, the Roman fort of Gariannonum (Burgh Castle) found itself suffering the opposite fate to that of Dunwich: no longer watching over the sea, or threatened by the sea, it lies today on a shallow hill above the river Waveney and Breydon Water, with crops growing not merely outside but inside its walls.

Sweeping round the hunched shoulder of Norfolk, we find a variety of sea defences, and other regions where the struggle has been abandoned. Some cliffs, like those between Mundesley and Trimingham, continue to be eaten away like the Dunwich ones, and several fields and houses have disappeared in our own century. Elsewhere

The Saxon cathedral at North Elmham, once seat of the Bishops of East Anglia, was built to an unusually large scale and at one time had two high towers.

there are breakwaters and concrete stockades, or steep protective walls like those which give Sheringham the appearance of an embattled fortress. Where the coast is flat, there are often great expanses of saltings, as at Stiffkey. Elsewhere, as at Cromer and Hunstanton, great vertical slices have been chopped from the chalk, at Hunstanton exposing different swathes of russet and white chalk and brown carr-stone.

A few miles off Happisburgh's agreeably sandy beaches, with their inner ridge of cliffs protected by zigzag groins that can be negotiated only by ladder, lie less agreeable sands. Despite the red and white warning lighthouse, many a ship has been wrecked here, and many a gallant rescue effected by local lifeboats, most famously that under the Cromer coxswain, Henry Blogg. In the churchyard lie the remains of many who could not be saved, including 119 crew of HMS *Invincible*, lost while on her way to join Nelson at Copenhagen. There are also graves of German airmen washed ashore in the Second World War – and inside the church, souvenirs of that same conflict, a number of pieces of shrapnel from an air raid embedded in the aisle pillars.

The most curious burial was that of Jonathan Balls in 1846. He asked that a plum cake, a poker, a pair of tongs and a Bible should be interred with him. After his death it was suspected that he had poisoned some acquaintances and might conceivably, by accident, have poisoned himself also. When his body and those of some of his supposed victims were exhumed, all were found to contain lethal quantities of arsenic. It was remarked locally that he would certainly need the fire-tongs in the life hereafter, and they were duly reinterred with him.

Further to the west, Salthouse was once a port with a wide channel to the sea near Cley, but found itself stranded when seventeenth-century marsh reclamation blocked the inlet.

The lake in the grounds of Holkham Hall was once an intruding limb of the sea. The Coke family had arduously reclaimed some 700 acres of marshland, but it was not until the late eighteenth century that Thomas William Coke – 'Coke of Norfolk', later to become Earl of Leicester – set about the even tougher task of creating fertile farmland from the local desert conditions. From a waste in which, according to his visiting friend Lady Townshend, 'all you will see will be one blade of grass, and two rabbits fighting for that', without previous farming experience he transformed the wilderness by digging marl from below the sandy surface and devising an improved rotation of crops.

An old rhyme tells of other shifts of earth, water, and fortune around King's Lynn:

Rising was a seaport town when Lynn was but a marsh;
Now Lynn it is a seaport, and Rising fares the worse.

The name of Castle Rising does not refer to any high ground or to the height of the building itself: it is either the home of Risa's people, or the home of people of the brushwood. The castle, with its lavishly decorated keep in an artificial hollow, was founded by William de Albini, Duke of Buckingham and Norfolk, who married Henry I's widow and became also Earl of Sussex and Arundel. Later it served for 30 years as a sort of open prison for Queen Isabella after the murder of her husband, Edward II, in 1327 and her son's subsequent seizure and execution of her lover in 1330.

Sea and wind can wipe away not merely tracks in the sand but whole coastlines. Tracks across the land are, in spite of weather and ploughing and industrial development, more lasting. Prehistoric paths can still be traced in surprisingly large numbers: some leave a distinguishable furrow across lonely uplands, others underpin later thoroughfares, still others are visible only as shadowy lines in aerial photographs. Centuries-old drove roads make their way over the borderlands between Scotland and England. Ridgeways, pilgrims' ways, drift roads for cattle and ancient trackways past hill settlements to ritual meeting-places or prehistoric markets for flint and stone tools – all form a web, broken in places but surprisingly resilient in others, over the face of the British Isles. They were planned to link up regularly with brooks or ponds so that flocks or pack animals could be watered. As well as easing the movement of cattle and sheep, many were used in medieval times for the transport of salt from coastal salt-pans.

In East Anglia the most distinctive route is that of the ancient Icknield Way, which served Celts and Romans and even in William the

The church of Happisburgh, seen here across a typically spacious Norfolk field of grain, is as important a marker to mariners as the lighthouse.

Conqueror's day was of such importance that it shared with Watling Street, Ermine Street and the Fosse Way the privilege of 'The King's Peace', guaranteeing protection to all travellers thereon. It links a chain of historic and prehistoric sites, crossing Salisbury Plain near Stonehenge and heading over the Chilterns and on through Hertfordshire and Cambridgeshire to cross the river Thet near the Iron Age earthworks of Thetford and skirt the Neolithic flint mines of Grime's Graves. A short distance from the Wash it has been swallowed up by time and tide. But when we read about King John crossing the Wash, it is obvious that in earlier times, before the drainage of the Fens, the estuary was narrower than it is now, and that shallow tides retreating a long way made its fording simpler. Hardly surprising, then, that after fading into the Norfolk littoral the Icknield Way is picked up again in Lincolnshire to the west.

Another ancient track is that of Peddar's Way, leading from the coast near Hunstanton in a fairly straight line towards Rushford in the valley of the Little Ouse. In some places it has disappeared below agricultural land, but even then there are faint streaks of it across some ploughed fields; it marks the parish boundary between Bardwell and Barningham. During the Iron Age this region was one of the most densely populated in Britain, and when the Romans came and converted the Britons to their ways this roadway remained important to all levels of society. Of the few Romano-British villas identified in East Anglia, the greater proportion lie close to this route. The Saxons abandoned it, perhaps fearing there might

Castle Acre bailey gate.

still be Roman-trained Celts who knew its course and its coverts better than they could, or perhaps for superstitious reasons. Considerable stretches may still be walked along: there is, for example, a substantial section signposted off the main road between East Dereham and Swaffham, about a mile and a half east of Swaffham.

One of the few places of any consequence touched by Peddar's Way is in Norfolk, some little way south of that Dereham-Swaffham road. Little more than a village now, Castle Acre is a palimpsest of successive races and cultures, and the junction of many half-obscured tracks. In our own time it has been a regular stopping-place for Easter pilgrims walking from Bury St Edmunds to Walsingham, some of them carrying crosses to be set in the garden of the fourteenth-century slipper chapel at Houghton St Giles. But long before Christian pilgrims trod this way the site must have been of great importance. It was only in the 1970s that the full extent of a large Roman settlement buried beneath later fortifications was appreciated. The remains of a huge motte-and-bailey castle built for William the Conqueror's son-in-law, William de Warenne, and the ruins of the Cluniac priory founded by de Warenne's son are still awe-inspiring. The castle bailey in fact encompasses most of the present village, with the thirteenth-century bailey gate still in place above the slope leading down towards the river Nar.

The situation does not seem a particularly vital strategic one, from either Roman or Norman viewpoints. But it retains, as much as any site in eastern England, an air of remarkable grandeur – and mystery. There are still innumerable puzzles to be solved, threads to be unravelled.

STRONGHOLDS

ONE HUMP OF MASONRY, with gaps through its middle like a Henry Moore or Barbara Hepworth sculpture, thrusts up from an earthen mound in parkland near West Grinstead in Sussex. It is all that remains of the Norman keep of Knepp castle. Below Bredon Hill the village of Elmley Castle in Worcestershire no longer has even a trace of a castle, but the name perpetuates what once existed here. Fragmented battlements above Kendal mark the birthplace of Catherine Parr, Henry VIII's last wife. The Newcastle upon Tyne was no longer new by the time Henry II decided to add one of his great keeps to it.

Few English counties are without some relic of Norman and medieval castles, associated with a worried king or with local or intrusive baronial families and thus with the whole history of the region. A few descendants of original castellans remain, even if the strain has been diluted by marriage. And the ruin of some fortresses, the 'slighting' by kings or rival factions, the abandonment of some and the restoration and refurbishing of others, all have their own individual dramas to be remembered in tranquillity.

Motte and bailey

The most primitive type of fort, whose principles and, indeed, physical reality underlie nearly all later and more sophisticated buildings, was that of a steep mound of earth flattened at the top. In digging out the earth for such a hillock, a trench

Bodiam castle in Sussex was one of the first to incorporate gun-ports, but its defences were never seriously tested by anything more than a Civil War threat to use cannon against them.

was formed around the base, playing its own part in the defences as a dry or wet ditch – the term 'moat' being a later corruption of the original 'motte'. The top of this mound was girdled with a wooden stockade, and some kind of protective tower would be raised within, first of wood and later of stone.

Establishing a permanent home for the local lord and his retainers was not practicable on such a summit. All supplies of food and ammunition had to be dragged up from below, sanitation was crude or non-existent, and unless the mound had been constructed above a reliable well – which would in any case necessitate driving a very deep shaft – water supplies were inadequate. The garrison, smiths, fletchers, farm labourers and serfs lived most of the time within another stockaded enclosure below the mound, known as the bailey. If enemies appeared, cattle would be driven in across an outer ditch over a drawbridge, which would then be raised. If the enemy penetrated the bailey, the defenders would flee to the motte and hope to hold out long enough for help to come or for the raiders to weary and go away.

Outlines of motte, bailey, and protective ditches are still clearly visible at Hallaton in Leicestershire, and in the large grassy mounds of Elsdon in Northumberland. In Shropshire alone the sites of over 150 such edifices have been identified, some so small and some so overgrown that they can be mistaken for prehistoric tumuli. At West Felton, near Oswestry, the whole shape of the medieval village and its roads was conditioned by the castle bailey, providing an interesting contrast to the nineteenth-century offshoot which grew up along the Holyhead road.

The shell keep of Restormel, Cornwall.

Thetford in Norfolk retains its 80-foot high motte in the centre of older earthworks; and there is a smaller recognizable one at Ongar in Essex.

At Berkhamsted, where William the Conqueror received the formal surrender of Saxon London, the motte and bailey, decked with traces of a shell keep, are all that substantiantially survive of his original castle with its wet moat – for centuries a favourite royal residence.

York had two motte and bailey castles, built in 1068 and 1069, the former now surmounted by Clifford's Tower of 1245.

Shell keeps

As acquisitive barons and royal castellans drove their roots more securely into their allotted terrain, not merely was the fort atop the mound strengthened to provide worthier accommodation and withstand longer sieges, but the exposed drawbridge of the bailey was provided with gatehouses to help it survive and, if possible, repel any assault. In later centuries these barbicans became virtual fortresses in themselves.

Hard packed as the earth of the artificial mounds might be, some were incapable of bearing too great a weight, and the most suitable stone addition was found to be a single-walled or shell keep, forming an elevated bailey with small huts or stone-walled living quarters inside. One of the best preserved of these is the twelfth-century circular shell of Restormel in Cornwall, which also has remains of an early stone gateway, and a chapel projecting outside the main fabric.

To reinforce the lower bailey, stone walls were added there also, sometimes continuing up the slope to join the keep. Carisbrooke, Isle of Wight, and Launceston in Cornwall are examples of this; and the original shell keep can still be found among all the later alterations and complexities of Arundel in Sussex.

The successive stages of construction and destruction at Arundel form an evocative architectural accompaniment to the social and political history of the country. Granted to Roger de Monte Comerico (a name which in due course became Montgomery and was bestowed on the family's possessions along the Welsh border) by William the Conqueror, it remained in the hands of his sons until one of them rebelled against Henry I, who acquired it for the Crown and bequeathed it to his widow. She married William de Albini, whom we have already met at Castle Rising in Norfolk. He opposed the dissolute and incompetent King Stephen, and so came into favour when Henry II succeeded to the throne. The 'Honour of Arundel' was granted to de Albini (or d'Aubigny) and his heirs forever. In fact the heirs ran out in the fourth generation when the male successor died without male issue. His sister married a Fitzalan, and for another three centuries the estate belonged to this family until its union with the Howards, of whom the present Duke of Norfolk, hereditary Earl Marshal of England, is a direct descendant. Each generation added to the castle. It suffered serious damage during the Civil War, its great hall – the centre of all castle activities – being completely destroyed, to be uninspiringly reconstructed in Victorian times. The marks of cannonballs from that Parliamentarian siege can still be traced on the walls of the barbican.

At Warwick, the Conqueror fortified in 1068 a motte and bailey which later in the century acquired a shell keep. In the fourteenth and fifteenth centuries were added the walls and towers we see today; more comfortable residential buildings appeared in the seventeenth century.

The shell wall of royal Windsor was built about 1170 on a Norman motte which originally carried a wooden tower. Henry II and Henry III both added curtain walls. Between their reigns, one of King John's few contributions was a night of the sulks before keeping his appointment at Runnymede to accede to the terms of the Magna Carta. Various royal whims and creative moods were indulged here. Edward III, founding in romantic mood the chivalrous Order of the Garter, put in hand such a massive rebuilding programme that it was grumbled 'hardly anyone could have any good mason or carpenter, except in secret' because of the royal priorities. Nevertheless his proposed private chapel dedicated to St George, in which the annual Garter ceremony is now held, was not begun until after his death, by Edward IV. Henry VII completed the nave, Henry VIII was responsible for the roof of the choir, and also for the castle gateway and the north terrace which became his daughter Elizabeth's favourite haunt. But we owe Windsor's modern character largely to the vision of George IV, whose collaboration with Wyatt on the exterior and commissioning of Lawrence to paint suitable pictures for the interior imposed on

The great tower of Portchester, Hampshire.

hitherto incompatible though splendid features an even more splendid over-all style.

Great towers

Wooden towers on artificial mounds were, at best, makeshift retreats of last resort. Even the stone shell keep was, by definition, only a fragile skin. Now it was the turn of the rectangular keep with thick walls designed to withstand enemy discharges of stones and fire from trebuchets, mangonels or other siege machines, protected by narrow window slits from which arrows could be shot but into which it was tricky to aim missiles from outside. Too heavy to be set upon any save the most solid mottes, these great towers were usually built within the bailey and entered by steps to a door on the first floor. Sometimes these stairways were little more than ladders which could be hauled up in case of emergency, but soon an additional reinforcement was included: an outer housing for the steps and entrance, equipped as strongly as the bailey's drawbridge gatehouse.

Portchester's great tower was set by Henry II within the walls of the old Roman fortress of the

John of Gaunt's great hall at Kenilworth.

Saxon Shore, and its height increased in two stages during the following century.

Other keeps were incorporated as an integral part of the bailey wall, and entrance to the upper storeys was often only from the parapet of such a wall. Smaller towers inset at intervals along the parapet would each have to be subdued by an attacker before he could grapple with the last refuge of the stubborn keep itself.

As these towers grew in solidity and size, more of the castle's everyday affairs were shifted in from the outbuildings of the bailey. Just as life in Saxon settlements had centred on the chief's wooden hall, so life in Norman and medieval castles was adapted to the ambience of the great hall such as one finds in Castle Hedingham keep, Essex. The lord usually slept in a chamber above the hall and had a private solar from which to look down on activities below. The sumptuousness of the hall and its entertainments indicated the lord's social standing.

John of Gaunt, uncle of Richard II and father of Henry IV, added to Kenilworth a great hall worthier of a palace than a castle. The whole structure, with few breaks a royal castle for many centuries, was protected by water defences whose dimensions were more those of a lake than a moat. Not content with this, King John had built towers and buttressed walls; not merely were the walls of the keep, known as Caesar's Tower, 14 feet thick, but buttresses were added up to the first storey to strengthen the corners against possible undermining by enemy sappers.

At Rochester a noticeable irregularity in the balance of the keep is due to the action of such subterranean burrowers. In essence the tower is almost the same as when King John besieged it in 1215, but one of its turrets is round, unlike its three squared-up companions. In John's day it matched the others, but his engineers tunnelled below its base and set fire to brushwood steeped in bacon fat in order to burn away the wooden props they had inserted to support their operations. As the props collapsed, so did the tunnel roof and the corner turret. When the damage was later made good, the replacement was one of the circular constructions which were then growing in strategic importance.

Round towers

Curved surfaces were increasingly used in keeps and bastions to eliminate the vulnerable angles of rectilinear fortifications. It was easier for assailants to weaken sharp corners than a smooth arc. Although great square towers continued to be erected, strengthened by buttresses and thicker walls, throughout the thirteenth century there was a growing tendency to rely on curved wall faces. These remained popular until the impact of cannon made a complete re-thinking necessary.

Pembroke castle has a round keep nearly 80 feet high, with four storeys, the entrance being on the first floor. It is in Wales but is in every sense an English castle: the Norman lords of the region built it to guard their Welsh holdings, and consolidated it early in the thirteenth century with this most imposing of all round towers. Along the Welsh Marches were several others, much smaller, set upon mottes. At Longtown in Herefordshire are remains of a contemporary tower on a mound in the shadow of the Black Mountains.

At Launceston in Cornwall a round tower was set within the shell keep referred to earlier.

At Launceston, Cornwall, a round tower has been set within the original shell keep on its motte, and linked with the reinforced outer bailey.

Circular bastions and gatehouse drum towers appeared in the defences of, among many others, Goodrich in Herefordshire, Dover, Whittington gatehouse in Shropshire, and Skipton in Yorkshire. The modern visitor will find other interesting features in Skipton. Its old castle moat is attractively incorporated in a shady canal running through the town; and within the castle gateway is a grotto of seashells and fossils collected by one of the Clifford family, the 'Sailor Earl' of Cumberland, on his travels.

On an unusually low-lying, unprotected site by the river Nene in Northamptonshire, Barnwell castle is built to a square plan with circular bastions which looks very much like an early sketch for the next development – Edward I's more complex Welsh fortifications.

Concentric castles

This next significant expansion in castle building happened in the late thirteenth century, and in

Wales rather than England. But, like those at Chepstow and Pembroke, they were essentially English castles erected at key points to keep the turbulent Welsh under control.

As well as hammering the Scots, Edward I mounted two major campaigns against the Welsh and was determined that there should be no major repetition of troubles along the Marches. At Rhuddlan, Caernarvon, Conway, Beaumaris, Kidwelly and other sentinel sites he used cylindrical barbicans and bastions in a sequence of defensive walls much more cunningly devised than any straightforward bailey wall, however sturdy. The idea was to set concentric circles of walls about the heart of the castle, so that even if an outer bailey or ward were overrun the enemy would still be faced with a daunting inner wall – and maybe yet another. Each inner wall was higher than its outer ring, so that while trying to seize the outer defences the attackers would be subjected to defensive fire from above. The heaviest fortifications would be those of the inner ward, with mighty gatehouses and corner towers. In addition to all the other hazards, the attacker would find that gateways through the successive walls were staggered, so that he had to hurry round within the ward – under fire the whole time – to assault the next entrance.

Greatest of all these castles in Wales, and one of the most magnificent in the British Isles, is Caerphilly. With its formidable fortifications and its complicated system of moats and lakes, it was virtually impregnable until the invention of long-range artillery. In one corner, a drum tower sliced through and leaning outwards recalls an attempt to destroy it during the Civil War.

Ghosts and echoes

Souvenirs of bitter campaigns, personal triumphs and tragedies, royal humiliations and deeds of valour linger in many a crumbling fortress. Prisoners' pitiful laments are scratched into stone walls; coats of arms over gateways or in ceiling bosses and panelling recall noble owners, and tell a more detailed story when the marshalling of different arms in the quartering of the escutcheon records marriages and high official appointments; and a faded cloak, a sheathed sword, an old refectory table can evoke the drama of the past more vividly than any well-annotated museum can do.

Not all the ghosts and old rituals are too solemn; which does not mean that they are not

significant. In 978 the young King Edward was murdered at Corfe castle by his stepmother, who with her son Ethelred, his successor, later did penance by granting the Benedictine nunnery at Shaftesbury rich endowments. Today Corfe's ruins, a testimony to a Civil War assault, are the scene of an annual ceremony when, every Shrove Tuesday, the Ancient Order of Purbeck Marblers install new members and kick a ball along the road to Swanage and back, asserting their traditional rights over the route to the harbour from which Purbeck marble was once shipped.

At Berkeley castle in Gloucestershire it is almost too easy to summon up the shade of Edward II. Below the room in which he was imprisoned by his wife and her lover is a shaft which might be taken for a well, but was in fact used as a pit for rotting animal carcases, from whose contamination captives in the chamber sickened and died. Edward II did not succumb speedily enough, and was finally despatched by a red-hot spit thrust into his entrails. In view of the enormity of her crimes, his widow's subsequent incarceration in Castle Rising, Norfolk, was fairly easy-going; but still there are local tales of remorseful screams resounding through the keep late at night.

Berkeley's earlier mementoes include one from the founder of the original Saxon fort here. The Godwin Cup is a silver chalice from which Earl Godwin, father of the Harold who met his death outside Hastings, took daily communion until, having one day forgotten his devotions, he met disaster. It is difficult, however, to think of his being very assiduous in his religious observances: in order to build here, he destroyed a convent on the site and murdered its nuns.

In June 1215, while King John was lodged at Windsor, the barons assembled at Berkeley, before their meeting at Runnymede. And displayed within the castle today are a sea chest and other items associated with Sir Francis Drake.

Furnishings and ornaments of many family castles tell much of the family's own story against a backdrop of mightier events. Hever in Kent was the scene of Henry VIII's courtship of Anne Boleyn. Sir Walter Raleigh built Sherborne in Dorset, which became the home of the Earls of Bristol for more than three centuries. Dunster in Somerset was in a thousand years owned by only two families. The Luttrells of Dunster held out for the Royalists during the Civil War, and

Fourteenth-century Bolton castle in Wensleydale.

behind the village inn bearing their name can still be traced the mounds from which the Roundheads bombarded the castle.

Many a building rings with echoes of the wayward Mary, Queen of Scots. When she fled from her opponents in Scotland to beg shelter from her cousin Elizabeth I, she proved a great embarrassment. Opinions were divided as to the greater danger: her abduction back to Scotland, or her remaining in England to foment trouble and assert her own claims to the English throne. For a while she was lodged in Carlisle, but this was dangerously close to the border, and she was moved to Bolton castle in Yorkshire. The Earl of Shrewsbury was ordered to prepare more palatial, but closely guarded, accommodation for her in his castle at Tutbury on the border of Staffordshire and Derbyshire – the preparations were made in such haste that he and his wife had to move all their own expensive hangings from their home in Sheffield castle.

Mary's final home before her death was at Fotheringhay castle in Northamptonshire. All that remains of her prison is the shape of the motte and bailey, but there is one other grim local relic: a farmhouse, once a medieval hostel, where Mary's executioner is believed to have spent the night before he met her at the block.

In the custody of Bolton castle is something more mundane, for which ordinary folk in the past have had good reason to be grateful. It is the Bainbridge horn, still sounded nightly between Holy Cross Day in September until the beginning of Lent. In earlier times this acted as a guide to travellers lost in the dark woods of Wensleydale, and although superseded by modern direction-finding methods its tradition is proudly maintained by a local family.

The majority of English monarchs were for centuries buried in Westminster abbey, though Richard I joined his father at Fontevrault save for his bowels, which were buried at Chaluz, and his brother John was buried by his own wish at Worcester save for his heart, which also went – in a golden cup – to Fontevrault. Edward IV and Henry VIII, however, ended at Windsor, and it was to Henry VIII's vault that the decapitated corpse of Charles I was brought one February

night in 1649 to be wrapped in lead and buried without any religious ceremony. George II was the last to be laid in Westminster abbey. After him, all Hanoverian descendants are to be found at Windsor, though Queen Victoria and her consort, Prince Albert, lie outside the castle itself in a garish mausoleum of her own devising. During the First World War the name of Windsor became truly royal, when King George V bowed to popular condemnation of all things German and relinquished his Hanover and Saxe-Coburg-Gotha names and titles.

Does anybody nowadays ever read Harrison Ainsworth's melodramatic novel, *Windsor Castle*, with the spectral Herne the Hunter forever haunting Windsor Great Park? To my youthful taste he was always a more congenial writer than Sir Walter Scott, though Scott certainly had an insatiable appetite for castle settings: *Peveril of the Peak* in Derbyshire, the tale of *Marmion* at Norham in Northumberland, and of course the saga of *Kenilworth*.

Castellated manors

Gunpowder and cannonballs were not the only reasons for the castle's decline in importance. The virtual end of baronial struggles after the Wars of the Roses, and England's growing power and prosperity in Tudor times, left little need for private fortresses within the country. Henry VIII indulged in one last bout of castle building when anticipating an invasion but, as we have noted earlier, these structures were not residential and not designed for lasting use once the immediate crisis was over.

Comfort began to take precedence over security. A warm and graceful residence was preferable to a chill stone box. Even within stone walls there had been various attempts to incorporate manor houses, often in the outer bailey, with the keep fulfilling its old rôle as the last refuge.

Stokesay, a Saxon manor house fortified in the late thirteenth century by a Norman wool merchant from Ludlow in Shropshire.

Stokesay in Shropshire embodies several successive phases of medieval life. An originally unfortified hall was strengthened in the late thirteenth century when its owner, a rich wool merchant, was given royal permission to crenellate – that is, to install battlements and provide himself with a token fortress. In the following century another hall was built, and in the sixteenth a gatehouse was added, though of little military value: it stands as an attractive half-timbered flourish, decorative rather than defensive.

Tattershall in Lincolnshire, built in the mid-fifteenth century, looks like a mighty rectangular keep, but its slim red brick construction and spacious windows were those of an impressive private residence rather than a fortification.

The manor house was becoming the favoured residence of the local lord or squire, though some retained assertive imitations of crenellation along demesne walls and rooftops. We find ourselves moving on to the elegance of Compton Wynyates, largely built with material from derelict Fulbrook castle, of Hatfield House and Audley End, and of edifices which call themselves castles but have long ceased to be so. Belvoir castle, home of the dukes of Rutland, was a ruin by the sixteenth century, but in the nineteenth century was re-equipped with turrets and towers, and crenellated with pseudo-Gothic exuberance.

At Wingfield in Suffolk, the last privately inhabited castle in the county has its fourteenth-century battlements joined to a delightful Tudor manor house.

It would seem that the last building in England to be specifically commissioned as a castle in the true sense of the word was Thornbury in Gloucestershire, and even this was not completed according to plan. Work started in 1511 at the behest of the Duke of Buckingham, but stopped 10 years later when he fell victim to the headsman's axe at Tower hill on a trumped-up charge of treason. What remains is a pot-pourri of fortification and fantasy, with remarkably ornate chimneys and spacious bay windows which would have proved easily destructible in any genuine assault or siege.

NORTHUMBRIA

NOT UNTIL THE seventeenth century could those living along the unstable border with Scotland emulate their more relaxed southern cousins, give up building solid fastnesses for themselves, their families, retainers and livestock, and turn to the more civilized pleasures of comfortable dwelling-houses with ample windows. Neatly symbolic examples of the transition can be found at Belsay and Chipchase, where in each instance castellated towers built in the fourteenth century were supplemented after the Union of the English and Scottish Crowns in 1603 by Jacobean manor houses.

By the early eighteenth century it was possible for one of the few local families of Norman lineage to commission Vanbrugh, who had already distinguished himself at Castle Howard in Yorkshire, to design the baroque Seaton Delaval Hall, near which the Delavals were soon profiting from their coal mines, a glassworks, and a harbour through which their products were shipped.

At Belsay another hall was built in the early nineteenth century, with fine gardens in the hollows from which the stone had been quarried. In order to complete his aesthetic pleasure, the owner then removed all his tenants from their village, demolished it, and housed them in a new one out of his sight.

Later in that century the inventive Victorian architect, Norman Shaw, created a picturesque country mansion, Cragside, on an awkward and challenging slope above the vale of the river

By the time of Lord Armstrong's death in 1900 his Cragside grounds covered 1,730 acres, planted with 7 million trees around a string of lakes and paths.

Coquet near Rothbury. It is a remarkable mélange of romantic effects, complete with timbered tower, moulded chimney-stacks, gargoyles, and ornamental flourishes in stone; but from a more practical point of view can boast of having been the first private house in the country to be lit throughout by electricity. Although a symptom of late nineteenth-century prosperity, when one could not merely live unperturbed in an unfortified house but surround oneself with pleasure grounds, hundreds of trees and rhododendrons, the money to subsidize all this came, as so many other things in the neighbourhood have done, from battle: Sir William Armstrong, later Lord Armstrong, who commissioned it, was inventor of the Armstrong gun and an armaments manufacturer whose business by the turn of the century rivalled that of Krupp.

Elsewhere, the most immediately striking features of human habitation in this region are nearly all related to a history of border conflict with Picts and Scots. At Corbridge the pele tower, one of many small defensive forts across the county, is made from the stones of an older defence – the Roman station at Corstopitum, south of Hadrian's Wall. In the town of Hexham, often attacked by the Scots and burnt to the ground in 1296, there must once have been a makeshift castle consisting of the Manor Office and Moot Hall joined by a curtain wall. The Manor Office was built almost entirely of Roman stones between 1330 and 1332. Erected on the orders of the Archbishop of York, it was the first building in this country to be conceived specifically as a prison and was in use until 1824. The first gaoler was a Hexham barber. In the base-

The Roman milestone on the Stanegate near Chesterholm (Vindolanda) is the only one in Britain still standing in its original position.

ment are preserved its old dungeon and stocks.

A little way north of Hexham is a place of less imposing aspect which nevertheless owes much of its appearance to what was filched from Hadrian's Wall. The farm buildings of Acomb village are obviously of Roman stone, contrasting with a rare example of early Northumbrian brickwork in the garden wall and entrance of Acomb House. Even the font in Chollerton church has been taken over from an altar to Jupiter. It is remarkable that after so many depredations any of the wall itself should still survive.

Hadrian's Wall

Before the Emperor Hadrian decreed in A.D. 122 that the northern limit of the province of Britain should be clearly delineated and defended along a line between the Tyne and the Solway, there had been intermittent attempts to establish barriers against Pictish marauders from their barbarian haunts. Remains of a high bank and ditch known as Scot's Dyke can still be traced across Yorkshire between the Swale and the Tees, and there is a chain of Roman camps all the way up the Vale of York. Iron Age hill forts such as Yeavering Bell, and the height of Witchy Neuk above the river Coquet, were reoccupied and strengthened with stone defences. Agricola's northern campaigns between A.D. 78 and 84 resulted in the marking out of a frontier which he felt could be held along the Stanegate, a road through the Tyne Gap linking camps and fortifications from the eastern side of the country to the west. At Chesterholm (Vindolanda) some ramparts and gateways are now conserved by the Department of the Environment, and here a Roman milestone stands in its original position, with the base of another a mile or so to the west.

Dere Street, wide enough to take two chariots or supply waggons abreast, was driven north from Corbridge to allow swift troop movements over the border, its route closely followed by the modern A68 past the hummocks of innumerable small hill forts; and the Devil's Causeway nearer the coast is another Roman road.

But Hadrian's Wall remains unchallengeably the most substantial testimony to Roman determination and Roman engineering. Its full length was 73 miles (80 Roman miles); originally its western section consisted only of an earthwork, and the eastern section of stone. For much of the way it made good use of the natural barricade of the Whin Sill's volcanic rock escarpment. At each mile stood a small fort or milecastle, with two watch-towers in between, and a number of detached turrets continued down the Cumbrian coast. Larger forts with garrisons ready to be deployed as required were set into the wall or some distance back from it. On the defenders' side of the rampart was a ditch known as the vallum, and between wall and vallum ran a military road.

The eastern extremity gives its name to Wallsend. Many traces have been obliterated by the growth of Newcastle-upon-Tyne and Tyneside industry – though the city makes amends by the scope of its University Museum, with relics from the wall and model reconstructions of major features – but here and there some fragments come to the surface. In Wallsend itself, a Methodist church has been built beside a few overgrown courses of Roman pavement. A suburban garden in Broombridge Avenue at Benwell preserves the outline of a temple to the god Antenociticus, and nearby is a brief slice of the vallum. Stony courses of the actual wall emerge at Denton Burn and Heddon-on-the-Wall, disappear, and really begin to come out in their full awesomeness beyond Limestone Corner towards Carrawburgh and Housesteads, where one gets the real feeling of what life must have been like for the legionaries in these bleak, hostile outposts.

Each of the main forts or supply depots is worth a visit. Corbridge, or Corstopitum, was established on the junction of Stanegate and Dere Street some 30 or 40 years before Hadrian ordained the construction of his wall. In due course it became a military supply and repair centre – a sort of REME depot of its time – whose importance lasted until the ultimate abandonment of Britain by Rome. Only the foundations remain, but they are solid enough to mark out a whole pattern of shops, storehouses, granaries, temples and military compounds. Some of the treasures unearthed on the site are displayed in the accompanying museum. As a front-line town only a few miles back from the wall itself, it must have faced many dangers in its time; but one wonders what its hard-bitten conscripts would have made of the modern sign which greets one on entry:

DANGER: KEEP CHILDREN UNDER CONTROL

And what would a centurion from the next major establishment along the wall, at Chesters, have thought of spending a leisurely weekend's leave in the admirable George Hotel by Chollerford Bridge half a mile away – or his legionaries of strolling along for a pint in the cosy public bar?

On the slopes above Fallowfield, between Hexham and Chollerton, lies a ridge of sandstone into which are chiselled letters immortalizing one PETRA FLAVI CARANTINI. It seems feasible that Flavius Carantinus may have been foreman of a fatigue party quarrying stones from this ridge for the wall.

Chesters (Cilurnum) is no mere ordnance base but a fort straddling the wall itself, with a road from the south crossing the North Tyne. The bridge abutments of this all-important thoroughfare survive in the form of huge stones, collapsing sideways yet still retaining enough of the original shape to make the thrust of the route quite plain. On the north bank the cavalry fort itself has impressive guardian gateways, accommodation for officers and men, bath-houses with hypocausts, a chapel, and regimental headquarters with a strongroom below the paymaster's office.

Along various stretches of the ridge it is possible to identify remnants of milecastles and turrets. There are examples at Denton Hall, at Brunton near Chollerford, and across the Cumbrian border at Banks East.

Housesteads (Vercovicium), about halfway between Chesters and another river crossing at Gilsland, was well guarded by ponderous gateways and guardrooms; and to the south incorporated a community of garrison families and retired soldiers, some of whom set up shops to serve the fort, including a tavern in which excavations have revealed below the floor a skeleton with a knife blade still in its ribs – unhappy victim, perhaps, of a drunken taproom brawl! There was also, as in many military settlements, a temple to Mithras, Persian god of light and fertility whose cult was carried by legionaries even to these dark and infertile outposts of Empire. A full-size replica has been reconstructed in Newcastle.

Buildings at Housesteads remained sturdy enough to serve as hideouts for a gang of horse and cattle rustlers who plagued the surrounding

countryside in the late sixteenth and early seventeenth centuries.

At Gilsland, the garden of the former vicarage is divided by a double height of wall, a narrow segment on a broader foundation; and, as at Chesters, there are remains of a bridge abutment by the river. It was here that Sir Walter Scott, romantically inspired by the historic surroundings, became engaged to Charlotte Margaret Carpenter at the Spa Hotel – now a convalescent home for miners.

Many times the wall was overrun, and many times repaired. But at last the Romans went; and their successors shunned their handiwork.

The first English kingdom

Although Angles and Saxons were eventually to accept the leadership of Wessex in administration of the country and resistance to invaders from across the North Sea, the first kingdom of any consequence was undoubtedly Northumbria. Even late on in the negotiations between these petty monarchies, Northumbria still proudly refused to enter into wholehearted alliance with Wessex.

After the remaining Romano-Britons of the north and north-east had been defeated by Anglian tribes, there were at first two small principalities in the region: Deira, with its capital at York, dominating a large part of Yorkshire up to the Tees, and Bernicia between the Tees and the Forth with its royal palace at Yeavering. In about 605 these united under Ethelfrith to form the kingdom of Northumbria, taking in considerable tracts of what are now Cumbria and Scotland, and in its heyday spreading as far south as the Mersey.

The capital was at Bamburgh, named after Ethelfrith's wife Bebba, though today's heavily restored castle on the coastal outcrop of the Whin Sill bears few traces of the Anglian fort save for its well, which was dug 145 feet down through solid basalt. Round this well Henry II was later to build one of his massive keeps: not from the hard local rock but with stones brought in by sea. In 651 Penda of Mercia, unable to subdue it by seige, tried to set fire to what was by now a fortified town rather than a single castle. The Venerable Bede records that Bishop Aidan, then

The sweep of Hadrian's Wall at Cuddy's Crag, near Housesteads fort, which was set into the wall itself to guard a vulnerable gap to the east.

living on Farne some two miles out from Bamburgh, saw the smoke and flame rising and offered up a prayer, whereupon

The wind shifted away from the city, and drove back the flames on to those who had kindled them, so wounding and unnerving them that they abandoned their attack on a city so clearly under the protection of God.

Unfortunately this immunity did not last. By the end of the seventh century Mercia was asserting itself as the more powerful kingdom. And then came the Norsemen.

First there were sporadic Viking raids such as that in 793 on the Holy Island of Lindisfarne and on other richly endowed religious communities at Wearmouth and Jarrow, and as far round as the Isle of Man and Iona. Over the decades the pirate attacks of individual Scandinavian chieftains seeking easy loot were concentrated into a more determined invasion until in 865 a 'great heathen host' conquered Northumbria and went on to subdue Mercia. It was during these all-out campaigns that Edmund of East Anglia was martyred.

When King Alfred the Great of Wessex finally reached a peace settlement with the Danish Guthrum in 886, it was agreed that the Danes should occupy a region known as the Danelaw, east of a boundary formed by the river Lea and Watling Street. Within that segment we find ourselves to this day using names bestowed on towns and villages by the invaders. The *by* ending to Grimsby, Whitby, and many others signifies a town or village, or even a substantial farming community. Sometimes the identification is with a natural feature, sometimes with a person: Thornby is a settlement by a thorn bush; Rugby that of Hroca's people, and Aislaby in County Durham that of Aslakr. Asgarby in Lincolnshire is obviously Danish through and through. *Toft* means a homestead, and *thorpe* a minor settlement, as in Astonthorpe near Aston in Yorkshire. And not only place names came into the language: the common Norse word for stone-walled circular pens into which shepherds round up their sheep, a stell (or stall), is used on the fells to this day.

Northumberland, as opposed to the broader kingdom of Northumbria, assimilated fewer Danes, their ways and their speech, than did the region which was to become Yorkshire, whose 'Ridings' derive from the Danish 'thrithings' or thirds. But they are to be found here and there,

St Wilfrid's original bishop's seat in Hexham abbey later became a frith stool ('frith' denoting freedom from molestation) for those seeking sanctuary. Right: *Corbridge pele tower.*

along with earlier and later accents; and the modern Tynesider's vowel sounds, and some slurred consonants, are remarkably similar to those heard in Jutland.

There is an early Danish cross in Middleton church, Yorkshire; and below Hadleigh church in Suffolk was buried the Danish King Guthrum, though not under the anachronistic canopy now known as Guthrum's Tomb.

The comparatively peaceful settlement of the Danelaw was by no means the end of strife for the north. After Northumbria had rebelled against William the Conqueror and offered the crown of their kingdom to Sweyn of Denmark, William burned and slaughtered his way through their land, and demolished large areas of York to make way for improved defences. Then Edward I's hammering of the Scots brought upon Northum-

bria much of the grief that Belgium knew under the combatants of the First World War. The paucity of towns and even of villages with any long history in these borderlands is due less to the bleakness of the landscape and climate than to its constant exposure to wars and brigandage.

Quite apart from royal and dynastic conflicts, even as late as the end of the sixteenth century an estimate of recent murders passed the 1,000 mark, with losses of property amounting to £100,000. On both sides of the evanescent border it was as common to go out pillaging as it had been for the Danes, centuries earlier, to harry the English coasts from their longships. In Wallington, the great house near Cambo, is a somewhat florid panel painting depicting the local custom of a lady serving her husband at table with a pair of spurs to hint that food supplies had reached a low ebb. On this signal it was usual for him to ride out with his retainers, steal whatever livestock might be available, and burn farm or village behind him in the hope of forestalling retaliation.

The defeat of the Scots under James IV at Flodden Field – where, near Branxton, a memorial grieves for the dead of both nations – did nothing to check Scottish incursions: indeed the bitterness of the defeat brought on more violent decades of marauding and murder. Powerful lords might strengthen their castles or beg royal permission to crenellate their homes. But they were not numerous enough to guarantee the safety of the entire population. Each community had to find its own most appropriate defence.

The shape of Northumbrian villages and large farms was markedly conditioned by this prime consideration. Village greens were spacious, and always within the village rather than on its fringe. The straggling, extended 'street village' of the Midlands and southern England was almost unknown. Tightly surrounded by a stockade of houses, the green served as a refuge when beasts had to be driven in from their grazing through openings then sealed off by lidgates. Heighington in County Durham is almost a textbook example of such a community.

But determined raiders might still break in, and then some stronger protection was needed. As a last resort, a castle had its keep. Echoing this on a smaller scale, in many a lonely village and even above the enclosed yards of farms there appeared pele towers. The Latin *palus*, a stake, first gave its name to the enclosure within the walls or stockade, but then came to denote the

actual building rather than the area it protected. These stone towers had accommodation for the most valuable animals in a vaulted basement, while farm workers or villagers took shelter on floors above. Where possible the tower was adjoined by a barmkin, or fortified courtyard, into which other beasts were herded. Since it was common for raiders to carry off not only cattle and valuables but, if the opportunity offered, some local dignitary in the hope of ransom or simply to kill him at leisure, such worthies installed their own towers. Parsons, in particular, needed a private refuge: the tower of Ancroft church is virtually a pele in itself; the Norman fabric of Kirknewton church was rebuilt during the early fourteenth century quite deliberately as a stronghold; and there are many fortified vicarages, as at Embleton and Elsdon, with their vicar's pele.

Another form of defence for people of consequence was the square bastle (from 'bastille') in which a local squire might hope to hold out until neighbours or his tenants could come to his rescue. Hebburn Tower is one of these, on the edge of parkland at Chillingham where one may inspect living examples of another historic strain – wild white cattle, the only pure descendants of the oxen which roamed this country 700 years ago.

A village which epitomizes the whole tenor of life hereabouts is that of Elsdon. Nestling below barebacked hills which are velvety in some lights, sinister in others, often seeming part of the cloudscape, it seems to be situated in a foolishly vulnerable position, long bereft of its Norman motte-and-bailey castle. Enemies could come over those hills with little warning; or, even more easily, could sneak up through the hidden clefts of the vale. Yet its accessibility is the main reason for its being here in the first place. When the English and the Scots were at peace, this was a junction of drove roads along which cattle would be driven from the north to the markets of the south. Elsdon village green was itself a marketplace. When there was either outright war or an outbreak of rustling by Scottish reivers, the green became a place of refuge surrounded by its houses, with the vicar's pele at the head of the slope.

On a track a couple of miles north of Elsdon are the remains of what was once another, lonelier pele tower known as Raw Pele, used now as a cattle shelter, which was also probably one of its original functions. In 1791 it had been occupied for some years by an elderly woman who used it as a general shop supplying clothes and materials to local farmers' and miners' wives. One morning she was found stabbed to death, with a blood-stained knife in the bed beside her. The murderer was soon identified as William Winter, one of a band of gypsies who lived on their wits. Some items stolen from Raw Pele were still in the possession of Winter and the women who accompanied him. Found guilty, he was hanged at Newcastle. The tarred corpse was brought back to the neighbourhood of the crime and hung from a gibbet set into the stone socket of Steng Cross, above the road between Elsdon and Morpeth. When the body had rotted away it was replaced by a wooden dummy, and today, known as Winter's Stob, has a wooden head still dangling from it.

Some surviving pele towers have been equipped with more spacious windows in place of their old slits. That at Cambo – the village where 'Capability' Brown of nearby Kirkharle went to school – has become the post office. Two have been turned into inns: the Craster Arms at Beadnell, with a coat of arms declaring 'While there's life there's hope', and the Blackbird Inn at Ponteland where the pele has been stylishly amalgamated with a neighbouring Jacobean manor house.

The most northerly fortification in England, and its most northerly town, is that of Berwick-upon-Tweed. Founded in the ninth century as Anglo-Saxon Berwick, a 'Barley Farm', it belonged sometimes to England, sometimes to Scotland, changing hands three or four times every century until 1483. Edward I enclosed it in protective walls, renewed within a smaller compass by Elizabeth I between 1558 and 1590 when she feared a combination of Scots and French against her.

In 1611 James I ordered a stone bridge to connect the town with Tweedmouth across the estuary. From the times of the Roman route of the Devil's Causeway, through Norman, medieval, Tudor and modern times this was always a key road to the north. The last splendid spanning of the river was by the Royal Tweed bridge in 1928; but perhaps a more impressive sight is that

The Hope Wallace Memorial stands on Maiden Way near Featherstone Common and castle and was erected in memory of a husband lost in the First World War.

of Stephenson's Royal Border bridge which, together with his High Level bridge at Newcastle-upon-Tyne, completed the railway link to Edinburgh from south of the Tyne – though at the cost of a large part of Berwick's Norman castle, ravaged to make way for the station.

In spite of the Union of Crowns and, in 1707, the Act of Union which formally made the two countries one, the Scots still had some shots in their locker. In 1715 there was an attempt by supporters of the discredited and discarded Stuart monarchy to overthrow George I. This was a miserable failure, but in 1745 the Young Pretender, Prince Charles Edward Stuart, grandson of James II, landed in Scotland and at first seemed to pose a serious threat to George II. He marched south as far as Derby and, although driven back and finally defeated by the Duke of Cumberland at Culloden, left behind him a legacy involving both construction and destruction. When Bonnie Prince Charlie was on his apparently triumphal progress down the west side of the Pennines, General Wade's main army was on the east. To cut the invader off, Wade had to attempt a dash across country by the old road through Ovingham and Hexham towards Carlisle. It was little more than a muddy trackway, and en route a bridge over a stream collapsed; and then another. During the post-mortem on the Jacobite insurrection it was agreed that a secure road from Newcastle to Carlisle was essential against any such future eventuality; and in 1751 Parliament passed an Act authorizing its construction. On Wade's recommendation, much of the route from Newcastle westwards was set upon the ready-made base of Hadrian's Wall or its accompanying military road – involving the greatest damage done to the wall before or since.

Lords and landlords

Certain family names have their living or lingering resonance in districts which will forever be associated with them, often harmonious in spite of past excesses or blunders, but sometimes with a sour undertone. Baronial and squirearchal influences have left their imprint on the shapes of fields, the positioning of villages and parish churches, and even on the conformations of our supposedly modernized towns and cities: a name on a monument, a street, or an inn; hatchments and marble tombs in ornate chapels; and the styles and costs of building schemes dictated by the enlightenment or greed of those inheriting magnates' properties in the heart of London.

There have been the influential Sidneys, Pelhams and Sackvilles of the south; the Norfolk Howards; the Cecil clan who dominated so much of Tudor and Jacobean political and social life, and remained deeply entrenched within the conclaves of the twentieth-century Conservative party; and four ducal dynasties huddled so closely together in Nottinghamshire as to have their estates dubbed the Dukeries.

Some families divided, the better to infiltrate and conquer. But many in Norman times, though apparently rich in widespread grants from the Conqueror, had their work cut out to maintain all their scattered establishments. It was rare for any one baron, no matter how favoured, to be given a succession of properties in one region: by distributing them around different parts of the country, a wise king made it difficult for any would-be rebel to assemble a sizeable feudal army in any one spot.

At one period there existed a Lord Dacre of the North and a Lord Dacre of the South. This came about when in 1440 a Fiennes of Herstmonceux in Sussex married a Dacre heiress from Gilsland and was allowed to assume her family title. Little credit was brought upon this branch when, in the time of Henry VIII, a young Lord Dacre of the South was brought to trial charged with having, during a madcap poaching expedition, murdered the gamekeeper of his Pelham neighbour. He was found guilty and executed on Tower Hill. During that same reign the Dacre who administered Hexhamshire acquired a reputation for ruthless efficiency in the matter of keeping Hexham's large gaol fully occupied.

After the Conquest a large area of Northumbria had been shared out between two Norman barons. The Baliol family possessions were soon strung out in a rich chain from Bailleul in France to Scotland. In the middle of the thirteenth century, John de Baliol founded Balliol college, Oxford, which was granted the revenues of almost half the town and surrounding lands of Stamfordham. His son John contested the Scottish succession and in 1291 was awarded the Crown by Edward I's commissioners in preference to rival claimants, among them a Robert Bruce whose grandson was later to achieve greater success. The family built the original castle at Bywell, and associated themselves with one of the two parish churches there. Bywell stands on the boundary of their estate with that of the Bolbecs, a boundary

marked for much of the way by the March Burn.

In 1165 Walter de Bolbec invited 12 White Canons of a Premonstratensian foundation in Leicestershire to settle on his land by the banks of the river Derwent. Here they built an abbey and named it after the order's birthplace, Blanche Land in Normandy, which in English duly became Blanchland. In what remains of the abbey church there are some interesting tombstones, among which we find the abbey forester with carved representations of an arrow, his sword, and his horn with a baldrick; and also a stone ornamented with the outline of a pair of scissors, the symbol once denoting a woman – an odd memorial to find in a male monastic community.

Until the Dissolution of the Monasteries, the abbot lodged in what is now a hotel, the Lord Crewe Arms. This conjures up the presence of another influential local family. At the end of the seventeenth century Lord Crewe, Bishop of Durham, married the heiress to the estates of Blanchland and Bamburgh (where there is also a Lord Crewe Arms), paying off mortgages on them and setting up a charitable trust for their administration. Blanchland village is near the old

Blanchland post office is built into a range of the old abbey, and retains a Victorian post-box with warnings against despatching unregistered coins.

Lead Road over the moors, and even in the monks' time they had found it worth while to operate a small refinery for the extraction of silver in which the local ore was rich. Crewe trustees in the middle of the eighteenth century rebuilt the village to house the miners. The result is an appealing picture in creamy brown stone, with roofing of heavy stone slates cut from Pennine sandstone. But who, other than the late Victorians, could have allowed the school, with its walls admirably matching the surroundings, to be roofed with nasty, thin, grey-green slate?

The hotel retains not only a fine vault to serve as its public bar, but historic associations with the first Jacobite rising, when Lord Crewe's nephew and niece by marriage supported the Stuarts and, so the story goes, the girl Dorothy had at one stage to rescue her brother from Newgate and hide him here.

The Greys, too, are to be found woven into the fabric of Northumbrian history. It was the four-

The Percy stone (or cross) near Otterburn.

critics were to accuse him of indecision in tackling the problems which led up to the First World War.

But without question the Northumbrian family most famed within and beyond its own borders is that of the Percys.

Their northern estates were founded by yet another of the Conqueror's adherents, William de Percy. A Percy was among the barons framing the terms of Magna Carta. In 1346 the Percys stood with the Nevilles of Westmorland and a feudal levy against an attempted invasion by David Bruce, who had been king of Scotland until driven out by Edward III and the Baliol pretender supported by Edward. Bruce hoped to take advantage of the absence of English armies in France, but was defeated near Durham and began 11 years of imprisonment. A ruined cross at Neville's Cross commemorates the battle.

Henry Percy's exploits against the Scots, including the re-taking of Berwick during one of its frequent shuttlecock spells, were rewarded by his being created Marshal of England by Richard II and, later, Earl of Northumberland. Nevertheless he and the Nevilles turned against Richard and helped put Henry IV on the throne, whereupon the earl was given the further appointment of Constable of England. His son, nicknamed Hotspur, married a Mortimer and won such favour that he came into possession of a number of Welsh castles and estates along the Marches.

In 1388 a Scottish contingent under the Earl of Douglas met English forces under Harry Hotspur near Otterburn. This battle of Chevy Chase inspired a ballad which has helped to confuse a number of issues. The outcome itself was confusing. Douglas was killed, but the English lost the battle and Hotspur was taken prisoner. Burial mounds of the dead can be seen near Elsdon. The commemorative obelisk some half a mile from the actual battlefield is known as the Percy Stone or Percy Cross: it dates only from 1777, and is set in the socket of an original pillar which at some stage mysteriously disappeared.

In due course Hotspur found himself on the same side as his captors when, in alliance with a Douglas and other Scottish malcontents, the Percys came out against Henry IV. Hotspur was killed at the battle of Shrewsbury in 1403; his father, Earl of Northumberland, died at Bramham Moor in Yorkshire in 1408. Henry V later restored the title to one of Hotspur's sons.

Another Percy's Cross stands near Wooperton

teenth-century Sir Thomas Grey, besieged in Norham, to whose rescue the gallant Marmion came. A Royalist Grey took Bamburgh during the Civil War, only to have the defences pounded away about him by Cromwellian cannon. Backworth House, in our day a golf club-house and miners' recreation centre, was built for an eighteenth-century Grey. Grey Street is not merely the most splendid street in Newcastle but surely worthy to stand beside Nash's original concept of London's Regent Street. In this century we have had Grey of Fallodon, who as Sir Edward Grey was the first British foreign secretary to break away from the almost obligatory use of French in all diplomatic proceedings and insist on speaking English. His international achievements before 1914 were considerable, though

An inscription on the 1816
'Farmers' Folly' column at Alnwick
dedicates it 'To Hugh, Duke of Northumberland,
by a grateful and united tenantry'.

– a 10-foot sandstone pillar with the family emblems carved into all four sides. Near here the Percys and Nevilles clashed in 1464. Their alliance against external enemies had long since

turned to mutual hatred, and in spite of Parliamentary decrees against Tynedale brigandage they indulged in private wars which devastated the borderlands. Naturally they took opposite sides during the Wars of the Roses, when the struggle between Yorkist and Lancastrian claimants to the throne resembled Chicago gangster feuds rather than any highly principled royal duelling. On that April day in 1464, when Yorkists under Sir John Neville met Lancastrians under Sir Ralph Percy at Hedgeley Moor, Sir Ralph met his death. As well as the Wooperton pillar there are other features associated with him: Percy's Well, at which he is said to have paused for a drink during the fray; and Percy's Leap, two stones marking the 12 yards he is supposed to have sprung after the blow which caused his death.

The Percy insignia of a lion with stiffly jutting tail appears in scores of diverse locations, and dominates the town of Alnwick, the family's principal seat. It is carved above the entrance to their castle, and on the Hotspur Gate which once guarded the main road into the town. But the lion is most conspicuous on top of an 80-foot column dwarfing the war memorial by the old Great North Road into Alnwick from the Morpeth direction. This is officially known as the Tenantry Column; but from the moment of its completion was dubbed 'Farmers' Folly'.

When England was at war with France early in the nineteenth century, shortage of imported food meant big profits for native farmers. The second Duke of Northumberland decided to appropriate a share of these profits by tripling and quadrupling his tenant farmers' rents. When England was at peace again, prices tumbled, but the most the duke would concede to the tenants was a 25 per cent cut. To show their appreciation, the farmers clubbed together to erect a column in his honour – but so many went bankrupt or had to abandon their farms that the money ran out, and the duke himself generously finished it.

MERCIA

WHATEVER FOLLIES or misfortunes afflicted the farmers of the North, for a long time they suffered less from the appropriations which were to transform the rest of the country, in particular altering the whole face of the Midlands. We tend to think of our familiar hedgerow patterns and tidily domesticated fields as being essentially English; but in fact this patchwork landscape did not really begin to come into being until the middle of the eighteenth century.

Field and forest
Geology, history, and the development of new farming methods have all played their part in the scene stretched out before us. We can still trace the lineaments of successive stages of this development. Dartmoor preserves examples of small circular Neolithic fields more than 3,000 years old, hacked out of the scrub and planted with grain, as on Standon Down. Later the light Celtic plough operated more easily in squared-up clearances; and we have seen their lynchets on the chalk uplands of the south. The heavier Saxon ploughs left their mark in longer open strips which established our dimension of the acre – the area of an individual strip being settled as a chain wide by a furlong in length, that is, 22 yards by 220 yards. This led to the ridge-and-furrow pattern still visibly underlying so many later techniques.

These medieval open fields, tilled communally or in separate strips, had not substantially altered by the beginning of the eighteenth century, save where a few powerful landlords had enclosed

A field and hedge pattern in Northamptonshire.

certain areas in order to exploit resources more systematically. In some regions there were also enclosures at the height of the wool trade for conversion to sheep pasture. This often meant ruin to small arable-farming tenants and to peasants arbitrarily deprived of traditional rights over common grazing land. Employment suffered: one man and his dog cost an employer less th a score of farmhands. There was a widespread lament that 'the sheep do eat up the men'. But a great deal of this expansion of sheep rearing was carried out on uplands unfit, in any case, for cultivation. Rich abbeys of northern England exploited tracts of land as spacious and as bitterly contested as some Wild West ranches: there were continual disputes between one order and another about their drystone wall boundaries, many of which can still be seen tracing out the old monastic territories.

Enclosure of other lands and the gradual encroachment on 'wilds' and 'wastes' usually came about through private negotiations between influential neighbours. But from the middle of the eighteenth century there was an acceleration of demands for private Acts of Parliament to establish hard and fast rights of enclosure, reaching a peak when England was at war with France and needed to 'Dig for Victory', as propagandists in a later war were to exhort us.

Open fields were divided up into rectangular working units and hemmed in by hedges, fences or stone walls. Agricultural experimenters advanced theories on the optimum size for satisfactory operation. Robert Bakewell of Dishley in Leicestershire was convinced that '50 acres of pasture ground divided into five enclosures will

go as far in grazing cattle as 60 acres all in one piece'. He grazed his beasts in one field until it was bare, then moved them on to the next, and so on in rotation. He collaborated on experiments with 'Coke of Norfolk', who expanded his own herds and flocks not only for their milk and meat supplies but because of the way they could enrich the soil. Bakewell's cross-breeding produced several distinctive new species, including long-wool Leicesters and the famous Dishley longhorn cattle. He put his best rams and bulls out to stud, charging so much to finance further work on his model farm that it was said of the animals they were 'too dear for any one man to buy and too fat for any one to eat'. The walls of his home were hung with pickled anatomical specimens to illustrate his lectures to visitors.

But one man's success in, as it were, mass production meant deprivation for others. For every one who profited from high prices and then from the growing demands of the new industrial towns, there were scores who had to leave the land and seek work in those same towns. Enclosure at Kibworth Beauchamp in Leicestershire, for example, turned nine-tenths of the land over to grazing. The parson was granted a large sector as glebe land in compensation for his loss of tithe, but for most of the local labourers the change meant loss of food and employment, and of their old gleaning rights.

For many there was not just a loss of livelihood but a loss of the very ways along which they had walked. Old footpaths between cottage and strip field or between hamlet and hilltop were blocked off by new barriers, while new straight lanes served the needs of exploiter rather than peasant.

Hedges were the most common type of barrier, save in hill country where woodlands were scarce and stone plentiful, resulting in the skilfully assembled drystone walls of Yorkshire, Derbyshire and the Lake District. A properly planted hedge grew inexpensively of its own accord and, with suitable trimming, increased and strengthened. The hawthorn was a favourite component, growing thickly and holding the other elements together, and proving especially useful in the control of cattle because of its thorns.

One can calculate the date of a particular local enclosure fairly closely without any resource to

Drystone walling was known in the West country from the Bronze Age onwards but is most characteristic of North country enclosures for sheep rearing.

parish or parliamentary records. A remarkably reliable ratio has been established which depends on the use of the various species of tree or shrub in a 30-yard length of hedge. If the average number of different species in a length is counted, and this figure multiplied by 100, the approximate age of the hedge will be clear. If the result is 1,000 or more, the chances are that the hedge is a rare Saxon survival. Lower numbers mean a more recent planting. Beside the entrance path to Great Hickle farm outside Dedham in Essex is a stretch of hedge which has been estimated as 800 years old. Significantly, it marked the old border of Dedham common land – and 'Hickle' is the corruption of an old word meaning a cattle pound, in this case obviously for beasts brought in from grazing on the common.

In our own time the tendency has been not to plant hedges but to grub them up so that modern machines can rampage unchecked across wider and wider areas. Some of the dangers of this are only just becoming apparent. Disturbing the balance of wild life in a hedge means disturbing, in the long term, the whole ecological structure of the neighbourhood. It affects drainage, the control of micro-organisms in the soil, and the very stability of the soil. Some huge farms in East Anglia may all too soon create dust-bowl conditions. After a very dry season a few years ago, followed by a gale force west wind, large stretches of coastal cliffs in the region were invisible behind streaming clouds of parched soil blowing out to sea because there were too few hedges to block it.

The destruction of the ancient meandering tracks often meant the decline of a hamlet. Once upon a time a small farmer or labourer went to work from a row of cottages backed by easily accessible field strips. Now such easygoing individualism was at an end. Many a prospering farmer abandoned his own home in the community and built an isolated farmhouse out in the centre of his enclosed fields. If he aspired to move up into the class of 'gentleman farmer' and ultimately be accepted as one of the gentry, he might eventually build a virtual manor and even empark it with a surrounding wall. It was not just the field pattern which was changing, but the whole social structure.

In the Midlands, the squires and those who were accepted into their company created an upsurge of interest in hunting as a sport rather than a necessity. Master and peasant had always chased wild animals for food or as vermin which had to be exterminated. For long only the king had had the prerogative of hunting deer for the fun of it; later certain favoured lords had been graciously allowed to establish their own deer parks. Forest law weighed heavily on the ordinary man for centuries. But those prohibited forests did provide refuge and illicit food for many who had fallen foul of the law.

Here we are in what is generally thought of as Robin Hood country. Like most great romantic legends, that of the chivalrous outlaw in Lincoln green is beset with contradictions. Although associated with Sherwood Forest, which once covered 200 square miles but is now reduced to a few wooded patches between Nottingham and the Dukeries, and reputedly born at Locksley in Nottinghamshire round about 1160, he is also claimed by other parts of the kingdom. In Yorkshire a thirteenth-century pipe roll refers to a 'Robertus Hood, fugitivus', and a Robin of Barnesdale was known to make frequent raids on the rich properties of Whitby abbey. When fleeing from enemies with his accomplices, he used a bay where boats were always kept in readiness for such an eventuality – now called Robin Hood's Bay. On a moor above the village are Robin Hood's Butts, supposedly the scene of the outlaws' archery practice, but prosaically shown by archaeologists to be prehistoric barrows.

All the legends are, however, at one on the matter of his death. While sheltering in Kirklees priory near Brighouse he was bled by his treacherous kinswoman, the prioress, until too weak to escape. At the end he had just enough strength to shoot one last arrow from the window and ask that he should be buried where it fell. A tablet marks the spot. The grave of his right-hand man, Little John, is at Hathersage in Derbyshire.

The cupola of Nottingham Council House has frescoes of Robin Hood and his merry men, and the bell of the clock is known as 'Little John'. There is a bronze statue of Robin outside Nottingham castle, and another – by Madame Tussaud's grandson – in the grounds of Thoresby Hall, in Sherwood Forest itself. A carved mantelpiece in the library at Thoresby shows Robin and Little John meeting at the hollow Major Oak, the 1,000-year-old original of which can be found at Edwinstowe. Also at Edwinstowe is the church where Robin and Maid Marian are supposed to have wed.

In Bromsberrow church in Gloucestershire has been re-set some seventeenth-century Flemish

The hollow Major Oak in Sherwood Forest.

glass with portraits of two outlaws, Adam Bell and William Cloudislee of Inglewood Forest near Carlisle, said in an old ballad to have been trounced in an archery contest by Robin Hood's father.

The huntsmen who first conceived the pursuit of the fox as a sport had long since given up bows and arrows, preferring to leave the final kill to a pack of dogs. In the late eighteenth century when this activity became popular there were still stretches of unimpeded countryside across which to chase. Enclosure made things more hazardous, but hedges and fences offered a stimulating new challenge, provided there were not too many trees to block a jump. Clearance of wastes and heathland robbed the prey of cover, so the obliging pursuers set about planting some for him, thus creating the blobs of covert and spinney so common in the Leicestershire landscape, including those of Thorpe Trussels, Lord Morton's Covert, and the Botany Bay covert. In Melton Mowbray, the present Council Offices were once a hunting lodge.

Evoking the authentic atmosphere of ancient forests is difficult today. Sherwood Country Park preserves what it can, but is inevitably haunted by modern trippers rather than historic ghosts. Hatfield Forest in Essex is also a conservation area, but in this case rings truer. The medieval hunting ground has survived almost unspoilt, complete with its original tree and plant life and with herds of fallow deer. Traditional coppicing methods of cutting hazel, ash and hornbeam on a strict 16-year rotation are still applied. And while many oak forests were denuded by charcoal burners, the early iron industry and shipbuilders, Hatfield has managed to retain many of its venerable oaks.

Lost villages

Abandoned settlements can, like ancient field patterns, be detected more easily from the air, when superimposition of later farming methods cannot entirely destroy shadowy boundaries and furrows of original conformations. Aerial photography has, paradoxically, enabled us to see deeper into the earth than we could possibly do from our own closer vantage point. But once a site has been located from above, it can often be traced in detail on the ground.

Even in apparently open country there are frequent tell-tale traces. Old tracks and footpaths converge from several directions on something which seems of no consequence – until one looks more carefully. The approach lanes widen into green hollows where village streets used to run. Within the small web of streets, or alongside a single main street, rectangular grassy platforms mark the outlines of long-lost houses.

Camden, in his *Remaines* of 1605, observed:

For every towne, village or hamlet hath made names to families ... and so many names are locall which doe not seeme so, because the places are unknowne to most men, and all knowne to no one man: as who would imagine *Whitegift, Powlet, Bacon, Creping, Alshop, Tirwhit, Antrobus, Heather, Hartshorne*, and many such like to be locall names, and yet most certainely they are.

In fact many such designations were taken from villages now lost or always so insignificant that only the inhabitants were or are familiar with them.

The disappearance of once thriving communities has sometimes been blamed on the ravages of the Black Death, in the seventeenth century. This wiped out about a third of the population, and in some districts may have left too few inhabitants for their rural occupations to be viable any longer. Surviving peasants were in a position to sell their labour to the highest bidder instead of remaining tied forever to one master. Some hillside farms were abandoned, leaving only different swathes of colour to remind us of their old boundaries. But a drift from many economically failing hamlets, especially where arable land had been turned over to sheep farming, had been gaining momentum long before the plague years. Undoubtedly some sites were vacated because of such factors; but others were depopulated because of the desire for seclusion on the part of monastic orders, leading to cottagers' removal to some spot farther off; and a few disappeared at the whim of magnates also seeking privacy. In the fifteenth century a squire of Holyoak in Leicestershire threw 30 tenants off their farms to make room for sheep. At Nuneham Courtenay in Oxfordshire a village was removed because it hindered the development of a new park. The first Earl of Dorchester in the eighteenth century also trans-

ferred an entire community from within the bounds of his projected manor park, but was enlightened enough to install them in the purpose-built village of Milton Abbas in pleasant woodland.

Throughout England the sites of about 2,000 deserted villages have been identified, with a good 150 in Lincolnshire, 125 in Oxfordshire, 100 in Warwickshire, and comparable numbers in Leicestershire and Shropshire.

Bescaby in Leicestershire ceased to exist when sheep and cattle took over the fields in the early sixteenth century, but contours of hump and hollow vouch for its location, and the moat of the old farmhouse is still there. Ingarsby was enclosed by its monastic owners, Leicester abbey, in the middle of the seventeenth century, but retains the tell-tale hollows of village streets and lanes between house platforms. Extremely eerie is Widford church, built plumb on top of an old Roman villa at the centre of what must in its time have been an extensive Romano-British farm, taken over by Saxon, Norman and medieval successors but now only a ghostly sketch of lanes and footings.

In Shropshire, Pickthorn was recorded in Domesday Book as an independent manor, but over the years was gradually reduced to a hamlet and then a single farm now standing on the edge of a large field serrated with memories. Some of the county's Marcher hamlets may have been abandoned in despair because of Welsh raids – Owen Glendower sacked Burfield, for example, and nobody thought it worth while re-settling – but although this harassment may have slowed down the exploitation of land hereabouts, it was rare for a place to be utterly deserted for such reasons. In one or two cases, indeed, the coming of peaceful co-existence along the border actually contributed to a decline rather than a revival: at Caus, near Westbury, a community which had grown up under the protection of Norman fortifications and supplied the town with its needs lost any reason for existence once the fortifications were no longer important. And in Shropshire, as elsewhere, communities which had grown up around lead mines moved on to fresh employment and fresh accommodation when the workings were written off.

Stuchbury in Northamptonshire is at the hub of footpaths radiating to neighbouring villages. Belonging to a Northampton priory until the Dissolution, it had impressive earthworks, fishponds, and a dam. At Great Newton the medieval watermill has long since disappeared, but its supply conduit can still be traced. And here, again, is a lonely church with no village to minister to. At one deserted site in Northamptonshire, where on either side of a cobbled street there are traces of successive buildings from early timber cottages to stone, we get a hint of another possible explanation for abandonment of certain places. Here at Faxton it seems that extensions of a drainage system had to be made during a period when, according to contemporary documents, there was a long run of increasingly wet seasons: the drainage may in the end have proved inadequate, and the inhabitants, unable to cope, decided to give up.

Battlefields

Central England has borne more than its fair share of struggles between baronial families, king against usurper, cousin against cousin. Foreign enemies could be thrown back from the coasts without reaching the heartlands. Internal rivalries all too often festered and spread out from the centre.

In Saxon times the central kingdom of Mercia expanded on all sides under two rulers, Ethelbald and Offa, the latter being the first to declare himself King of the English. Wessex and Northumbria he could not annex, but they were forced to acknowledge him as senior partner. Along his western flank he built Offa's Dyke, a great earthwork intended not so much as a defensive barrier – which would have been difficult to man and fortify along its entire course in the efficient Roman fashion – as a visible boundary between Mercia and Wales. The Welsh did not lightly accept this demarcation, and on various occasions destroyed large sections of the wall. In spite of these depredations there remain substantial stretches which one can follow by footpath, including a section near Oswestry and one near Knighton, where a stone records the year of its foundation, 757.

As the Normans shared out their spoils, their estates and those of their successors sketched out the first vague blueprints of the later system of counties or shires. What are now administrative regions combining the old 'hundreds' (theoretically one hundred hides of land) were for long regarded as personal property by contentious nobles. What we generally call the Wars of the Roses, erupting intermittently from the end of

The construction of Offa's Dyke shows considerable engineering skill in the contours it follows, and has much in common with the northern Antonine Wall.

the fourteenth century almost until the end of the fifteenth, are more appropriately known as the Cousins' War, since the strife began largely through quarrels between Edward III's immediate descendants, and was fuelled by the ambitious noble families into which some of them married. The roses were those of Lancaster, represented at the start by the usurper Henry IV, and of York, represented by Edward IV, also a usurper. The tangle of relationships and mutual treacheries is such as to bewilder even the most attentive reader, and whatever reappraisals may in recent years have been made by novelists of Richard III's motives and character, it was eventually a great relief to have Henry VII on the throne, opening the great era of Tudor prosperity and national achievement.

The battle in which Edward IV defeated the

Lancastrians in 1461, thus driving Henry VI from the throne, is commemorated at Towton, in Yorkshire, by a stone cross. Another cross marks the spot where Lord Dacre was killed: his body lies in nearby Saxton church. Later attempts by Henry, by now virtually an imbecile, to make a comeback were finally scotched at the battle of Barnet and at Tewkesbury in May 1471, where Bloody Meadow saw the end of Lancastrian hopes. Edward had Henry murdered in the Tower of London, though the official statement declared that he had died of 'pure displeasure and melancholy'.

Kirby Muxloe castle, four miles west of Leicester, is one of the rare fortified dwellings begun during the Wars of the Roses, with the definite intention of installing cannon. Its instigator, the Yorkist Lord Hastings, did not live to see it completed, however: loyal to Edward IV, who had made him Chamberlain of the Royal Household, he was at once accused of treason and summarily executed when Richard III seized the throne.

Richard III met his own death in 1485 on Bosworth Field, two miles south of Market Bosworth in Leicestershire. On the site of the battle, Ambion Hill Farm at Sutton Cheney has an exhibition complete with battle models, a film theatre, and a battle trail which takes in King Richard's Field and King Dick's Well at which he is supposed to have drunk before the fight.

At Eastwell in Kent there is a curious entry in the burial register on 22nd December 1550 concerning one Richard Plantagenet, who is thought to be buried in an unmarked grave to the north of the church. A story has been handed down that Sir Thomas Moyle of Eastwell Park took into his employ a young man claiming to be the illegitimate son of Richard III and to have fought at Bosworth beside his father, after which he hid from pursuers and took up the trade of bricklayer.

There was further Civil War across the land when Charles I tried to set himself up as absolute monarch, dismiss Parliament, and raise money for himself by illegal imposts. On 22nd August 1642, having incensed all moderate opinion by trying to arrest five members of the House of Commons, he raised his standard at Nottingham and forced on a reluctant country a struggle which even his opponents wished could have been averted.

Battle was first joined at Edgehill, near Kineton in Warwickshire, ending in a stalemate. Two commemoration stones mark the site. Two years later at Marston Moor in Yorkshire the Royalists were routed by Parliamentary forces, much of the success being due to a cavalry force under Oliver Cromwell, a Puritan squire from Huntingdon.

Charles's really decisive defeat did not come until the battle of Naseby in Northamptonshire, in 1645. He obstinately continued the struggle, denying the authority of anyone else in the land; but never again did he find troops of a calibre to match the New Model Army built around the nucleus of Cromwell's cavalry. At Naseby there is a museum on Purlieu Farm with a miniature layout of the battlefield and some relics from the scene. Other relics, including armour and weapons, are housed in Abington Park, Northampton. Althorp House in the same county was the scene of Charles's last game of bowls when, visiting from Holdenby, he received word of Parliament's decision to remove him into closer custody at Hampton Court. These new restrictions were less stringent than might have been expected. Charles escaped to Carisbrooke Castle on the Isle of Wight and, though disappointed to find that its governor was not the secret Royalist he had been led to believe, managed to resume sly negotiations with the Scots in the hope of enlisting their support. They did in fact rally to his cause, with fatal results for many of them and for the king himself. Charles was beheaded outside his Whitehall Palace on 30th January 1649. After the execution the king's shirt, a pair of silk drawers, a watch and a monogrammed sheet which had been draped over his body were, by his own last wishes, presented to a loyal follower, John Ashburnham, who had been with him to the end. These were taken to Ashburnham church, near Battle in Sussex, and kept there so that sufferers from scrofula, the 'King's Evil', might touch the relics in hope of the traditional cure. In 1830 some items were stolen from the church, and the remainder taken into safe keeping in Ashburnham Place.

The Prince of Wales had fled to France after the débâcle of Naseby, but after his father's execution decided to assert his right to the succession. In 1650 he set out for Scotland, and on New Year's Day in 1651 was crowned King Charles II at Scone. He rallied a largely Scottish army about him and marched south, hoping to collect other volunteers on the way. But Cromwell met him at Worcester and inflicted a crushing defeat. Fleeing once more, Charles hid for a time

The cairn over Dick's Well, Bosworth Field, is maintained by the Richard III Society in memory of the drink the king took here before his defeat in 1485.

The Peasants' Revolt in 1381 came about after the introduction of legislation to prevent farm workers from asking higher wages because of the shortage of labour. Although the revolt was crushed after much fighting and looting through the streets of London, and after the betrayal of Richard II's promises to the leader, Wat Tyler, the poll-tax which had been a main source of the trouble was dropped, and landlords behaved a bit more circumspectly towards their human beasts of burden. The Pilgrimage of Grace, which started from Hexham in 1536 and acquired thousands of supporters in Yorkshire and Lincolnshire, was provoked by the Dissolution of the Monasteries, but its instigators were equally concerned with the agrarian miseries caused by Tudor enclosures. In return for a promise of a fair and honest enquiry into their grievances, the pilgrims' leader went to London to meet Henry VIII, and was cheated as Tyler had been: accused of treason, he was hanged at York. In 1549 Robert Kett's protest against magnates' rapacity in Norfolk came to the same ignominious end.

By the nineteenth century the workers in the fields were finding, like other labourers, the advantages of combining against exploitation. But although membership of Trades Unions had been grudgingly legalized, six farm labourers of Tolpuddle in Dorset who tried to form a group in alliance with Robert Owen's Grand National Consolidated Trades Union were arrested on a charge of administering illegal oaths. Sentenced to seven years' transportation to New South Wales they were released within two years after a vigorous public campaign. The 'Martyrs' Tree' under which they discussed their aims stands close to a memorial shelter on Tolpuddle village green, and six cottages for the aged have been named after them. In the churchyard is a headstone to John Hammett, the only one who settled in Tolpuddle after his return: the others, disgusted by the petty hostility of their neighbours, emigrated to Canada.

at Boscobel House in Shropshire. Later he told how he had been forced to climb into an oak tree to avoid his pursuers, who were 'going up and down in the thicket of the wood, searching for persons escaped, we seeing them, now and then, peeping out of the wood'. The so-called Royal Oak in the grounds has been grown from an acorn from the original, and Royal Oak Day is still celebrated on 29th May, the date of Charles's restoration to the Stuart throne. The Old Ship inn in Brighton marks the other end of his escape route: safety was bought with the pension granted to the captain of the lugger, later renamed *The Royal Escape*, which carried the king back into exile across the Channel.

There have been internal battles other than those of contentious kings and nobles. In every century, peasant dissatisfactions with the oppressions of such royalty and nobility have threatened to burst out in rebellion; frequently they did so.

Another agricultural conflict came to a head in our own century. From the earliest days of the Christian church in England it had been customary for the faithful to offer a proportion of their output, in produce or in labour, to support their priest. This tithe was in due course to be legally established as 'a tenth part of the increase yearly arising from the profits of lands, stocks upon lands and the industry of the parishioners payable for the maintenance of the parish priest by

everyone who has things titheable'. At first dues were paid in kind: incumbents of prosperous parishes and abbots of richly endowed monastic foundations collected farm produce and rural handiwork into their spacious tithe barns, striking examples of which survive at Bredon in Worcestershire, Tisbury in Wiltshire, and – the two mightiest of them all – Great Coxwell in Berkshire and Abbotsbury in Dorset.

As time went on, it became more practical for payment in kind to be replaced by a monetary contribution. In 1704 a fund known as Queen Anne's Bounty was set up to administer the tithes confiscated by Henry VIII after the Dissolution of the Monasteries; and in 1925 a new Act made the fund responsible for collection of tithe rent charges. These charges were fixed in relation to the prevailing price of corn, but also carried a surcharge to provide for the day when tithes would be altogether abolished – which seemed to many hard-pressed farmers to be a long time in coming. During the depression of the 1920s and 1930s farmers were expected to continue paying tithes on a theoretical profit when many of them were struggling along at a loss. Catholics or Nonconformists felt especially bitter at having to contribute to the upkeep of the Church of England, whose religious views they did not share; and farmers had every justification for complaining that no other trade or profession was similarly taxed.

Some rebels refused to pay. The commissioners empowered to collect the tithes then sent in gangs of hauliers to remove livestock, by force if necessary. The 'Tithe Wars' spread through East Anglia, parts of the Midlands, and into Kent. When goods were seized and put up for auction, friendly auctioneers connived with neighbours to sell them back at a pittance to their original owners. The commissioners put a stop to this by insisting that the receipts had to equal the tithe figure outstanding. It soon became difficult to get any market to accept anything suspected as being distrained tithe goods.

In 1936 an Act was passed to phase out tithes within 60 years, which to most farmers still seemed far too long. Many continued demonstrating, but patriotically ceased doing so when the Second World War came. Since then, Queen Anne's Bounty and the Ecclesiastical Commission have amalgamated into the Church Commission; and tithe redemption payments have been collected through the Inland Revenue.

Two memorials in Suffolk recall the skirmishes over cattle and sheep being dragged from their farms: one at Elmsett near Hadleigh, and one at Wortham, where the novelist Doreen Wallace and her husband also had their furniture bundled out of the house because of their refusal to contribute to a church whose views they strongly opposed.

Words and Music

Echoes of old sadnesses ring on through the lines of John Clare, the peasant poet of Helpston in what was at the time of his birth in 1793 a Northamptonshire village, later finding itself in Huntingdonshire, now a part of Cambridgeshire. Clare was no lover of boundary changes, as his bitter writings about enclosures show, and the madness which drove him ultimately to an asylum in Northampton would surely have been inflamed by this administrative juggling. His laments for declining villages are not so well known as the Goldsmith poem once dinned into so many schoolchildren's ears – 'Ill fares the land, to hast'ning ills a prey, Where wealth accumulates, and men decay' – but are the heartfelt utterances of a true man of the soil, writing from knowledge rather than tidy sentimentality:

> Ye banish'd trees, ye make me deeply sigh –
> Inclosure came, and all your glories fell:
> E'en the old oak that crown'd yon rifled dell,
> Whose age had made it sacred to the view;
> Not long was left his children's fate to tell;
> Where ignorance and wealth their course pursue,
> Each tree must tumble down – 'old Lea-Close Oak', adieu!

Clare's cottage is preserved at Helpston. He is buried in the village churchyard, outside which a rather over-fussy cross has been erected in his memory.

Clare lived in his madness to the age of 71. Another country lover who also regretted the passing of old ways but recorded them in prose rather than verse, Richard Jefferies, lived to be only 39. Abandoning early ambitions to be a novelist, he concentrated on noting the changes in village life and old crafts, and expressing warnings about increasing mechanization. 'The

A stone obelisk commemorates the battle of Naseby at which Oliver Cromwell led the most famous and most devastating of his cavalry charges.

In the Middle Ages the 200-foot long thatched tithe barn at Tisbury in Wiltshire stored produce exacted by the landowning abbesses of Shaftesbury abbey.

next generation of country folk', he observed, 'will hardly be able to understand the story of Ruth.' At Barbury on the Wiltshire Downs a sarsen stone carries his epitaph:

> Richard Jefferies
> 1848–1887
> It is eternity now.
> I am in the midst
> of it. It is about
> me in the sunshine.

Nostalgia seems to run through so much pastoral poetry. It is impossible even to see the names of Clun or Knighton on a signpost, or to walk under the shadow of Wenlock Edge, without recalling A. E. Housman's melancholy tone of voice. Although born in Worcestershire, he appropriated the Shropshire towns and villages and landscape as his own, misting them with his deeply ingrained pessimism yet somehow filling that mist with an unforgettable music. One of the many odd things about this odd, withdrawn scholar was his utter indifference to music itself. He was never in the least impressed by the song cycle, *On Wenlock Edge*, in which some of his lyrics were admiringly set by the Gloucestershire-born composer, Ralph Vaughan Williams.

A truly local musician was Edward Elgar, born at Broadheath in Worcestershire and deriving much of his inspiration from walks and cycle rides through the sylvan countryside. At his birthplace there is now a small museum with many personal relics. He, like Vaughan Williams after him, contributed liberally to the annual Three Choirs Festival which takes place in rotation at the cathedrals of Hereford, Gloucester and Worcester.

Further back in history, but close enough in space, two places are associated with Dr Samuel Johnson. His birthplace in Lichfield is now a museum, and not far away in the Market Square are statues of the 'Great Cham' and his indefatigable companion and biographer, Boswell. On the plinth of Johnson's own statue a relief panel recalls an incident at Uttoxeter. His father once asked young Samuel to look after a bookstall in Uttoxeter market, but the young man was ashamed to be seen doing so, and refused. In later life it was his refusal which ashamed him the more, and he returned to stand in penance on a rainy day in that marketplace, where there is another sculpture to immortalize the gesture.

One of Johnson's more protracted tasks was the preparation of an annotated edition of the works of William Shakespeare. And if we are to glance, however briefly, at the creative artists of the region we cannot avoid the writer who will be forever associated with the name of a once-great Warwickshire forest – in which the village of Meriden has a cross declaring it the very centre of England. Shakespeare's mother, Mary Arden, claimed descent from the eleventh-century Arden family. She was born in a Tudor yeoman's house at Wilmcote, where some of the original farm buildings have been refurbished as a museum of local crafts and relics, including a cider press, farm implements, and poacher's traps. From Wilmcote Mary went to wed John Shakespeare at Aston Cantlow, and in 1564 she produced a son, William.

Stratford-upon-Avon, where John was a burgess of fluctuating fortune, one of whose duties was to act as bailiff during visits by troupes of strolling players, flaunts the dramatist's name and supposed likeness in so many corners and on so many façades that one may be forgiven for growing sceptical about the accumulation of attributions. But William Shakespeare was assuredly born and baptized here in 1564, his home in Henley Street is fairly well vouched for and has been restored to house relics and documents; and he went to school in the local free grammar school established by the Guild of the Holy Cross. He died at New Place shortly after being visited by Ben Jonson and Michael Drayton, and was buried in Stratford church – though there are many theorists who prefer to believe that the plays were written by someone else, now lying in a grave elsewhere though as yet unidentified.

In 1582 William had married a pregnant woman some eight years older than himself, probably at her insistence – which detracts somewhat from the prettily romantic legends surrounding Anne Hathaway's cottage at Shottery. The cottage was in any case not Anne's but that of her stepmother, with whom Anne went on living after the death of her father in 1581.

William and Anne had two daughters and a son. Their granddaughter Elizabeth ultimately inherited the whole estate, including Shakespeare's books and manuscripts. For 20 years she lived with her second husband, Sir John Barnard, at Abington Park, Northampton, dying childless. Who inherited the priceless manuscripts is not known, but it seems more than likely that the widower sold them off for what they would fetch. One cannot help wondering if there might not be, somewhere, a jealously concealed hoard of Shakespearian drafts, annotations, and even perhaps some personally revealing, unpublished work.

Spires, Sanctuaries and Scholars

IN ENGLAND, AS IN THE REST of Europe, much evidence remains of the early links between religious and educational foundations. Our great cathedrals, originally shrines to house the bones of early Christian saints, encompass within their mighty spaces not only centuries of changing architectural styles but the history of the early church and the rise of learning which accompanied it.

In 596 Pope Gregory I, distressed by the prevalence of paganism in Anglo-Saxon England, charged a monk named Augustine to leave Rome and attempt the restoration of Christianity to that remote country. Augustine and a small band of followers landed near Richborough, as Romans and Saxons had done before them. A nineteenth-century cross in Saxon style marks the spot where he preached his first sermon before King Ethelbert of Kent, whose Christian wife smoothed the way for the missionaries and

Above: *Saxon chapel, Bradford-on-Avon, Wiltshire. Founded in the late seventh century by St Aldhelm, this tiny church was once used as a school and cottage. Left: Celtic cross, Mawagan-in-Pyder, Cornwall, in the grounds of Lanherne. This is one of the most elaborate Cornish crosses, depicting Christ crucified.*

encouraged their establishment of a centre at Canterbury – the Cantwareburh or 'fort of the people of Kent' – in the little chapel of St Martin which Ethelbert had given her on their marriage. Traces of Roman brickwork, later embodied in the expanded medieval church, testify that this is almost certainly the oldest continuously used church in England. In 601 Augustine was elevated to the archbishopric of Canterbury and primacy of England.

After the martyrdom of Thomas à Becket on the altar steps of the cathedral in 1170, Canterbury became the main English goal of pilgrimages, and both the Downs trackway from Winchester to Canterbury and the old Roman road of Watling Street have become known as the Pilgrims' Way. These paths were in fact of much earlier origin, and although they might well have provided a ready-made route for devout travellers, there is little evidence of their having been exclusively adopted by pilgrims; but Chaucer's *Canterbury Tales* and the notion of such a holy thoroughfare are now indissolubly blended.

Just as Augustine was associated with the foundation of Canterbury, the Northumberland hermit St Cuthbert inspired the building of Durham, the great Romanesque cathedral of the north. He was appointed bishop of Lindisfarne, and after his death the monks of the island produced the exquisitely illustrated pages of the

Lindisfarne Gospels in his honour. The threat of Viking raids led to St Cuthbert's remains being removed and eventually finding a resting place in a wooden shrine built on a high, rocky peninsula above the river Wear. A monastery was created around this shrine and in 1093 work began on what was to become Durham Cathedral. 'Endless the miracles that were wrought' at the shrine before its despoliation by Henry VIII during the dissolution of the monasteries.

There are survivals of Norman (or 'Romanesque') influence in other such edifices, and the Normans also encouraged monastery building: the later influx of Cistercian orders led to the construction of abbeys such as Rievaulx, Tintern and Fountains and of other contemplative establishments. In England the mention of a monastery automatically conjures up visions of gaunt yet splendid ruins, unroofed, with fragments of great arches and gaping windows, usually photographed in mysterious mists or against a background of lonely hills at twilight. The idea of

Above: *Greensted-juxta-Ongar, Essex.*
The only surviving log church in the country, with nave timbers which may date from 850, once sheltered the remains of St Edmund. Right: *Earls Barton church, Northamptonshire. Primarily Saxon, the west tower is a mighty, unbuttressed edifice. The arch of the doorway is probably Norman, however.*

these buildings as thriving homes of a busy, devout community is hard to grasp. They have so many of the attributes of the contrivedly picturesque, like some magnate's self-indulgent architectural folly. Yet their priors and abbots were once among the most influential men in the land, and their population equal to that of several major towns put together. In the Middle Ages it was said that if the abbot of Glastonbury were to wed the abbess of Shaftesbury, any child of their marriage would be richer than the king of England.

The abbeys were by their very nature private. Cathedrals were awe-inspiring, but rarely served

more than the local populace or, from time to time, bands of pilgrims. For the greater number of people working on the land – which meant most of the population in the days before industrialization – mendicant friars or a parish priest offered the only devotional tuition they might expect. Early Saxon churches were seldom more than small wooden chapels, not reinforced in stone until the later days of Alfred the Great. They were simple in form, consisting basically of a nave for the congregation and a sanctuary in which the priest officiated at the altar. Later a chancel was introduced between nave and sanctuary, integrated by many subsequent builders with the sanctuary itself. With an increase in the

Above: *Durham Cathedral, Galilee Chapel.*
This forms part of the Lady Chapel which was set a long
way from its usual place behind the high altar by St
Cuthbert, who hated women! It houses the tomb of the
Venerable Bede, church historian. Left: *Canterbury*
Cathedral, the Crypt. More lofty and spacious than any
previously built in England, it escaped the fire of 1174
and remains perfectly preserved. Its glory lies in the
carved capitals of the columns (left, above) which are the
best preserved Early Romanesque sculptures in the
country, depicting fabulous creatures.

size of congregations, churches were enlarged by extending the nave or adding aisles alongside the nave. Cruciform churches, with a tower between nave and sanctuary, spread to north and south with the arms of transepts stretching out from the tower. Some rich individuals built family chapels on to the church; and as trade guilds grew in strength they, too, founded chantries.

The influence of the Renaissance turned builders and architects away from the Gothic towards a rethinking of classical styles, especially after the Restoration. Instead of housing a complex of aisles, chantries, transepts and recesses, the church became a simple well-lit hall dominated by the pulpit. Sir Christopher Wren's undivided spaces in which the entire congregation could see and hear were a more genial outcome of the strict Palladian style favoured by

Inigo Jones and his disciples.

Memorials and associations in churches or churchyards are a study in themselves. We all have our favourites. Brasses, more plentiful in England than any other country in the world, record not just distinguished knights and their ladies but changing fashions in armour, ecclesiastical and civilian dress, through medieval times and on into the late seventeenth century. There was rarely any attempt at portraiture, the features of the subjects being stylized; but great care was taken in the clothing and heraldic devices. The earliest brass in England is Sir John d'Abernoun's of Stoke d'Abernon in Surrey, dating from 1277, which shows him holding a lance. A diminutive, rather cuddly little lion rubs against his ankle. The second oldest is that of Sir Roger de Trumpington at Trumpington near Cambridge, his feet resting on a hound.

In the early Middle Ages contemplative monks chose sites for their hermitages which would deter visitors or persecutors, and might gather a few favoured disciples about them. In this way, in the thirteenth century, disciples of scholars who had sought peace in marshy, insalubrious surroundings formed the nuclei of Oxford and Cambridge universities, our oldest seats of learning.

Oxenforde came into being some time in the eighth century when St Frideswide's nunnery

Above: Lincoln Cathedral from the river Witham. With its memorable silhouette, it is an outstanding example of the Early English style. Left, above: Iffley church, Oxford. A magnificent building, lavishly decorated with sculpture typical of the late twelfth century, it is one of the best preserved village churches of that time. It was built as the gift of a rich patron. Left, below: Fountains Abbey, Yorkshire. The finest of ruins conjuring up a picture of Cistercian monastic life.

was established near the river crossing. The first teachers to arrive were clerics with their own groups of theological students, some of them friars burning to impart new learning and philosophies from the Continent. Students did not at once form colleges, but lived in halls of residence at their own expense or on the charity of others. Tuition was almost exclusively religious, and the earliest endowments stipulated that this was to be the whole purpose of the place.

There are still niggling arguments as to which college can claim to be the pioneer, but on the whole the honour has been generally conceded to University College, founded in 1249 by the bishop of Durham 'for the maintenance at Oxenforde of ten needy Masters of Art studying Divinity'. Balliol and Merton followed.

Although its university charter also concentrated on the education of pupils for the priesthood, Cambridge's first true college, Peterhouse, was established in 1284 by the bishop of Ely with the express intention of encouraging nonmonastic students 'in the pursuit of Literature'. Its hall and buttery are relics of the original building.

While the concept of university teaching for clerics, with a leavening of the arts and humanities, might appeal to royal, noble and religious benefactors, it was a long time before anyone took very seriously the idea of education for the masses, and the whole tenor of teaching remained primarily religious. Towards the end of the seventeenth century a number of individuals and organizations founded schools with charitable intent but still with discipline and godliness as prime requisites. In 1698 six tradesmen founded the Grey Coat School in Westminster. They

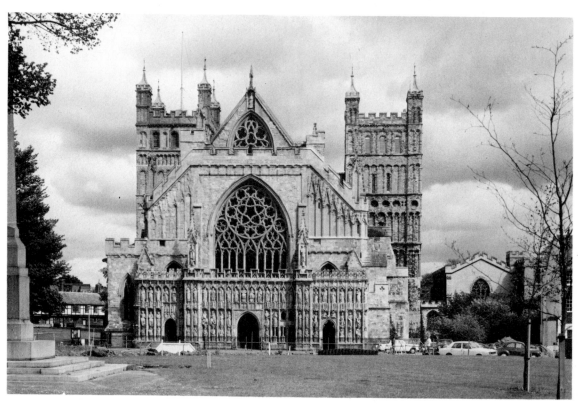

engaged a full-time master, took in a dozen boys and girls, increasing the number as funds permitted.

Any advances in general education were, until almost our own time, left mainly to private enterprise and compassion. What, then, of the so-called public schools – what schooling, and for what public? The most famous of these had in fact started as charitable endowments promising help to the needy. Winchester, founded in 1394 by William of Wykeham, bishop of Winchester, avowed its purpose as a 'perpetual college of poor scholars' clerks', including a set number of choristers. Like Eton, it embodied the idea of free places and tuition for the under-privileged – *paupères et indigentes* – and when Eton brought the phrase 'public school' into common use it was with the meaning that it was available to scholars from any part of the country and not merely from the institution's immediate locality.

Less exclusive schools with local endowments and local interests – the grammar schools – also began with a strong leaning towards the classics, and interest in the wider spread of the humanities was late in developing. Founded in the sixteenth century for the teaching of Latin, the language of the Western Church, the grammar schools have nowadays been absorbed into the 'comprehensive' system, the term causing as many arguments as 'public' schools. Subtractions from the first plans, additions to them, and arguments over the whole principle have swayed this way and that ever since, according to the political party in power at the time. This chapter is not one which can be rounded off with a neat summing-up: the very word 'education' is still one which baffles and will go on baffling the English.

Above: *Ely Cathedral, the West Front.*
In the Early English style, it dominates its flat Fenland setting with a west tower rising high and broad, and a central Gothic octagon and lantern. Left, above: Tintern Abbey, Monmouthshire. This famous ecclesiastical ruin was founded in 1131 for Cistercian monks and completed early in the fourteenth century. Left, below: Exeter Cathedral, the West Front. One of the few cathedrals which is architecturally of a piece. Begun c.1275, its distinctive west front dates from 1327.

Above: *Ledbury Grammar School,
Herefordshire. Among many fine examples of black and
white buildings in Church Lane, this school was built
around 1500.* Right: *King's College Chapel, Cambridge.
One of the major examples of English medieval
architecture, completed in 1515. Elaborate fan-vaulting
provides a magnificent roof, the stained glass is the most
complete set of church windows surviving from the time of
Henry VIII and the screen and choir stalls are the purest
wood carving in the Early Renaissance style.*

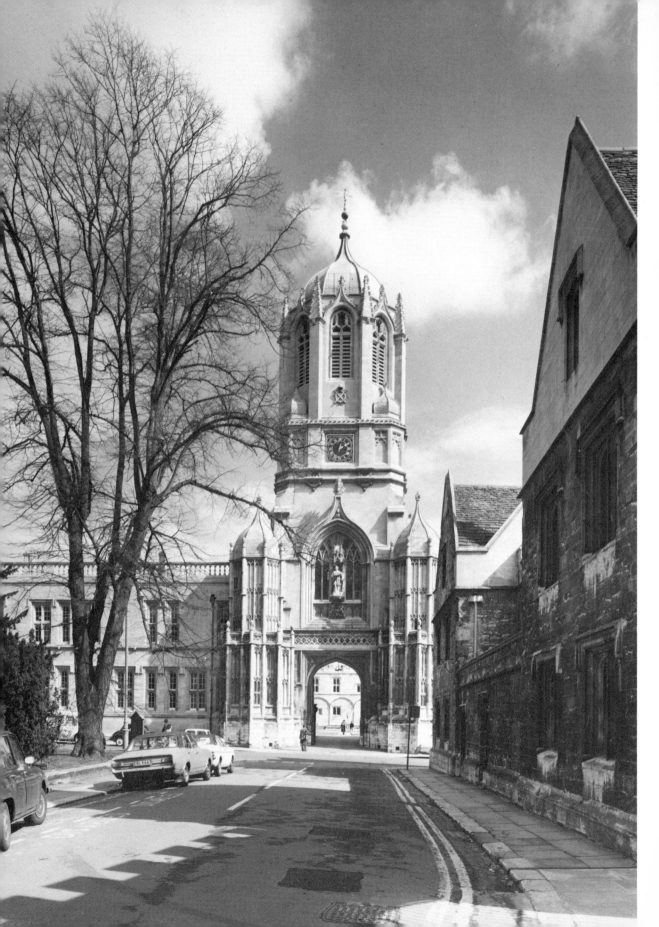

Above: *Grey Coat School, Westminster, London.*
It was founded in 1698 as a boarding school for 70
children. Its centre with lantern of 1701 was destroyed in
the war but has now been restored to a twentieth-century
version of the Queen Anne style. Left: *Tom Tower,*
Christ Church, Oxford. The tower stands in the centre of
the long façade of the college, on the west side of Tom
Quad. Architecturally its lower part is Wolsey's, its
upper part the work of Christopher Wren, 1681–2, in
Gothic style.

LANDS RECLAIMED

AT ONE SIDE OF Holme Fen Nature Reserve in Cambridgeshire an iron post sticks up some 14 feet from the ground, serving no immediately obvious purpose. This was brought here from the Crystal Palace after the Great Exhibition of 1851 and sunk into the peat at a time when the wide neighbouring expanse of Whittlesey Mere, then England's largest freshwater inland lake, was being drained to provide new farmland. When the post had been driven down to rest on the more solid clay below the peat, only its top was visible. Today we see it entirely exposed. It offers stark proof of Fenland's historic problem: how to drain the soil and keep the waters in check when by that very draining you shrink the land like a squeezed sponge and thereby invite the waters back again. Even under modern controlled conditions the land is continuing to sink at a rate of about an inch a year.

Draining the Fens

Peat forms mainly in regions of ample rain and poor drainage. The creation of the Fens began between the two limestone ridges slanting across country from the Dorset coast, when in the swathe of clay separating them there accumulated silt and decaying matter deposited by ancient rivers. Only a few solid outcrops rose high enough to form islands above this unstable bog. The decomposed substance of the peat accumulated acid because of an insufficiency of soluble limestone to neutralize it. Mixing this squelchy surface layer with lime is the most effective way of controlling the acidity, releasing surplus water and producing a workable loam; but it took many centuries of trial and error to achieve the balance

Above: *In 1490 Bishop Morton of Ely, founder of the original Hatfield House in Hertfordshire, cut the 40-foot-wide drainage channel of Morton's Leam.* Left: *Holme Fen post.*

which makes the present-day arable land of the Fens so fertile.

Pre-Roman attempts to establish communities in these waterlogged wildernesses must have been fitful, and were abandoned when increased flooding in the Iron Age made the region quite uninhabitable. The Romans took advantage of a slight but significant shift of land and water levels soon after their arrival and, with their usual thoroughness, tried the first comprehensive development and drainage of the area. Groups of their new subjects were installed on islands above the bogs and meres. Aerial photographs reveal large settlements joined by roads laid along embankments. The 60-mile canal of the Car Dyke was cut between Ramsey and the river Witham at Lincoln, probably in Hadrian's time, helping to catch water running down from the shallow western slopes and divert it into the Witham and the Nene. It also provided transport. The suggestion by several historians that Fenland was an imperial estate obliged to supply eastern and northern military requirements is confirmed by the extension of the Foss Dyke to complete a navigable route all the way from Cambridge to the key garrison at York.

Records after the Roman withdrawal are scanty, but there does seem to have been a land subsidence or some shift in tidal patterns which brought water flooding in more vigorously. For hundreds of years there remained only a watery desert, though still with a few surviving islands to which the Anglo-Saxons added their suffix *ey* or *ea*, as in Ramsey, Whittlesey, and Shippea. Some silt ridges, locally known as roddons, built up above the peat, providing foundations for most of the houses we see today. But on the whole it took a surefooted, experienced local man to find his way safely along the few reliable tracks through the bogs and around the vast pools. Upthrusts such as Ely, the 'Eel Island' indicatory of the staple local diet, provided refuges for the rebellious Hereward the Wake, who was able to harry William the Conqueror's supporters in Peterborough and Ely itself until well on into 1071. In William's time an attempt was made to drain Deeping Fen, but it proved a failure.

A ridge in Holland, near the south coast of Lincolnshire, had been settled with some success

The woodwork of Wicken Fen windmill has been restored, but the ironwork comes from the original pumping mill which once fed main drainage dykes.

in the seventh century. By the beginning of the twelfth, villages linked by the embankments known as droves were learning the advantages of cooperation. Here and further south attempts were made at communal enclosing and draining; but it was too easy for one parish to squabble with a neighbour over responsibility for this wall, that breached bank, and even more over the sharing out of tasks after a flood.

Out of the anonymity of the early Fenland dwellers and experimenters a few names begin to emerge which are on the map today. Bishop Morton of Ely is commemorated in his pioneering channel of Morton's Leam, a 14-mile cut designed to take water from the Nene near Peterborough to Guyhirn instead of letting it follow a more circuitous, undisciplined course. In the time of James I his Lord Chief Justice, Sir John Popham, created Popham's Eau for carrying water to an outfall at King's Lynn.

And then come the most significant names of Adventurers' Fen and the Bedford Level. Individual dabblings with the region's natural hazards were bound to prove abortive. To finance an overall scheme it was necessary to persuade a number of investors to venture their capital in return for a share of what profits might accrue from lands reclaimed from the water. In 1630 the Earl of Bedford, inheritor of the abbey estates of Thorney and Whittlesey, having obtained a royal charter for the conversion of certain areas into part-time pasture, joined with 13 other 'Adventurers' to employ the Dutch engineer Cornelius Vermuyden.

The basic theory was to cut channels which would feed water from tributary conduits downhill to the Wash, and provide them with sluices to prevent any reversal during high tides. 'Washes' between the main drains might be allowed to flood during winter, but could be profitably grazed in summer. Wider expanses might be turned into permanent arable land. Unfortunately Vermuyden's complex schemes were not completed before some of the Adventurers began to run short of money. Charles I stepped in, but his methods of tax collecting had already threatened to bring him down, and the Civil War stopped any further investment for a while. Then, both during the Commonwealth and after the Restoration, further Acts were passed, and Vermuyden continued his work.

To the straight drain of the Old Bedford River, which he had driven from the Great Ouse

Stretham Old Engine, only complete survivor of early
nineteenth-century Fenland steam pumping engines, cost
£2,900 in 1831; its building, another £2,050.

from Adventurers' Fen and restored to working order in Wicken Sedge Fen, so that it still plays a part in controlling the water levels there in the old style. Under the aegis of the National Trust, Wicken has been preserved as representative of primitive Fenland conditions. Here the undrained peat stands six to eight feet higher than the drained lands about it – quite a contrast to the earth surrounding the Holme Fen post. Sedge and reed are cut for thatching as they always used to be, and there are specimens of an original lode and of a 300-year-old drove which used to serve as a path for those working the fen.

Even the power of windmills was not enough to guarantee continued improvement. In 1820 the first of many steam pumping engines was introduced at Ten Mile Bank. One built in 1831 is preserved at Stretham by the Old West River, with a scoop wheel capable of raising 124 tons of water a minute. This in its turn was superseded in the 1920s by diesel and then electric pumps; but Stretham Old Engine has summoned up the energy to assist in a few emergencies since then.

In its engine-house are collections of peat samples and what is called bog oak, a local speciality which is often not oak at all. Sometimes seen in great lumps by the roadside like some warped monster heaved out of the primeval slime, bog oak consists of waterlogged roots of trees which, often impregnated with salt, died in the peat. When the peat drained and shrank, these twisted shapes rose to the surface as iron-hard as timbers long immersed in the sea – and as dangerous to the Fenland farmer's plough as flints have been to the ploughmen of East Anglia or the South Downs.

One of the most modern manifestations of the need to be forever vigilant over the waters is to be seen at Denver Sluice. Vermuyden's first sluice has given way to great new gates, guarding his old waterways and new ones in the Great Ouse Flood Protection Scheme which was completed – if such a task can ever be said to have been completed – in 1964.

What benefited many sections of the populace did not always spell improvement for others. The more effectively the overall drainage of the region improved, the more was the livelihood of some individuals and communities threatened. Fenland fishermen and wildfowlers lamented the disappearance of their meres and marshes and streams, and hence the disappearance of the food and income on which they depended. They were

at Earith to Denver, he added in parallel the New Bedford River or Hundred Foot Drain. Morton's Leam was refashioned, and a web of old and new lodes was woven: a lode being one of the smaller waterways combining drainage with thorough-fares for barge traffic between villages. Vermuyden's own name was bestowed on the Vermuyden River (more commonly the Forty Foot Drain). The geometric tapestry of his and subsequent work makes an Ordnance map of the region identifiable at once: even at the most casual glance it is unmistakable.

One major snag had soon made itself obvious. When the peat was efficiently dried out, it contracted, causing the ground level to sink. Downhill drainage failed when 'downhill' turned back on itself. Hundreds of windmills and horse mills, sometimes working in pairs, had to be installed to pump water from the minor cuts into the main dykes. One of these windmills has been moved

by tradition hunters, not farmers. For many families the changeover could not have been an easy one.

At Wisbech we have an interesting example of a port once busy with prosperous coastal traffic and the Baltic timber trade. Now, because of changes in the ebbs and flows of tides and rivers, partly natural and partly provoked by man, Wisbech finds itself 13 miles upstream from the Wash along the narrow, twisting river Nene. This river has served as a main drain in the local system from early times: a drain in every sense, since for long it also served to dispose of the town sewage.

From the 1820s onwards there were continual arguments about the construction of new docks and improved navigation of the Nene. Shoals and bends impeded the flow of tidal water and the movement of ships. But it was protested that any works of improvement 'which have for their object the admission of a larger quantity of tidal water will prejudice the fresh water supply of Thorney and under certain conditions to the Middle Level also'. Nevertheless a Drainage Act in 1852 authorized the strengthening of the river banks, dredging and straightening, and the provision of a new pivoted iron bridge. Protesters were a bit abashed when, in November of that year, floods seriously damaged the banks and rendered the existing stone bridge unsafe.

The progress of the river works and the whole appearance and atmosphere of Wisbech in the 1850s are wonderfully recorded in the calotypes of the pioneer documentary photographer, Samuel Smith, whose evocative scenes can rewardingly be set beside present-day scenes for comparison.

Wisbech in Smith's time was planning, as did so many Victorian communities, for an expanding future. But in the end the expenditure on improvements was far greater than had been estimated; once railway lines had been laid across the Fens, the town was robbed of much of its coastal trade; and ambitious schemes for a more easily navigable waterway to Peterborough came to nothing. Today the town, with its surviving riverside warehouses and its fine Georgian merchants' homes, handles a respectable quantity of Baltic timber as of old, and despatches cargoes of bricks from the brickworks whose tall chimneys stand red and dusty between here and Peterborough – but belongs more to its surrounding orchards, nurseries, market gardens and canning factories than to the maritime world.

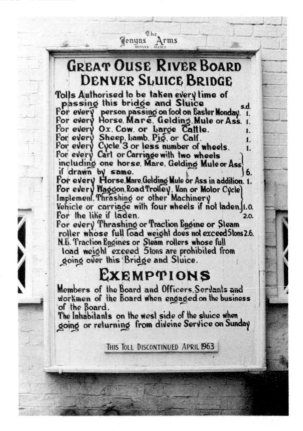

The old toll board for crossing Denver Sluice has been preserved on the wall of an inn now frequented by sailing enthusiasts and anglers.

The Eastern Association

A plaque on the Huntingdon Research Centre marks the site of Oliver Cromwell's birthplace. His grandfather once owned the George Inn, a short distance away along what used to be the Roman Ermine Street. His father is buried in All Saints' Church. Oliver, born in 1599, went to the old grammar school, occupying part of what had been a twelfth-century hospital – opened as a Cromwell museum by the Speaker of the House of Commons in 1962 – and then to Sidney Sussex college, Cambridge. He himself entered the House of Commons in 1628 as Member for Huntingdon, and later he stood for Cambridge.

With an austere hatred of royal absolutism, and suspicious of Charles I's leanings towards Catholicism and his attempts to rally European Catholic monarchies to his aid, Cromwell threw all this weight into the conflict which split the country after 1642. He raised a troop of 'godly

men' and trained them on his own farmlands near St Ives, where his statue now dominates the marketplace. Rallying friends and neighbours from the Fens and East Anglia, he united county recruiting and supply committees into the Eastern Association, and produced such successful fighting units that the whole New Model Army was duly fashioned around his methods.

Royalist mockers derided the Parliamentary soldiers as Roundheads on the strength of the puritanically close-cropped hair of some of them; and the more romantic designation of Cavaliers is usually bestowed on Charles's followers because of the short-lived superiority of his cavalry. In fact, many of the gentry who supported Parliament wore their locks just as long as their opponents'; and under Oliver Cromwell could soon field far more skilful horsemen.

Nevertheless it was undoubtedly the most severe Puritan element which came to dominate the councils of the Commonwealth after Charles I had been defeated and executed. Theatres were closed, dancing was proscribed, and church attendance on Sunday was strictly enjoined on the whole populace. Old Church of England incumbents were dismissed from their places. One rector who refused to quit his living had his household furniture and 'five very good horses' seized, and after being charged with the heinous crime of having rung the sanctus bell was dragged from his pulpit and led out with one of his captors mockingly beating a frying-pan.

Although Cromwell himself always advocated 'liberty of conscience' in all matters spiritual and temporal, and even during his virtual dictatorship as Lord Protector tried to restrain the excesses of some of his associates, for too many this meant liberty for those of their own persuasion, with concessions for Quakers and Jews but none for Roman Catholics or the majority of Anglicans.

One of the least attractive features of the Commonwealth interregnum was the zeal with which iconoclasts, officially enjoined to destroy all 'graven images' as a lingering contamination of Popery, went about their business of smashing statues, fonts, and stained glass. Even while the Civil War had been still in progress, the Earl of

Peckover House, home of a Wisbech banking family who later amalgamated with Barclays, was built in 1722 and extended by their millionaire descendant, Algernon Peckover, in the nineteenth century.

Manchester had commissioned William Dowsing of Laxfield in Suffolk as Parliamentary Visitor to demolish all superstitious pictures, images and inscriptions.

Dowsing threw himself wholeheartedly into this vandalism. At Hadleigh he destroyed '70 superstitious pictures', including all the church's stained glass. At Bramfield he happily recorded the demise of '24 superstitious pictures: one crucifix and picture of Christ: and twelve angels on the roof: and divers Jesus' in capital letters: and the steps, those to the rood-loft, to be levelled.' At Mildenhall, axes and hammers chopped down some wooden figures, and although the angels in the roof were too high for the wreckers to reach, they peppered them with small shot and even with arrows. Faces on fonts were obliterated, or whole figures chopped away – as on the Seven Sacraments font at Southwold. The huge church at Blythburgh required so much work that Dowsing housed his men and stabled their horses there during the proceedings: remains of the tethering rings are still to be found in the nave pillars, and the brickwork of the floor around the pillars has been trampled. After removing brasses, breaking and throwing away statues, attacking the angels in the roof with musket fire and smashing the stained glass windows, Dowsing must have taken away the church plate, as it was never seen again. As a final insult he presented the churchwardens with a bill for his services. Dowsing lived to a ripe old age and was buried in Laxfield in 1679. His grave has never shown any sign of becoming a place of pilgrimage.

Others resorted less to physical violence than to verbal dissent, denunciation and adjuration. Not content with a State religion which preached austerity but theoretically allowed freedom of inner interpretation of the Gospels, in keeping with Cromwell's tolerant 'Fear lest error might step in is like the man who would keep all wine out of the country lest men should be drunk', there was a proliferation of sectarians each determined to outdo the next in the extremity of his views. There were Calvinists, Levellers, Diggers, Fifth Monarchy Men who announced the imminence of the Second Coming of Christ and offered themselves as the best qualified to prepare the country's administration for that event, Quakers, Ranters and Muggletonians, who claimed the gift of prophecy and the God-given power to lay curses on all who opposed them.

One who listened to a number of Nonconformist doctrinaires and became obsessed with a sense of personal sin was John Bunyan, son of a tinker and small landowner near Bedford. The boy was born in 1628 at Elstow, where the Moot Hall is now a Bunyan museum. Conscripted into the Parliamentary army, he was subjected not only to military discipline but to the religious disquisitions which were part of everyday conversation. When he married in 1649 – 'as poor as poor might be, not having so much household stuff as a dish or spoon betwixt us both' – his wife did at least bring with her two of her father's religious books, which had a great influence on Bunyan. Increasingly worried about his own chances of salvation, he joined a local Baptist community, began preaching in the neighbourhood, and wrote polemical tracts against Quakers and other sects which in his eyes were all wanting in one essential or another.

When Cromwell died and his son proved incapable of sustaining the Protectorate, Charles II was called back from exile by a country weary of Puritan gloom and sectarian eccentricities. The Church of England was restored with its bishops and Prayer Book, and Nonconformist preachers driven from their parishes. A reconstituted Parliament set about expunging the Puritan influence. A Five Mile Act forbade any Nonconformist minister to live within five miles of his previous parish or even to visit it. Many secret meetings were nevertheless held. For example, the erstwhile vicar of Ovingham in Northumberland continued to address his congregation in the secret attic of a thatched house at Horsley, near Hadrian's Wall. When more tolerant times came, what is now the restored Congregational church was built next door, and the surreptitious meeting-place became the Manse.

John Bunyan was among those who suffered for their refusal to conform. Arrested as a 'common upholder of several unlawful meetings', he was sent to Bedford gaol and spent most of the next 12 years there, with only brief intermissions. In 1672 Charles II, who had signed a secret treaty with France pledging himself to announce his conversion to the Roman Catholic faith as soon as was practicable, offered a Declaration of Indulgence to make things easier for the Catholics with whom he was covertly in sympathy, and, perhaps to mask his true purpose, also eased the penalties on Nonconformists. Bunyan was released from prison.

But by now Parliament was largely in the hands of orthodox Anglicans who deplored any attempt to ease the lot of Dissenters, and in retaliation they pushed through even more stringent legislation, categorically denying the doctrine of transubstantiation – a calculated slap in the face to Catholics – and excluding from universities and from any significant office those who would not take the sacrament according to Anglican rites. John Bunyan, who had been invited by his old congregation to preach to them in a disused barn, found himself back in gaol for six months, during which time he wrote most of *The Pilgrim's Progress* – or, to give it its full title, *The Pilgrim's Progress from this World to that which is to come.* This symbolic narrative of Christian's journey, with a burden on his back, from the City of Destruction towards the Celestial City, embodies all Bunyan's ideas and fears in the shape of allegorical personages and places. Although few of his other writings are easy to assimilate or, indeed, offer much enlightenment even to the most devout reader, this one book is of such intensity and universal appeal that it has been translated into more than 100 different languages and dialects.

The site of the old gaol is marked with a pavement slab on the corner of Silver Street, Bedford. One of its doors is preserved in the museum of Bunyan relics in the Mill Street barn where he used to preach, and the bronze outer doors of this museum carry bas-relief scenes from *The Pilgrim's Progress.*

Another son of the region was Samuel Pepys, born in 1633, who went for a short period to that same Huntingdon school which Cromwell had attended some decades earlier, and in due course to Magdalene college, Cambridge. Lodged in Magdalene are the volumes of his fascinating diary, so difficult to decipher because of the deliberately obscure shorthand he adopted. In associating his name primarily with these racy, gossipy journals, we tend to overlook his invaluable work under both Charles II and James II as a reformer at the Admiralty in the teeth of stuffy tradition and obstruction.

Pepys frequently returned to the family home at Brampton, now in Cambridgeshire, near the

Oliver Cromwell attended Huntingdon grammar school, converted in 1565 from a Norman hospital, across the road from the church where he was christened and in which his father is buried.

mansion of Hinchingbrooke House built by Cromwell's great-grandfather. On one occasion he is reported to have buried his money in the garden there when fearing either the Plague or a possible Dutch invasion. In 1842 an iron pot of silver coins was discovered by the garden wall, and may well have been part of his hoard which he forgot to recover.

Recluses

The Fens were not the only tracts of England waterlogged for much of their history. Far across country in Somerset, much of Sedgemoor is still below sea level, and when its swamps were settled in Iron Age times the villages had to be built on stilts to keep their thatched huts above the floods. Access and exit were by means of wooden causeways to firmer ground. Peat formed here in the same way as in the Fens, and helped to preserve fragments of the circular hut villages of Meare and Godney, now in the museum at Taunton and the Tribunal at Glastonbury.

Attempts at drainage began early in the fifteenth century but made little progress until the reign of Charles I, when there was woven a network of main drains and ditches, known in this part of the country as rhines.

Those with a bent for solitude – hermits, ascetics, anchorites and other religious solitaries – have frequently chosen such settings for their fasting and meditation. In some instances there are indications of their taking over pre-Christian religious sites. Glastonbury, associated with the 'Isle of Avalon' and so much of the mythology of King Arthur, sits above the Somerset marshes near an impressive Iron Age earthwork which seems indefensible as a fort but could well have been a Celtic sanctuary and meeting-place. Christian settlers perhaps shared their predecessors' taste for such eerie wildernesses; or perhaps were

The dog-tooth arch above the ruined altar of Crowland's Benedictine abbey, damaged by Danes, Henry VIII's commissioners, and Cromwellian artillery.

determined to cancel out earlier pagan rituals with the resonances of their own.

The dank islet of Croyland (now Crowland) in the Lincolnshire Fens attracted, in a mood of self-chastisement, Guthlac, the son of a seventh-century Mercian, who gave up a military career to become a monk. Educated at the abbey of Repton, he decided to seek seclusion for his deeper soul-searching, and was rowed to Croyland by a boatman who recommended the bleak place as ideally suited to his needs. Plagued in his hermitage by marsh fevers and by the insults and boorishness of such few human beings as eked out a living in the vicinity, Guthlac prayed for aid – and was miraculously presented with a three-thonged whip to fight off his persecutors. On the west front of the abbey there remains a carving of this whip in his hand; and the abbey's coat of arms combines St Guthlac's three whips with St Bartholomew's three knives. The floor of the original hermitage was excavated in 1908 and, though covered in again, is marked by a metal plate in the south aisle of the abbey church.

The foundation itself was the gift of Ethelbald of Mercia in gratitude for St Guthlac's prophecies, advice and prayers, given when the prince sought refuge on the island from a cousin and rival who sought to remove him from the Mercian succession. It is said, proudly though with little verifiable evidence, that Hereward the Wake was later buried here.

Boundary markers of the old abbey can still be found around the fringes of its jurisdiction. At Brotherhouse, bordering on Spalding, St Guthlac's Cross in the toll-house garden carries an inscription whose translation declares: 'This rock, I say, is Guthlac's utmost bound.'

The strange triangular Trinity Bridge once enabled villagers to cross dry-shod over the waterways formed by a division of the river Welland – not to mention the all-too-frequent flooding of the streets in later times. There are still traces of the base of a preaching cross at the apex of the bridge, at which an annual ceremony is still held.

THE HAUNTED BORDERS

SLAUGHTER BRIDGE on the river Camel in Cornwall carries, together with a nearby stone slab called Arthur's Tomb, the legendary resonance of the battle of Camlann at which King Arthur was mortally wounded. Contesting the authenticity of this tomb, Glastonbury sets itself up as Arthur's last resting-place, standing above the Vale of Avalon to which he was borne away to be immortally healed. Glastonbury monks in 1190 recorded the finding of the sixth-century grave of both Arthur and his queen, Guinevere. In 1278 this tomb was opened in the presence of Edward I and Queen Eleanor, who took the bones out of their respective caskets, wrapped them in silk, and rehoused them in a sumptuous black marble tomb which stood in the choir until the Dissolution of the abbey in 1539. The base of this demolished shrine was rediscovered in 1934, and the site is now marked by a plaque and concrete surround.

The once and future king
Originating in the Celtic fringes of our homeland, this most persistent and pervasive of all British legends has acquired more national and local embroideries than narratives of any other ruler, real or fanciful: Wales, Cornwall and Brittany all claim the authentic settings, but the name and exploits of Arthur echo right up England to Arthur's Seat in Cumbria and across the border to Arthur's Seat in Edinburgh, Ben Arthur in

Legend says that the Rollright Stones can never be accurately counted, that no human force can shift them, but that they go of their own accord at midnight to drink at a stream in the nearby spinney.

Dumbartonshire, and yet another Arthur's Seat in Angus. Like Robin Hood, he seems to have been wherever his admirers would have wished.

In all its manifestations the basic story belongs to medieval romance, serving as the theme for French and English fashions in chivalry and courtly love, with a touch of mysticism where the Church related it to the allegorical quest for the Holy Grail. But there was no King Arthur in the Middle Ages: no Round Table, and no roster of knights errant riding out to rescue fair damsels; no shining Walt Disney castle for them to return to. If there ever was a living Arthur, he must have been a harassed Romano-British chieftain trying to stem the Saxon invasions after Rome had abandoned Britain. There may well have been several such chieftains organizing resistance in different parts of the country, with all their achievements and failures and legends coalescing over the centuries into one symbolic figure.

Picking out possible truth from colourful fantasy is an arduous task. One of our few points of reference would seem to be Mount Badon, at which it is recorded there was a major British victory against the Saxons in about A.D. 500. But where was Badon? Badbury Rings in Dorset provide one conjecture; Liddington Castle near Swindon another; and one chronicler places it near Bath. Whatever its location, it does seem that the battle brought several years of peace and that some leader named Arthur was largely responsible – though the Arthur mentioned in a ninth-century history of Britain describes him as a general rather than a king.

Legend makes this hero the son of Uther Pendragon, himself one of the sons of the Emperor

Constantine III. Uther fathered Arthur on the wife of the Earl of Cornwall, having impersonated the earl with the aid of the wizard Merlin. The boy's birthplace was Tintagel castle. In fact the ruins of this castle do not date back to the only period in which an authentic Arthur could have lived. There was an early Celtic monastery here, but no record of a castle until the Normans set up a motte and bailey during the troubles of Stephen's reign. This was reinforced a century or so later, but fell into decay and was neglected until nineteenth-century devotees of Tennyson's *Idylls of the King* revived interest in it. The seer Merlin, who trained Arthur during his childhood and foretold many of the triumphs and tragedies of his reign, is remembered in Merlin's Cave below Tintagel; and there is a Merlin's Rock associated with his prophecies near Mousehole quay.

Arthur's royal court and his Round Table are always located in a many-towered Camelot. And this Camelot is often linked with Cadbury, not a fairy-tale palace but a massive Somerset hill-fort where excavations have revealed layer upon layer of human settlement. There are traces of Stone Age, Bronze Age, Iron Age and Roman occupation. Somewhere around 500, just the right time to fit the Arthurian story, there was another phase of fortification and the building of a large hall on the summit. Later the Saxons also took possession. The flat top on which the hall was built is now known as King Arthur's Palace, and one of the wells is King Arthur's Well. Somewhere in the depths of the mound is said to be a golden gate beyond which Arthur sleeps until awakened in the hour of England's greatest peril. But how does the idea of this secret chamber fit in with the bones of that burial at Glastonbury? Certainly there was a physical link between the two places: remains of a causeway have been traced, now inevitably known as Arthur's Causeway and included by some in the accruing legends as the path along which the dying king was carried to Avalon.

But he is also said to be at rest in a cave below Hadrian's Wall. And near Dorstone in Herefordshire is Arthur's Stone, marking his grave – or perhaps the grave of a rival king who died in combat with him.

The Round Table hangs in Winchester castle. Malory, whose *Morte d'Arthur* was the encapsulation of many earlier legends and the inspiration of many later writers, saw Winchester as Camelot. Henry VII, basing much of his claim to the throne

The wording around the Tudor rose claims 'Thys is the rownde table of Kyng Arthur with xxiv of hys namyde knyggtes'.

of England through Welsh descent from Arthur himself, subscribed to this view, and had his first son baptized Arthur at Winchester. Married young to Catherine of Aragon, Arthur died at the age of 16, leaving his widow to become the wife of his younger brother, Henry VIII – a marriage which was to have so many fearful repercussions. As to the Round Table itself, it is unlikely to have been made before the thirteenth century and was later embellished with the Tudor rose and designs boosting the Tudor claims to Arthurian ancestry.

The interested traveller can hardly fail to find other allusions wherever he goes. Typical are the Table Men rock near Land's End, a tomb slab supposed to have been the scene of a thanksgiving feast after Arthur, in the company of several Cornish chieftains, had defeated an enemy onslaught; St Michael's Mount, boasting itself the last outcrop of the lost land of sunken Lyonesse in which 'the last great battle of the West' was fought by Arthur; and Dozmary Pool on Bodmin

Moor, the lake into which Sir Bedivere threw Arthur's sword Excalibur at the end.

The Devil at large

Dozmary Pool plays a part in other local tales, including that of the villainous Jan Tregeagle. A seventeenth-century magistrate who misused his position to acquire a tidy fortune, Tregeagle was rumoured to have sold his soul to the Devil, murdered his wife and children, and then bribed his way to burial in consecrated ground. Summoned from the grave, his evil spirit was set the task of emptying Dozmary Pool with a perforated shell, a tedious job whose monotony was relieved every now and then by the Devil and a pack of headless hounds arriving to chase him across the moor.

The Devil's appearances in folklore are almost as frequent as those of King Arthur, and as widespread, though with less noble connotations. In Herefordshire he once tried to make himself a fishpond by damming Orcrop Hill weir, but dropped some of the stones on Garway Hill, where they now lie as the White Rocks. Another stone, said to bear his fingerprints, lies on the bank of Semer

Dozmary Pool, Cornwall, is said to be the last resting place of King Arthur's sword; but Richard I in 1191 presented a supposed Excalibur to Tancred of Sicily, claiming it had been preserved in Glastonbury abbey.

Water in Yorkshire, where he dropped it during an exchange of missiles with a giant. Following a bet with an Exmoor giant he constructed during one night a bridge of huge stone slabs known as Tarr Steps, or the Devil's Bridge. And in that same part of the world, during the freezing winter of 1855, he left a trail of footprints 100 miles across country, up the sides of barns and haystacks and along roofs.

Children have often been courageous enough or foolish enough to evolve dances or rituals meant to summon up witches or demons. At Westleton in Suffolk they used to dance widdershins round the Witch's Stone. In Bungay in the same county, near the north porch of St Mary's church is a stone thought to have been here for 2,000 years, round which until quite recently boys and girls used to skip 12 times while pretending to invoke the Devil. Whether on one occasion

The builder of these early nineteenth-century cottages at Veryan, Cornwall, chose a circular shape so there would be no corners for the Devil to hide in.

some few hundred years ago this proved too successful, or whether some temporary canine madness was to blame, it is impossible now to tell; but one Sunday in broad daylight a huge black dog raged into the church and tore out the throats of some worshippers. Such an animal appears in the town sign, stabbed by forked lightning and said to represent the Devil – or perhaps Black Shuck, the legendary hellhound with blazing eyes of the Suffolk coast and marshes. Some sort of fiendish mischief was also wrought at Blythburgh in 1577, when a storm brought down the steeple and blew in the north door. Some members of the congregation swore that they had been burnt by the Devil's breath; and there are still scorch marks to be seen on the door.

Fortunately Satan seems rather ill-equipped for most of the wicked tasks he undertakes. At Rudston in Yorkshire he tried to destroy the church by hurling a huge monolith at it, but the stone fell short and now stands in the churchyard – the tallest standing stone in England. He was more successful at Graveley in Hertfordshire, where he brought down the church steeple; but even there it is said that he was actually aiming at Stevenage. The lumps of earth he dug from six holes in a nearby wood all went wide, and now form the Six Hills. These round barrows were once thought to date from the Bronze Age, but it has been shown that they were in fact Roman burial mounds.

Other missiles which fell short are the Devil's Arrows near Boroughbridge in Yorkshire, mementoes of the Devil's failure to annihilate the inhabitants of Aldborough, a mile or so away. Perhaps his fiendish temper spoilt his aim here and on other occasions.

Every now and then his wrath was directed against an individual rather than entire communities. There are several versions of his encounters with St Dunstan who, as a blacksmith, made horseshoes – always believed to have special powers in warding off evil. One story has it that the saint once shod the Devil's cloven hoofs, burning him so badly that the poor arch-fiend rushed away and shunned horseshoes for ever after. Dunstan was working at Mayfield in Sussex when the Devil, disguised as a woman, came to tempt him. But the saint spotted a cloven hoof below the hem of the dress and, snatching red-hot tongs from the forge, pinched his guest's nose so that the Devil once more screamed and fled. Either this or a similar episode is thought to account for the name of Tongdean Farm on the South Downs. The original tongs are housed in the Convent of the Holy Child at Mayfield. Or so it is said: their workmanship shows them to be far too late for this tenth-century archbishop.

Many an ancient ditch, cleft or embankment calls itself the Devil's Dyke. Three of the most impressive are at Wheathampstead, Newmarket, and Brighton. The one behind Brighton is another example of infernal ineptitude. Enraged by the sanctity of the Sussex Wealden churches, the Devil decided one night to dig a channel from the sea through the Downs in order to drown the lot of them. But all it took to frighten him off was an old woman holding a candle up to her cottage window to see what the commotion was, thereby setting the cocks crowing in the belief that it was dawn and so driving the bungler away.

Others have given Old Nick a bad time of it. In Norfolk and Suffolk there are several representations of Sir John Schorne, who succeeded in catching the Devil in his boot. In Cawston church Sir John is honoured with a place among the saints on the screen.

Sometimes the Devil's spitefulness did work. The standing, leaning and collapsed stones of the megalithic circles and avenues at Stanton Drew in Somerset have the sad reputation of being petrified sinners who danced to the Devil's fiddle from a Saturday night on into the Sabbath. Here they must remain until he deigns to return and strike up the music again. Similar legends cling to a number of Cornish stone circles each known as the Nine Maidens. One of the best examples is at Boscawen-ûn near Land's End where, as with the Merry Maidens on the other side of St Buryan, each stone in the ring represents a girl who danced on a Sunday, and a stone set apart from the rest is identified as the piper.

Dark echoes linger also in the limestone crevices of the Rollright Stones on the border of Oxfordshire and Warwickshire. Here a king setting forth for conquest fell foul of a witch to whom this land belonged. She transformed him and his men into stone and herself into an elder tree. The King Stone is set apart, and the King's

One of three fluted monoliths of millstone grit, the 'Devil's Arrows' near Boroughbridge, probably relics of a Bronze Age sanctuary of the Brigantes.

men are drawn up in a stone circle, while some distance away another cluster of stones (clearly the remains of an ancient burial chamber) is known as the Whispering Knights because the wind rustling through them is believed to whisper prophecies. In days gone by it was a local custom for young men and women to meet here at certain times of the year for a special picnic; and when the elder tree was in blossom, all would gather round the isolated King Stone while someone cut the tree, and as the sap oozed out it was said that the King's head moved.

A haunted battlefield

While Charles II was still in exile in Holland, one of his mistresses produced an illegitimate son, James. After the Restoration the boy was created Duke of Monmouth. He was a popular and efficient soldier, and towards the end of his father's reign there was strong Protestant support for having him declared successor to the throne,

The marshy battlefield of Sedgemoor in Somerset, in one of whose ditches the defeated Duke of Monmouth cowered until his tearful eyes gave him away.

rather than Charles's Catholic brother James, Duke of York. When Charles died, however, Monmouth was in Holland, where he had fled after being suspected of complicity in a plot to kill his father and uncle. The Duke of York became King James II in February 1685.

In June of that year the Duke of Monmouth was encouraged by Protestant elements to sail for England and assert his claims to the throne. Landing at Lyme Regis, he rallied several thousand west-countrymen to his standard and at Taunton proclaimed himself King. But James's forces were ready for him. Battle-trained veterans of Tangier and other campaigns met Monmouth's peasant army on the misty plain of Sedgemoor and cut it to pieces. Monmouth was captured, and executed on Tower Hill. Such of his followers as survived the battle were mercilessly hunted down, their families driven from their homes, and anyone suspected of the slightest sympathy with the rebels condemned at the 'Bloody Assize' of the

sadistic Judge Jeffreys to death, torture, flogging or transportation.

In Lyme Regis the house where Jeffreys dined after sentencing 12 to hang is said, whenever there is no one in residence, to be haunted by his wretched ghost, eternally gnawing a bloody bone.

At Locking, a little way inland from Weston-super-Mare, the barking of a dog betrayed its master's hiding-place and so led to his being apprehended and hanged. The widow grabbed the dog and hurled herself with it down the well. From time to time she goes wailing across the district with the dog under her arm.

On the battlefield itself the defeated rebels still sometimes shout defiance, their spirits hang in the air or drift away like glowing wills-o'-the-wisp, and horses charge while men flee into cloudy nothingness. Every 5th July the phantom Duke of Monmouth rides madly away, deserting them as he deserted them in 1685.

Dame Alice Lisle, 70-year-old widow of one of those who had voted for Charles I's execution, was tried on a charge of treasonably sheltering two fugitives and condemned by Jeffreys to burn at the stake. After a wave of protest the sentence was commuted to that of beheading in Winchester marketplace. Occupants of Dame Alice's old home at Moyles Court in Dorset have frequently heard the rustle of her gown and footsteps across the floor.

Although James II was still in power, his triumph proved short-lived. Having alienated the majority of his people and government by anti-Protestant measures and by intrigues with France, he faced another invasion through the West country. This time his own daughter Mary was involved: she and her husband, William of Orange, were invited by Parliament to become joint sovereigns. When 'The Glorious Revolution' of 1688 began at Torbay there was some reluctance on the part of local inhabitants, with their terrible memories of the Monmouth aftermath, to join the newcomers. But this time there was no Sedgemoor. William's forces advanced unopposed, James fled the country, and after his one attempt to regain the Crown at the battle of the Boyne in Ireland there was an end to the Catholic Stuarts and, with William III and Mary, the effective beginning of 'the Protestant Succession'.

Little sympathy was felt for one terrified fugitive. James II's Lord Chancellor, the infamous Jeffreys, tried to flee the country dressed as

On his way from Brixham to Exeter, William of Orange is said to have held his first impromptu council outside Parliament Cottage at Lincombe, Devon.

a sailor, but was recognized and caught near Wapping Old Stairs on the Thames. He was thrown into the Tower, and died there.

Dances and processions

Although the Stuarts were gone, some affectionate memories and superstitions remained in certain minds and hearts. After Charles I's execution there was for a time a brisk trade in curative handkerchiefs soaked in his blood on the scaffold. When there were still vague hopes of a Jacobite restoration, a toast was commonly drunk to 'the little gentleman in black velvet' – the mole into whose hole William III's horse put a foot, so throwing the king and leading to his death.

At Castleton in Derbyshire there is an annual procession on Oak Apple Day associated with Charles II's concealment at Boscobel. But there are other threads of older origin. The Garland King who rides within a wicker cage interlaced with flowers and leaves is another version of the fertility figure of the May King, and of that Green Man known through so much folk lore. It has additionally been suggested that his strange cage, which at the end of the day is hoisted to the

top of the church tower and left there until the vegetation has shrivelled, may hark back to Julius Caesar's reference to a Celtic tribal custom of making just such wickerwork cages into which human sacrifices were packed and set on fire.

Many local customs and annual fêtes have been appropriated by the Christian church and invested with new significance, without losing the undertones of the old. Fertility rites become harvest festivals; pagan celebrations of sun gods and earth spirits become church holy days; but the veneer is often a thin one.

Our old acquaintance the Devil rears his clumsy head again at Helston in Cornwall. He was returning from one of his visits to the neighbourhood with a huge slab of granite to block the gates of Hell. The archangel Michael, patron saint of both the town and the county, engaged him in combat and forced him to drop the stone in the courtyard of the Angel Inn. This Hell Stone of Helston is now set in the wall of the old coaching inn dedicated, like the parish church, to St Michael.

On his feast day, 8th May, a revel which used to be known as the Servants' Ball begins at seven o'clock in the morning and goes on well into the hours beyond twilight. It has had a variety of names. In the late eighteenth century it was referred to as a Faddy, became the Floral Dance, and now is more usually called the Furry Dance. There are undoubted floral associations, maybe derived from some pagan celebration of spring: before the dancing starts, young people go into nearby woods to collect branches of beech and sycamore. 'Furry' links two concepts: the Celtic *feur* or fair, and the Latin *feria* or holy day – in this case unquestionably St Michael's day.

When the sprigs have been carried into the town in a procession featuring – so far from Sherwood Forest! – Robin Hood and his Merry Men, children start up a dance. This is taken over at noon by the Mayor in full regalia, after which two natives of the place lead their friends and neighbours through the streets, all dressed in their best. Once it was customary to weave in and out of houses and shops during this sort of Cornish Conga, but in recent years these diversions have been eliminated.

Another dance starting early in the morning and threading its course through village streets is the Horn Dance of Abbots Bromley in Staffordshire, held annually on Wakes Monday, the first Monday after 4th September. The participants dress in Tudor costume, six of them wearing heavy reindeer antlers and accompanied by a jester, a bowman, a hobby-horse rider and Maid Marian (an inexplicable hermaphrodite who would surely have puzzled Robin Hood), supposedly to celebrate the grant of hunting rights in Needwood Forest. The origin of their ritual movements, pursuits and mock stag battles must, however, stem from something much deeper in history. There are obvious parallels with the prehistoric symbolic hunting and fertility ceremonies which one sees painted on the walls of the Lascaux caves. The horns themselves, three pairs painted blue and three white, are kept all year round in a chapel of the parish church, but have a pagan ring to them. It has been piously suggested that they were trophies brought back by a Crusading member of the Bagot family of neighbouring Blithfield Hall from the Holy Land – an odd place for reindeer, surely? More plausibly there is a story of their having come with the Vikings.

The maypole at Aldborough in Yorkshire, repainted and topped with a crown for the coronation of Queen Elizabeth II in 1953.

The Vikings loom large again at Minehead in Somerset. Their attacks on the little estuary town were so frequent and ferocious that the inhabitants decided to answer fear with fear, and built a longship in the form of a terrifying sea serpent. The next gang of raiders fled ignominiously. A distorted replica of the serpent appears in the Hobby Horse which emerges on the evening of May Day and prances about the neighbourhood for the next three days to the accompaniment of drum and concertina. Beneath the floral ribbons and framework there is more than a hint of some half-forgotten spring fertility ritual.

A number of church processions derive from similarly clouded sources. The beating of bounds in spring goes back to pagan practices of beating the earth to awaken it and start the crops germinating. Rogation Days (asking days) follow pre-Christian patterns of pleading with God, or the gods, to bless the fruits of the earth and protect them from parching and pestilence. The Roman Lupercalia, an annual festival of purification and sanctification related to the legend of Rome's founding by the sucklings of a wolf, involved a ritual dance around the altar on which dogs and goats were sacrificed. Afterwards, flayed shreds of the victims were carried around the city and the sacred places. From this came 'church clipping', in which parishioners encircle their church while holding hands, dancing three times in and three times out and singing a traditional hymn.

When we think of round dances we can hardly forget the encircling of the maypole. The rite was another of those offered in phallic homage to the god of fertility. The pole itself, garnished with flowers and ribbons, was usually of birch and in most towns and villages was raised on the green or in the marketplace the evening before May Day. London retained several permanent maypoles – the name of St Andrew Undershaft embodies the 'shaft' standing close by the church, pulled down in 1517 when City apprentices rioted against their merchant employers. During the Commonwealth the whole idea of May Day celebrations was frowned on, and the maypoles were proscribed until the Restoration. One of those replaced was a tall cedar shaft in the Strand, later removed to serve as a support for a Royal Society telescope in Isaac Newton's day. Others, replaced or renewed when necessary, still keep their place in remoter towns and villages. One painted in spiralling red stripes stands on the green of Welford-on-Avon, Warwickshire. The lord of the manor at Temple Sowerby, Westmorland, is in duty bound to renew the village maypole if it deteriorates. The 100-foot specimen at Barwick-in-Elmet, Yorkshire, is taken down by specially appointed polemen every three years for repainting. And the town of Aldborough in Yorkshire offers a fine historical summary: capital of the tribe of the Brigantes; Roman town with mosaic pavements some of which find their way into the local inn; preserving a battle cross commemorating a clash in 1322 between Edward II's forces and the rebellious Earl of Lancaster at Boroughbridge; and the tall, quivering maypole.

So the process of assimilation went on and will probably continue to do so. Celtic water sprites intermarried with Saxon and Norse gods. The Romans, sprawling across the known world, enforced some doctrines and blended others together. At Bath they left a fine gilt-bronze head of their goddess Minerva, but an equally fine stone representation of Minerva's protégée Medusa combined with a Celtic water divinity's daughter to form the dual deity Sulis-Minerva. The patron spirit of the Brigantes was elevated to the status of the goddess Brigantia complete with Minerva's spear and shield and the wings of Victory. Pagan horses cut out of chalk downs were linked with the legends of St George and so became Christian symbols. And when some figures or formations proved too recalcitrant to be taken into the family of the faithful . . . why, then they were condemned as works of Satan, in Devil's Jumps and Devil's Dykes and Devil's Punchbowls and Devil's Quoits.

One wonders what nomenclature the future (if there be one) will invent for our own fabrications: Satan's Suburb, Dictator's Ditch, the Dancing Drug Addicts, the Concrete Skeletons? Doubtless man will prove no less ingenious than before.

INDUSTRIAL REVOLUTIONS

RICHARD ARKWRIGHT'S ORIGINALLY hand-operated spinning frame of 1769 is preserved in the Science Museum, South Kensington. At Helmshore in Lancashire is a mill whose fulling stocks and spinning machinery were driven by a waterwheel. There are bigger waterwheels at Foster Beck mill in Yorkshire, and the Killhope crushing mill in County Durham; and the mightiest of them all at Laxey in the Isle of Man, used for driving pumps in lead mines. One of the Cornish engine houses at Botallack clings precariously to a cliff, high above lead mines which reach far out below the sea. At Coalbrookdale in the Severn valley, the furnace where Abraham Darby first smelted iron ore with coke in 1709 lay preserved, like some ancient tomb, under a burial mound of waste until excavated in our own time. And the Tanfield Tramway in County Durham has left us Causey Arch, the oldest railway bridge in the world, built in 1727 to carry wooden tramlines high above the deep cleft of a stream.

These are just a few of the monuments which, scattered far from one another, yet combine to form the foundations of our present age. We tend to lump them too indiscriminately together under the heading of the Industrial Revolution: there never was a single, identifiable revolution; many things in many places contributed to bring about a variety of changes, and these in themselves created further needs, patterns and complexities.

Textile manufacture created the first large-scale factories in England. Richard Arkwright of Nottingham built the first water-powered cotton mill above the river Derwent at Cromford in Derbyshire in 1771.

Manpower to steam power

From ancient times until just over 200 years ago textile manufacture was a largely domestic occupation. Families spun by hand and wove by hand. Among the earliest real factories were the fulling mills, at first small communal buildings beside running water which then expanded, particularly in the West Riding of Yorkshire, into larger units as other hand-work processes became mechanized. Allerton Hall on the outskirts of Bradford still has some old weavers' cottages about its courtyard. Near Hebden Bridge is a small mill which once employed only a score of workers in sylvan surroundings, and at Hepstonstall above it is a cosy group of cottages; but the town itself now presents the familiar mill-town scene of large factories, chimneys, and congested back-to-back terraced houses. Piece Hall, opened in Halifax in 1775 as a trade and bargaining centre, is a far cry from Lavenham's half-timbered Guildhall. In Leeds, Burley Mills recall the profits to be made from military requirements during the Napoleonic wars, and show how the actual weaving was also being pulled in close to the fulling mill – no longer a matter of outworkers carrying on a trade in their own time on their own premises.

The great innovations, however, came more quickly in the cotton industry. In 1768 a Blackburn weaver, James Hargreaves, invented a spinning machine which he called a 'Jenny', after his wife. It could spin a number of threads at once: over 100, by the time he had perfected it. A year later Richard Arkwright produced in Nottingham a water frame capable of spinning a fine yarn which could also be pressed and twisted to an

125

A flax mill waterwheel near Pateley Bridge, Yorkshire.

Goadby-Marwood in Leicestershire a power loom, models of which were put into operation in Doncaster and Manchester. Weavers afraid of losing their livelihood burnt down the Manchester mill. But there was no holding back the new methods, where rows of looms in a factory could be driven by one long shaft turned by a waterwheel. Human hands were now needed only to tend the implacable machines.

Running water had already been used to operate other early industrial processes. In Queen Elizabeth's time her jeweller, Sir John Spielmann, had been granted a licence to collect waste as raw material for the manufacture of paper, and founded a paper mill at Dartford in Kent. His name in German means a jester, and his use of a jester's figure in the watermark of his paper probably gave rise to the word 'foolscap'. Other mills appeared along the banks of the Darent and Medway, convenient not only as a source of power but, following the demand in later centuries for imported basic materials, as waterways for incoming Baltic and Canadian logs and wood pulp. Today more than a quarter of Britain's paper is produced in these North Kent factories.

In Northumberland there are remains near Haughton Castle of a paper mill built in 1788 which operated for about a century before being abandoned. Remains of its water supply channels and the drying room are still identifiable. Soon after it was built it began to produce paper for forged assignats, the currency used in republican France. When the Duke of York launched his unsuccessful campaign in the Netherlands in 1793, he took a supply of these forgeries with the intention of spreading them around and depreciating the enemy currency. One of the moulds for this process is preserved in the Black Gate Museum, Newcastle.

The next step in the textile industry was to find a driving power which did not confine the mills to watercourses which might be difficult of access or, in times of drought, be reduced to a trickle or even dry up altogether.

A Dartmouth blacksmith, Thomas Newcomen, had found a way of using steam to drive machinery for pumping water out of mines. His first engine was set up in 1712 at Dudley Castle in Staffordshire, soon to be followed by many others in coal mines and the engine houses in Cornish tin mines. A reconditioned example has been given a home in a specially built engine house in Newcomen's birthplace, Dartmouth, and remains of a typical

improved firmness. It had a drawback: its action was too heavy to be operated by human hands. The earliest models were horse-driven; but then Arkwright moved to Cromford in Derbyshire, built the first water-powered cotton mill above the river Derwent in 1771, and attracted workers by setting up a factory village for them. The era of mass production and industrial townships was dawning.

The techniques of Hargreaves and Arkwright were combined in Samuel Crompton's 'mule', producing the finest thread yet. Crompton was cheated of the fruits of his inventive mind and died in poverty; but others prospered. It is salutary to note that the wool mill at Helmshore speedily turned its attention to cotton, and still has machinery based on the original mules.

All these new spinning devices increased output of thread enormously. But as yet there was no corresponding machinery for weaving, and the hand-loom workers could not cope with such increased supplies. It was left to a clergyman, Edmund Cartwright, to design in his rectory at

Remains of a mine engine house at Botallack, Cornwall.

set of granite buildings for pumping machinery, including the boiler house and a substantial section of chimney stack, are to be found at Wheal Busy near Porthtowan, Cornwall.

The engine was invaluable to the miners, but could not be modified for use with other machinery. Also it was wasteful: its principle of creating a vacuum in the cylinder by first heating that cylinder with steam and then injecting cold water to condense the steam meant too much expenditure of fuel and energy in the heating and re-heating cycle of the operation. This problem was solved by James Watt, a mathematical instrument maker at Glasgow University, when repairing a model Newcomen engine. He devised a separate condenser for cooling the steam, so avoiding wasteful fluctuations of temperature in the cylinder itself, and after going into partnership with the Birmingham manufacturer Matthew Boulton in 1775 built engines for mines, breweries and cotton mills.

The growth of these mills powered by steam was accompanied by the hurried building of cheap neighbouring houses for the workers, rarely with much concern for the true welfare of those workers.

Few had quite the quality and – by the standards of those times – the comfort and cleanliness of Styal, a village started in 1784 in Cheshire by the Quarry Bank mill owner Samuel Greg to attract hands for his factory, which, starting as a water-powered cotton mill, had steam machinery added in 1800. A few timber-framed agricultural cottages remain today, flanked by the terraces of Greg's factory colony. He also provided a shop, and took over a farm to provide its supplies. The whole complex, including his own house next to the mill, is now cared for by an independent trust under the wing of the National Trust.

Provision of shops by mill and mine owners was not always as advantageous to employees as one might suppose. These tommy shops or truck shops – 'truck' meaning the payment of wages in kind rather than in cash – were all too frequently monopolies which required the workers to accept smaller rations of food and goods in lieu of money than the money itself would have bought elsewhere, and which further debased supplies by adulterating sugar with sand, flour with chalk.

Quays at Newnham on the Gloucestershire banks of the Severn were supplied in the early nineteenth century with coal, timber and slate from the Forest of Dean by a tramway which incorporated the earliest known railway tunnel (1809).

Even after the Truck Act of 1831 made it an offence to pay any proportion of wages in kind, many owners still tried to force their employees into their own shops, which might be the only ones in the near neighbourhood. At Cramlington, near the collieries of Seaton Delaval, pitmen clubbed together to send one of their number regularly into Newcastle to buy in bulk; they were soon able to build a cooperative shop, warehouse and stables, traces of which remain in the village. But the acknowledged founders of the Co-operative Society movement were the Rochdale Pioneers, a group of 28 cotton weavers who opened a store in Toad Lane, Rochdale, and spread their ideas across the whole country.

Coal and iron

To construct the new engines there was need for increasing quantities of iron, and iron of a higher quality. The industry of the Weald of Kent and Sussex had been dwindling because of diminishing supplies of timber to provide charcoal. The Forest of Dean, too, was continually torn by disputes between iron-founders and foresters, who in the seventeenth century built a courthouse at which their conflicting interests could be argued out. This Speech House, though now a hotel, is still used for official sittings of the Verderers' Court.

It needed 200 acres of trees to make enough charcoal for a year's operation of one furnace. Experiments in the use of coal had been unsatisfactory until Abraham Darby was lucky enough to find the local Shropshire 'clod coal' particularly well suited for the production of coke for iron smelting. At first he produced only pig iron for casting. His son improved the process and began to produce bar iron. The family business prospered, making iron rails for tramways and iron parts for engines, until in 1777 Abraham Darby III rebuilt the old furnace in order to cast sections large enough for the world's first cast-iron bridge, giving its name to Ironbridge Gorge.

At Broseley, also in Shropshire, John Wilkinson opened new ironworks which produced borings and castings of the quality and accuracy essential to the Boulton and Watt development of steam engines. In 1783 Henry Cort took another step forward with his methods of puddling pig iron and rolling it into bar iron.

Industry could now get the quantity and quality of iron it needed. But, in the terrible relationship of supply, demand and capacity which resembled that of the spinning and weaving problems of the textile trade, who was to produce the tonnage of coal now required for smelting?

Although charcoal had for centuries been the staple fuel, coal had been known for just as long. As far back as Roman times it had been used in Britain, as proved by the fragments found in an Antonine building at Corstopitum and now displayed in the Corbridge museum. When men found it close to the surface, they grubbed it up gratefully. Early mines were little more than a scratching of the surface, or drift mines gouging into hillsides – the private probings of miners with old family privileges such as those of the Forest of Dean. As demand intensified the diggings had to be driven deeper, and there was a need for cheap labour to carry the product out of the tunnels and to a despatch point; and so underpaid women and children were brought in to supplement their men's work.

The nearest thing to mechanical lifting of coal from the depths was provided by a horse-gin, where a horse plodded round a circular track to turn a drum which lowered or raised ropes and their loads up and down a mine shaft. Once the raw material reached the top, tramways on wooden rails carried horse-drawn waggons (or chaldrons) to distribution centres, nearby factories or foundries, and ports: in the north-east, the coastal staithes were fed lavishly by the collieries surrounding Newcastle-upon-Tyne, justifying the old saw about the futility of taking coals to Newcastle.

A specimen of a horse-gin survives at Wollaton Hall in Nottingham.

Mechanized winding gear followed, together with a number of safety devices which, in spite of every subsequent technological advance, have not guaranteed absolute immunity from the perils of fire-damp explosions, or the collapse of pit-props and the entombment of pitmen.

Coal supplied the fuel to make iron, which supplied the machinery to draw up more coal to make more iron; and both coal and iron had to be shifted from place to place. Inevitably the means of transport became iron machines on iron rails.

Road, canal and railway

Until the middle of the eighteenth century the roads of England had been little better than long-trodden lanes, unsurfaced and frequently impassable in bad weather, more accustomed to the trudging of human and animal feet than to the rolling wheels of carriages. When travellers began to demand speedier and more comfortable transport for themselves, and merchants more secure thoroughfares for their commercial loads, attempts were made under local supervision to improve conditions. But for a long time there was little co-ordination. Parishes had always been charged with the responsibility of maintaining certain roads for the safe passage of the king and his officers; they were rarely assiduous in this task, and were all too ready to use disputes over shared responsibility with neighbouring parishes as an excuse for doing as little as possible.

A feudal lord of the manor had been supposed to care for road bridges within his domain, and the Church declared that the building and maintenance of bridges was a good deed helping towards salvation. Medieval guilds sometimes assumed responsibility for particular bridges and stretches of highway. In many cases small chapels were set on such bridges so that the traveller might pause for prayer, including a prayer for the souls of the builders. There are such bridge chapels at St Ives in Cambridgeshire, Bradford-on-Avon in Wiltshire, and two in Yorkshire – one at Rotherham, and a richly carved one above the river Calder at Wakefield.

In the eighteenth century a number of Acts of Parliament were passed to allow the construction of turnpikes, to be paid for by dues collected from travellers at bars and toll cottages, such tolls to be discontinued when the basic expense had been cleared and the parish could take over routine maintenance. Enclosure roads provided access to these main roads for farm waggons, though not many such feeders were surfaced until the end of the nineteenth century.

Toll cottages are still easily recognizable, even when converted to other uses. They were constructed so that windows could command views to either side, and occasionally even take in a side road at a junction. The shape was usually octagonal, sometimes with side windows in a large

Thatched toll cottage outside the village of Stanton Drew in Somerset where travellers' dues were collected.

ally be handed over to local authorities often took a long time to be fulfilled. When a turnpike trust could control the main roads in and out of a market town, it was in no hurry to relinquish its rights. In order to avoid a whole sequence of exactions, drovers continued to use ancient trackways where, in addition to free passage, their animals had the advantage of being able to feed and drink along the way. Farmers tried to get to market along side roads and back roads. When they had the power, the turnpike operators sealed off entries and exits so that traffic was forced to use the paying route. In the middle of the nineteenth century it was protested in Camberwell that 'every road, every alley, every passage has its "bar". One part of the parish – where the more humble classes of the community dwell – is completely isolated, and the back districts are cut off from all intercommunication by the Turnpike and Ticket System.'

Nevertheless, whatever its abuses, the system did provide the means of paying for new developments in road building. And, as the country-wide network was gradually rationalized, better directions were provided for travellers, and distances calculated more scientifically. After the adoption of 1,760 yards as the standard mile, Trinity Hall, Cambridge, set up between 1725 and 1729 the first milestones in England on the road from Barkway to Cambridge. They can be identified by the crescent emblem of Trinity Hall, and one near Trumpington may have utilized a stone of Roman origin. Under the shadows of modern metal signs with their current international symbols can still be found scores of older waymarks: fine lettering in the bridge over the Swale at Richmond, Yorkshire; several old Great North Road milestones in the verges of what is now the A1; a column giving Brighton's original name of Brighthelmstone on the road between Sheffield Park and Wych Cross; an East Hoathly stone combining the Pelham buckle, emblem of a local knight who accepted the surrender of King John of France at Poitiers in 1365, with Bow Bells representing London 50 miles away; a cast iron example at Kilmersdon in Somerset; and a Telford milestone near Shrewsbury.

Thomas Telford was one of the giants of the days when there was a clamour both for new roads and for canals. He built over 100 bridges and 1,000 miles of road in Scotland alone; and canals, docks and bridges throughout England and Wales, including the incomparable Pont-

porch; or in some instances could be round. There is a perky thatched toll cottage outside the village of Stanton Drew in Somerset, and at Chard in the same county another with an attractive overhanging roof; one on the A5 at Montford Bridge in Shropshire; and a typical bridge toll house by the river Tamar at Gunnislake in Cornwall. In my own lifetime I can remember a private toll still operating along the Military Road a little way out of Rye, the cottage now a snug little residence. Some toll bridges still operate, such as that across the Trent at Dunham, and the Glenside toll at Saltburn. At Sandwich, to soften the blow, toll for crossing the Kentish Stour is collected at the fine medieval barbican.

Unfortunately a number of speculators seized the chance of filling their own pockets through the turnpike trusts, and further losses were incurred through the fingers of dishonest collectors at the bars and cottages. The avowed intention of charging tolls only until roads could economic-

cysyllte aqueduct and the Menai suspension bridge. His roads were laid on the principle of uniform stones for the foundation, with smaller, irregular pieces on top so that traffic would compact them and their grit into a tough, solid mass; and he insisted on good drainage. He straightened and deepened canals, simplified time-wasting lock systems, and was in charge of the last major canal project in the country – the Birmingham and Liverpool Junction route.

Canals had for long rivalled the roads in their transport of heavy loads. Barges on inland waterways could move masses of material more smoothly and economically than was possible in carts and waggons on ill-made trackways. But natural watercourses did not always proceed in the right direction: their bends had to be straightened out, their banks shored up, and towpaths for horses driven through any number of natural obstacles. Then navigable rivers could also be joined by straight, newly-dug channels or canals.

In 1759 the Duke of Bridgewater wanted to move coal from his Worsley mines to Manchester at a cheaper rate than the road hauliers demanded. He engaged James Brindley to dig a canal; and this Derbyshire farmer's son, virtually self-taught as an engineer after a sketchy apprenticeship, not only did so but solved the problem of crossing the Irwell valley by means of an aqueduct at Barton which was regarded as one of the wonders of its age. A later route to Runcorn and so to the port of Liverpool was so well designed that passenger boats soon began to ply along it. Brindley visualized an ultimate 'Grand Cross' system of waterways linking the major ports of London, Liverpool, Hull and Bristol, with a number of important branches to Midland manufacturing towns.

One of these industrial centres, where Josiah Wedgwood was transforming the pottery industry with a blend of high quality and mass production, was the Burslem region. His processes required china clay from the west and flint from the southeast, which meant that transport costs loomed high in his budget. Bringing raw materials in by waggon or packhorse was expensive; and the despatch of finished products to London or the ports acquired an additional burden of loss through breakage. Barge conveyance along tranquil waters would solve both problems. Wedgwood commissioned Brindley to devise the Trent and Mersey Canal. One of its marvels was

the Harecastle tunnel in Staffordshire, near Kidsgrove, almost 3,000 yards long. Many years after Brindley's death Thomas Telford, charged with relieving this bottleneck, had to admit that he could think of nothing better than driving a parallel Harecastle tunnel. When the railways came, following roughly the same obvious route, the line from Macclesfield to Norton Bridge had to go through the same obstruction.

Brindley's early work on a water-driven mill can still be seen at Leek in Staffordshire, and the main line of the Bridgewater canal survives, as does the junction of his Trent and Mersey canal with the Staffordshire and Worcestershire at Great Haywood, and one of his aqueducts.

But there is something ominous about that railway tunnel driven above the Harecastle canal tunnels. The canals could mostly compete with the roads, at any rate when it came to shifting freight. Now both highway and waterway were to be outpaced by the iron way.

At Longton in Staffordshire a charitable trust has preserved the old bottle ovens of the Gladstone Pottery.

James Watt had dabbled with the notion of applying his experiments in steam power to the driving of waggons, but had abandoned it. The breakthrough came in 1801 when Richard Trevithick, son of a Cornish mine manager, took his work with mine engines an inspired step further into the construction of the first steam locomotive to draw passengers; but he had to contend with wooden rather than iron rails, made mistakes in the promotion of his invention, tried some rash sorties abroad, and died in poverty. The first true steam locomotive was William Hedley's *Puffing Billy* (to be seen in the Science Museum, South Kensington), used on the colliery tramway at Wylam in Northumberland.

From a cottage at Wylam the son of a colliery fireman, George Stephenson, had every opportunity of studying colliery steam engines in action. Two years after his appointment as engineer at Killingworth in 1812 he designed a locomotive to move loads of coal, and then in 1825 created *Locomotion* (preserved on Darlington station), which drew the first mixed loads. This claims to have been the first true railway in the world, and near the station is a plaque commemorating the sale of the first passenger railway ticket. But in fact it was rather a mix-up; a lot of its traffic was horse-drawn, some goods trucks were hauled by a stationary engine, and different trains ran under the aegis of different companies paying tolls to the owners just as on the turnpikes.

Stephenson himself had made his mark. He was soon employed by the promoters of the Liverpool and Manchester railway to advise on the practicability of joining the two cities by crossing the appalling bog of Chat Moss. These businessmen had expected to use stationary engines at strategic points along the route. Stephenson went all out for locomotives and, in the Rainhill trials of 1829, convinced all doubters with his *Rocket* – whose remains, accompanied by a faithful replica, can be found in the aforementioned Science Museum at South Kensington. The opening of the railway was marred by the death of William Huskisson, whose honourable Parliamentary career brought him less fame than his melancholy distinction of having been the first person to be run over and killed by a railway engine.

Not that Stephenson had any rooted prejudice against stationary engines. A stroll along the towpath north of the Regent's canal westwards

Plaque beside the Regent's Canal towpath in London.

from Camden Lock brings one to a dulled plaque on a brick wall behind which rust the remains of his hauling device to drag trains up the long slope from Euston station before they could be left to the power of their locomotives.

Queen Victoria came to the throne 12 years after the opening of the Stockton–Darlington railway. In 1842 she became the first sovereign to travel in a railway train, and in July 1847 accompanied her Prince Consort to Cambridge for his installation as Chancellor of the University, in a train luxuriously fitted out for them by 'the Railway King', the over-ambitious speculator George Hudson. By the time of her Golden Jubilee the country was criss-crossed by the lines of dozens of different companies, and the commonest of commoners were being offered the cheap travel, family outings and seaside excursions which were to cause a major shift in English social life and attitudes.

William Cobbett had once complained of the pernicious speed of stage coaches, bringing Brighton within daily commuting distance of London. Now the railways cut the time amazingly. Brighton and other south coast towns became popular rather than exclusive holiday resorts. Blackpool began to draw its thousands from Yorkshire and Lancashire, though some travellers still set themselves apart from lesser folk: wealthy Manchester merchants hired special saloon coaches in which only members of their club could travel from Manchester to Blackpool or the Lake District. Felixstowe in Suffolk was a small fishing community before the railway came: over the years its population rose from 2,000 to 20,000. In 1871 Clacton was still a rural Essex community of only just over 1,000 people; by 1881 it had doubled; and then came the railway in 1882, and by the turn of the century the town had some 7,500 residents, many of them catering for London excursionists and holidaymakers.

The opening of a line to Acle in Norfolk in 1881 and then an extension of other lines from the North and the Midlands led to the opening up of the Norfolk Broads. It was possible to spend a week on a wherry, with the services of a man and boy, for 30 shillings a week each. In 1870 hardly anyone had thought of visiting the Broads for diversion. By the 1890s there were over 1,000 people a week afloat during the season.

Living museums

It might be said that all England is one vast open-air museum. Nobody needs to go indoors to study glass cases or neat arrays of static exhibits to learn what has brought us where we are. Just visiting Stourport is enough to show how a township is born because of an immediate local need. Every hamlet, town or city has its own *raison d'être*, and this can usually be traced through its lineaments. Stourport might not have been there at all, though, if it had not been for the hostility of the townsfolk of Bewdley. When James Brindley wanted to link his Staffordshire and Worcestershire canal section to the river Severn he thought first of Bewdley as the obvious ready-made port. But he was brusquely told to take his 'stinking ditch' away – and did so, settling on a junction of the Stour and Severn where, until he arrived, there had been nothing but a lonely inn. Soon there were docks, offices and warehouses.

On the Grand Union canal in Northamptonshire a warehouse has been adapted as a waterways museum near the Stoke Bruerne lock system and Blisworth tunnel; and to the north, near Market Harborough, are the spectacular lock 'staircases' of Foxton, lifting the canal through two sets of five locks.

Sticklepath in Devon has a museum of rural industry, including a corn and cloth mill later converted to a tool factory. There are hammers and other machinery driven by waterwheels, and on the banks of the stream can be found remains of a serge mill. At Avoncroft, near Bromsgrove in Worcestershire, an open-air museum of buildings includes a windmill and nail and chain

Preserved tracks of the Kent & East Sussex railway.

making workshops. Some of the machines of James Nasmyth, who invented the steam hammer in his factory at Patricroft, are on display at Monks Hall in Eccles, Lancashire.

The last steam train in England ran on 11th August 1968 from Liverpool to Carlisle. Halfway through its journey the Stanier locomotive drawing it was replaced by the Britannia Pacific *Oliver Cromwell*, which is now kept in immaculate condition at Bressingham Gardens, Norfolk, in company with the *Royal Scot*, and steams up and

Restored mine shaft at Blists Hill museum, Shropshire.

heights, the dizzying Hounsgill viaduct near Consett, County Durham, has been incorporated in a public footpath.

One of the most comprehensive museums yet conceived is also in Durham, under the sponsorship of the county councils of Durham, Northumberland, Cleveland, and Tyne and Wear. At Beamish, old buildings from all over the region have been assembled – and will continue to be added to – including relevant furnishings and machinery. A complete railway station was dismantled and reassembled here, with coal drops, a cast-iron footbridge from the middle of the nineteenth century, and a Class C locomotive and rolling stock of the old North Eastern Railway. Another footbridge leads to a town which over the years will grow into a replica of a typical north-eastern market town, complete with period shops and a Victorian bandstand. Near a re-created colliery is housed a working model of Stephenson's *Locomotion*, and a complete row of pit cottages has been transferred here from Hetton-le-Hole, furnished in late nineteenth-century style.

A miner's cottage with more famous associations is in Victoria Street, Eastwood, Nottinghamshire. In 1976 the district council restored and opened as a museum the birthplace of D.H. Lawrence, whose novel *Sons and Lovers* is a largely autobiographical narrative of his early life, when his hard-drinking father worked in nearby Brinsley pit.

At Beamish a trip can be made across the grounds in old tramcars. But for those who still nostalgically recall the trams which until well after the Second World War ran through so many British towns, the most representative collection is to be found at Crich in Derbyshire, in an old quarry originally opened by George Stephenson to supply limestone for the Ambergate kilns. The rails of his mineral railway were removed in 1959 to restore the Talyllyn line in Wales; tramlines took their place, with a choice of more than 50 cars including some from Blackpool, Gateshead, Leicester, Sheffield – and even one from Prague, sent here just before the Russians invaded Czechoslovakia in 1968.

It was appropriate that when the Ironbridge Gorge Museum opened around the furnaces and machinery of Abraham Darby's Coalbrookdale it won not only the British Museum of the Year award but also the main European award. Along this part of the Severn valley from Coalbrookdale

down a length of track carrying visitors on its footplate on Thursday and Sunday afternoons throughout the summer.

The railway museum at York has an imposing collection, but the engines are at a standstill. To cover any appreciable distance behind a working steam locomotive one needs to visit preservation society tracks such as those of the Bluebell Line in Sussex, the Kent and East Sussex railway starting from Tenterden, the 18 miles of the North York Moors line between Pickering and Grosmont, or the Nene Valley railway from Wansford in Cambridgeshire.

Some of the original tracks and embankments are being put to other uses. Local authorities have converted many stretches into footpaths and bridleways. The one-time Potteries loop-line has become a 'green way' weaving through Tunstall, Burslem and Hanley. The High Peak Trail in Derbyshire follows the course of the remarkable railway which once linked the Peak Forest canal at Whaley Bridge with the Cromford canal, and can be joined from a car park and picnic area near the Black Rocks. For those with a head for

The world's first cast-iron bridge at Ironbridge Gorge.

furnace site to Blists Hill open-air museum are the most evocative relics of early industrial days. Symbolically, the clock tower above the Coalbrookdale Company's warehouse is made of cast iron. Around Darby's first furnace are ranged examples of the ironwork it produced. The iron bridge itself still stands, saved from danger of collapse in recent years when the banks shifted and the stone abutments threatened to squeeze the ironwork out of shape. At Blists Hill a mine shaft has been restored, three blast furnaces are being shored up, work has been resumed by the original Coalport pottery, and across the site runs a section of the Shropshire canal ending at the top of an inclined plane for raising and lowering tub boats between the canal and the river below. There is also a section of road built according to Telford's specifications, with a reconstructed toll cottage beside it. The new town above the valley has, worthily, taken to itself the very name of Telford.

He would probably have been horrified by the amount of traffic on our modern roads. A sad little testimony to the perils of such traffic can be seen in Harborne churchyard, Birmingham, where there is a tombstone in the shape of a tyre, commemorating a girl killed by a motor-car in 1936.

The present slips away so swiftly into the past that even certain aeroplanes are becoming period pieces. The Shuttleworth Collection in Bedfordshire preserves early planes and fighters of both World Wars. On Southampton Water can still be seen the slipway at the old Vickers Supermarine factory where R.J. Mitchell worked on his seaplanes, one of which won the Schneider Trophy, before he went on to develop the Spitfire. The Shuttleworth Collection includes a working Spitfire. In Kent, a restored Hurricane and a Messerschmitt are on display at Chilham Castle's Battle of Britain Museum, and at Brenzett on Romney Marsh a smaller museum cared for by enthusiastic amateurs has accumulated relics of crashed aircraft from the Ashford, Tenterden and Marshland area.

In the collection at Duxford airfield in Cambridgeshire sits the prototype Concorde, already a museum piece: it flew in here but can never fly out again, the runway having been severely truncated after its arrival.

IN Memory OF
JOHN PEEL OF
RUTHWAITE. who died
Nov. 13th 1854. aged 78 Years,
Also MARY, his wife, who
died Augt. 9th 1859, aged 82
Also JONATHAN their Son
who died Jan, 21st 1806.
aged 2 Years.
Also PETER their Son, who
died Novr 15th 1840.
aged 27 Years.
Also MARY DAVIDSON their
DAUGHTER who died NOV. 30th
1863, aged 48 Years.
Also JOHN their Son who died
Novr 22nd 1887 aged 90 Years.

CROSTHWAITE

CUMBRIA

IN 1847 THE FIRST RAILWAY via Kendal to a terminus at the hamlet of Birthwaite, originally designed as a trade branch from the main Lancaster to Carlisle line which would continue to Ambleside, in fact opened up another holiday region to the English public. 'The manufacturers of Yorkshire and Lancashire', wrote *The Times* only three years later, 'are carried by shoals to the lakes of Cumberland.' Birthwaite changed its name to Windermere, and before long there were pleasure steamers to Lake Windermere and Coniston Water. The original Windermere steamer *Dolly*, put into service in 1850, still makes occasional demonstration runs on the lake – perhaps the oldest surviving powered vessel in Britain still in working order.

In one of two odes on The Kendal and Windermere Railway, William Wordsworth expressed his horror:

Hear YE that Whistle? As her long-linked Train
Swept onwards, did the vision cross your view?
Yes, ye were startled; – and, in balance true,
Weighing the mischief with the promised gain,
Mountains, and Vales, and Floods, I call on you
To share the passion of a just disdain.

He protested that railway entrepreneurs were luring the humbler classes away from home and that, if this went on, 'for the profit of shareholders and that of the lower class of innkeepers we should have wrestling matches, horse and boat

The Caldbeck gravestone of the huntsman whose summoning of his hounds caused the frequent complaint, 'The sound of his horn brought me from my bed.'

races without number, and pot-houses and beer-shops would keep pace with these excitements.'

The Poet Laureate loved the lofty thoughts aroused in him by the tarns and mountains of the Lake District where, according to a Cumberland saying, 'God ran out of space and had to start piling up the rocks.' He was not keen to share these with others, save by the written word.

Mountain riches

Wordsworth, born at Cockermouth in Cumberland in 1770, really ought not to have found the intrusion of mechanical monsters into his native region too disconcerting. Picturesque as the Lake District may have been, and romantic as he preferred to regard it, it had for centuries supported a great deal of industry: as far back, indeed, as Neolithic times. High up on the bleak Pike of Stickle a cave hacked out of the mountainside was clearly once a production centre for stone axes, specimens of which have been found here and right down to the south coast – though 4,000 years ago there was no railway to transport them to such distant markets. Trackways high in the mountain passes show where the ancient trade routes ran; Bronze Age settlers continued to use them and have also left traces of themselves in stone circles such as those around Long Meg near Little Salkeld, at Castlerigg near Keswick, and at Swineside near Broughton-in-Furness.

There are also a few Roman routes which the modern traveller can follow. Although there was no comprehensive attempt to colonize and civilize this somewhat remote region in the full Roman manner, defence against the Scots, the need to keep an eye on the unreliable Brigantes tribe, and

The legionary fortress of Hard Knott castle, built early in the second century, still has substantial remains of granaries, bath house, and parade ground.

the possibility of attack from or even an eventual assault on Ireland, led, well before the building of Hadrian's Wall, to the setting up of forts such as those at Watercrook near Kendal, Galava at Ambleside, and the fine example of Hard Knott fort above Eskdale. From Ambleside the military road through Hard Knott Pass reached the coast at Ravenglass, guarded by the fortress of Glannaventa with its 13-foot high walls. On the fells above Melmerby are remains of the paving of the Maiden Way.

In the end it was not the Irish themselves who invaded but, long after the Romans had gone, Norsemen who had taken over large tracts of Ireland. They established themselves on the Cumbrian coast and spread inland. There are no lasting Roman names in the region, but plenty of Norse ones. The common ending of *thwaite*, as in Brackenthwaite, Stonethwaite and Applethwaite, denotes a forest clearing or low-lying meadow, usually prefixed by some self-explanatory geo-

logical or agricultural identification. *Side* and *seat* derive from a word meaning a mountain pasture, as in Ambleside, Oughterside and Summerseat, the latter having probably been used only for summer grazing. And, as on the east coast, the *by* defining a town or small defended settlement is found in, for example, Asby, Raby, and Melmerby. Celtic and Norse combine in Mallerstang: bare hill and boundary mark.

With their passion for monastery endowment, the Normans granted vast acreages of farm land and sheep pasture not only to local abbeys such as Calder, Seaton, Lanercost, St Bees and Furness, but to rich foundations on the other side of the Pennines such as Fountains. Early monastic enclosure by miles of drystone wall, supplemented by sturdy drystone pounds for animals, and even some emparking so that abbots and their friends might go hunting, were followed in the eighteenth century by the enclosure of thousands more acres of 'waste', still as a rule with those interminable walls.

Fell and dale farming was always a bleak business here. Small farmers huddled with their families into 'long houses' with an extension

The Pike above Penrith was built in the eighteenth century as a watchtower and beacon, last used during an invasion scare in Napoleonic times.

to accommodate livestock under the same roof. While the men eked out their living, the women spun and wove to supplement their meagre income. Independent yeomen farmers with land of their own were referred to as 'estates men' or 'statesmen'. Apart from the few manor houses of wealthier families, their homes are the most individual surviving examples of Lakeland architecture.

But there was a greater wealth in these hills. Old mine workings – which should be approached with care – can be distinguished around Grasmere and on Helvellyn, and there are tunnels and spoil heaps of copper mines near Coniston. Lead had been mined from the western slopes of the Pennines throughout the Middle Ages, but reached a peak towards the end of the sixteenth century. In Queen Elizabeth's time the Company of Mines Royal, charged to 'search, dig, try, roast and melt all manner of mines and ores of gold, silver, copper and quicksilver', imported a number of skilled German miners into the Keswick region. At first resented by the local populace, they established their community on Derwent Island in Derwentwater, and named one of their first

important mines Gotes Gab (God's Gift), which soon became Goldscope. In it was employed an engine with a double waterwheel to lift the ore and pump water out of the workings. There is a display of local historic mining tools in Keswick museum.

After about 100 years the Mines Royal ceased to operate, but there was still material to be extracted and exploited. Plentiful 'pipes' of blacklead or graphite were found in the Borrowdale fells near Seathwaite. Used in the manufacture of cannonballs and pottery, and providing the basis for a local lead pencil industry, this graphite was so much sought after and fetched such a good price that, in spite of all official precautions and penalties, there was an equally thriving trade in smuggling. Remains of an old hut just below the summit of Great Gable are thought to mark a smugglers' rendez-vous, and the George Hotel in Keswick plays the same part in local tradition as do the gin, lace and brandy smugglers' inns in

Keswick museum, in the heart of a lead-mining region worked from the sixteenth century to the late nineteenth, has a display of miners' tools and barrows.

eastern and southern England. As in most efficient 'free trading' operations, there was a two-way traffic: a great deal of contraband came ashore near Ravenglass from the Isle of Man.

Much of this industrial activity had demanded a great deal of charcoal in smelting processes, and the forests suffered here just as they had suffered elsewhere. Traces of charcoal hearths, or pit-steads, remain in Glemara Park, Ullswater, and in the Upper Troutbeck valley. On these wide circular platforms cut out of the hillside would be built camp-fire constructions of wood which, covered with straw and sand, would be ignited in the centre and then maintained at a rate of slow combustion so that the flame would never actually burn up the wood. At one time the iron workings, so rich that even now the rocks near Esk Pike can play havoc with a compass, were threatened with collapse when their furnaces were restricted so that supplies of charcoal could be guaranteed to the Mines Royal processes – just as, in Surrey

and Sussex, glassmakers were driven out of business so that charcoal could be reserved for cannon manufacture.

Even when seams were worked out in later years, there was still a call for charcoal in several gunpowder works of the region: the remains of one of these can be found at Elterwater below Little Langdale.

The Cumbrian coalfield may not have competed with those of Lancashire, Yorkshire or Northumberland, but by the end of the eighteenth century it was important in the smelting of local iron ore which went to the Barrow-in-Furness shipyards. In this century Colonel Senhouse, a lord of the manor, had developed coal mines and docks for handling their product at one of the Roman coastal forts, renaming the place Mary-port after his wife. Today the commercial harbour has become merely a fishing and sailing centre.

One pleasing relic of all the industrial activity in Eskdale is the 7-mile stretch of mineral railway from Dalegarth to the coast at Ravenglass. In 1915 its gauge was reduced from 3 feet to 15 inches by Bassett-Lowke, the well-known engineering modeller, and passengers are now drawn behind engines named after local rivers.

Charcoal and coal, lead and copper and iron: they have by no means had their day, but the buildings and processes of today and tomorrow are making a significant appearance in the Cumbrian landscape. Whitehaven has its cement and phosphate works, Carlisle its ring of factories. And not far from the ruins of Calder Abbey now stands Calder Hall, the world's first atomic power station, opened by Queen Elizabeth II in October 1956, with Windscale atomic research centre beside it.

A Romantic Revolution

Wordsworth House in the main street of Cocker-mouth was the birthplace and childhood home of the poet, and his garden and terraced walk are still intact. The grammar school desk on which as a schoolboy he carved his name is preserved at Hawkshead; Anne Tyson's cottage where he lodged can be found in Red Lion Square; and in Hawkshead Court-house is a museum of the local rural life which entranced him as a child and brought him back to Lakeland after his travels abroad.

On his last summer vacation from Cambridge, William Wordsworth at the age of 20 had gone on

After escorting Coleridge on a 'picturesque tour' of the Lake District in 1799, William Wordsworth settled with his sister at Dove Cottage, Grasmere.

a walking tour of France, Italy and the Alps. It was not merely their scenic beauty which fired his imagination, but the tang of revolution in the air – revolution both political and artistic, as the chill neo-classical intellectualism of the early eighteenth century succumbed to a passionate romantic revival in painting, prose and poetry. In 1795 he and his sister Dorothy met Samuel Taylor Coleridge, lived close to him and his wife for a while in Somerset and travelled with them to Germany. The two men collaborated on a volume of *Lyrical Ballads* whose declared aim of turning away from fashionable mannerism towards simplicity and warm romanticism aroused the scorn of many critics. One of Wordworth's contributions was *Lines composed above Tintern Abbey*; the most celebrated of Coleridge's, *The Rime of the Ancient Mariner*.

But the county of Wordsworth's birth drew him back. Here, if anywhere, was just the landscape to appeal to those whose new obsession was the romantic and picturesque, its essential ingredients defined by Dr John Brown, an early Lakeland tourist, as 'Beauty, horror, and immensity'.

In 1799 Wordsworth and his sister took a cottage at Grasmere called Town End, now Dove Cottage, near which is now a small museum whose display of village life and personal relics includes his shaving mug and snuffbox. In 1802 he married his cousin Mary, and after living in various places and travelling on his sinecure job as distributor of stamps for Westmorland, settled at Rydal in the sixteenth-century house of Rydal Mount, which contains first editions of his work.

They had plenty of visitors. Thomas de Quincey, later to write *Confessions of an English Opium Eater*, came frequently and for a time lived at Dove Cottage. The friendship with Coleridge continued, and Coleridge introduced Robert Southey into the circle. Somerset born and bred, Southey duly settled at Keswick. In 1813 he became Poet Laureate – an appointment which passed on his death in 1843 to Wordsworth, no longer a political radical but an enemy of the French Revolution and all he had once admired.

A wrestler's successful throw at Grasmere Sports, held annually in August together with sheep-dog trials and hound-trailing.

The friendship of the three men, their sharing of aims, and their residence in Lakeland led to their being dubbed contemptuously 'the Lake Poets' by the *Edinburgh Review* – which itself suffered some vitriolic attacks from Lord Byron.

In 1800 Coleridge had taken Greta Hall, Derwentwater, but was driven by the dank climate to take laudanum and opium in such copious quantities that even de Quincey, himself an addict, later condemned its ruinous effect. Southey, collaborator with Coleridge on a satire, *The Devil's Thoughts*, had to take over Greta Hall while his friend went abroad, failed to find a satisfactory occupation, and returned to stay with the Wordsworths before being taken in and cared for by James Gillman, a surgeon of Highgate, until his death in 1834.

Coleridge is buried far south under the vaults of Highgate school chapel. His oldest son Hartley

is buried, like Wordsworth, in Grasmere churchyard. Dora's Field near Rydal, given by Wordsworth to his daughter, still produces its 'host of golden daffodils' every spring. Southey is buried at Great Crosthwaite on the outskirts of Keswick.

Also in Great Crosthwaite churchyard lies its one-time vicar, Canon Rawnsley, who in 1895 was a co-founder with Octavia Hill and Sir Robert Hunter of the National Trust, which preserves so much unspoilt land and historic property which might otherwise have been lost for ever. Its first acquisition was a stretch of woodland along the west bank of Derwentwater; since when it has taken into its care over 70,000 acres within Lakeland alone. (Its first purchase of a building was the fourteenth-century clergy house at Alfriston in Sussex.)

Another literary arrival in Lakeland was John Ruskin, who, after some other idealistic experiments made possible by a comfortable income and then a large inheritance from his wine merchant father, encouraged the rejuvenation of a hand-made linen industry in Langdale. In 1871 he moved to Brantwood on the east bank of Coniston Water, his home until in 1900 he died and was buried in Coniston churchyard. His coach and boat are still kept at Brantwood, and the local museum which he founded contains personal relics and many of his drawings.

Tennyson, too, who inherited the laureateship from Wordsworth, lived for a while near Coniston at Tent Hall.

Beatrix Potter first visited the Lakes as a child, repeatedly came back, and in 1896 discovered Saurey to the west of Windermere, where she eventually bought herself a farm. She applied herself successfully to sheep farming, but it is for the children's stories she wrote and illustrated, starting in 1902 with *Peter Rabbit*, that she will be best remembered. After she had married an Ambleside solicitor in 1913 her writing deteriorated, but her interest in the land and wild life never faded. At her death in 1943 she left the farm and extensive surrounding land to the National Trust, and later they acquired further fields and, in 1976, the neighbouring Tower Bank Arms inn.

Walking, riding, wrestling, racing

In his disapproval of 'wrestling matches, horse and boat races without number', Wordsworth shows himself less wholeheartedly committed to local people and local ways than he often tried to make out. One doubts if he would have enjoyed, even once a year, the Grasmere Sports which in 1852 began an annual celebration of Cumbrian pastimes and contests. There are bouts of Cumberland and Westmorland wrestling, in which contestants lock hands across their opponent's back and then struggle either to break that opponent's hold or get any part of his anatomy other than his feet to touch the ground. It is not a matter of successive throws or 'catch as catch can', but of 'first down's the loser'.

Fell racing is an endurance test which appeals to the hardy on both flanks of the Pennines. Near Burnsall bridge in Wharfedale is a notice recording the fastest time for a mile climb of 1,000 feet up the fell as 12 minutes 59.8 seconds, an achievement unmatched since 1910.

Rock climbing in England really began in earnest in the Lake District in the nineteenth century. The favourite challenges are those of Langdale Pikes, Scafell – England's highest mountain – and Great Gable, where a comparatively simple track for beginners follows the route of an old slate-mine tramway. Fell walking rather than direct assault on the awesome slopes is more to the taste of most visitors, provided they have come equipped with sturdy boots, warm clothes and a modicum of commonsense. Helvellyn, imposing as it may appear from Patterdale village below, is another height which can be tackled by a resolute walker.

Riding to hounds was not as popular on these tricky slopes as in the clear Midland fields. The Lakeland habit was to chase along on foot – just as arduous at times as the most competitive fell racing – and one of the most celebrated of its devotees was John Peel, a 6-foot yeoman born and living most of his life in Caldbeck. He eloped to Gretna Green to marry, and fathered 13 children, 11 of whom lived to attend his funeral in 1854, when he was laid in Caldbeck churchyard. His pack of hounds inspired a friend, John Woodcock Graves, to compose words – impromptu, it is said – to an old Cumberland air which became the regimental march of the Border Regiment.

In our own time there have been triumphs and disasters hereabouts. Sir Henry Segrave, knighted in 1929 after breaking the world's land speed record in Florida, was killed when his speedboat overturned on Windermere. Sir Malcolm Campbell took the land speed record from him shortly afterwards, continued to break his own records, and on Coniston Water in 1939

Townend at Troutbeck was the home of well-to-do statesmen, or estatesmen, so called because of local family tenant rights amounting virtually to freehold.

made the fastest speedboat trip so far. Sir Malcolm's own son, Donald Campbell, took the water speed record on Coniston in 1959, and both land and water speed records in 1964; but in 1967, attempting yet higher speeds in a new jet-propelled boat, somersaulted and sank to his death in Coniston.

Is there no nook of English ground secure
From rash assault? Schemes of retirement sown
In youth, and 'mid the busy world kept pure . . .
Must perish . . .

One wonders what Wordsworth would have made of power boats on Windermere – 'boat races without number', indeed! – of a valley being drowned under Thirlmere reservoir, and of Forestry Commission conifer blankets, picnic sites, caravan parks and a lakeside motorway.

THE BACKBONE

ON ASCENSION DAY every year the people of Tissington in Derbyshire display the handiwork of several preceding days. Each of the village's five wells is decorated with a screen up to 10 feet high, bright with coloured patterns or pictures and usually a solemn text or motto. The mosaic is made from flower petals, grasses, pebbles and crushed stone carefully pressed into a coating of clay on a wooden backing.

The origin of such a custom is obscure, but was most likely connected in pagan times with rituals in honour of water nymphs, especially those guarding springs and wells. That such practices were widespread is shown by the tenth-century Christian proscription of the worship of fountains. In the Peak district, rugged and inhospitable to strangers, the tradition may nevertheless have continued long after canonical disapproval had been voiced. A glance at a rainfall map shows that these limestone heights are among the wettest in England; yet the rock is so porous that most of the surface water seeps rapidly away, and without benefit of modern reservoirs and modern pumping devices earlier communities had to ensure the reliability of their precious wells by propitiating the appropriate spirit.

When the Black Death struck the land, Tissington was the only village in the Peak to escape unscathed, and attributed this to the purity of its water. The well-dressing ceremonies, now in Christian guise and accompanied by Biblical texts, were openly resumed, though it was not until the early nineteenth century that the designs became pictorial. After a lull, the custom was

Well-dressing at Wormhill.

taken up again with renewed vigour and more ambitious presentation after the Second World War. Most Peak villages now have their own well-dressing ceremonies, spaced out through the summer in order to avoid clashing with one another, and to allow groups from one place to visit rivals elsewhere and feel smugly superior or envious, as the case may be. The Church maintains its own symbolic hold on the festivities, trying to ensure that the blessing of the local well takes place on the saint's day of the local parish church. Pagan echoes have not altogether been subdued, however. Among other adjuncts to the old rites, Stafford Morris Men dance the offertory in Tideswell church one Sunday morning in June.

Quite apart from the everyday provision of fresh water, many wells have had mystical curative powers ascribed to them. There are any number of places and streets in England called Holywell – in Cornwall, Dorset, Cambridgeshire and Warwickshire, to select only a few. A Lady's Well at Holystone near Rothbury in the vale of the Coquet is traditionally associated with St Ninian; that at Elmswell in Suffolk was long believed to work miracles in the curing of eye ailments. St Anne gave her name to many wells: though in some cases the name was there before in its pagan form of Black Annis, the fertility spirit with an appetite for human flesh, especially that of children.

There was once a Holy Well in London, taken over by a Mr Sadler in the seventeenth century and advertised as a medicinal spring, Sadler's Wells, round which he built a small concert-room where his clientele could listen to music while taking the waters.

During the eighteenth century there was a great

fashion for taking the mineral waters at various spas, as English venues set up in opposition to the dominance of Spa in the Ardennes. With a tradition going back to the Romans, Bath had always been in the forefront; but after Tunbridge Wells had become a favourite resort of Charles I's queen, Henrietta Maria, the attractive row of The Pantiles was laid out to provide a spacious walk to and from the spring – still visible, though little visited now – and soon it was not merely the mineral water but music, gossip, and the contortions of dandies like Beau Nash which helped counteract 'the colic, the melancholy, and the vapours'. Epsom in Surrey had tried to compete after the discovery of springs rich in magnesium sulphate; but they ran dry, and in any case would have been driven out of business by the eventual discovery of cheap extraction of 'Epsom Salts' from sea-water. Cheltenham fared better with its alkaline spring, and one can still take the waters in the evocative atmosphere of the restored Pump Room.

Towards the end of the eighteenth-century Richard Rigby, when Paymaster General, sought to create a smart watering-place from scratch at Mistley in Essex, but had to give up when some of his financial misdemeanours came to light. All that remains of his unfinished scheme is a fountain topped by a swan, and two lonely-looking towers designed by Robert Adam to ennoble the village church whose nave has since been demolished.

In Derbyshire, thermal springs had been discovered at Buxton by the Romans, and have continued to flow. They rise from a mile below the surface to an outlet in the Natural Baths at one end of the graceful Crescent built in 1874 by the fifth Duke of Devonshire, where visitors once took bathing cures. This building is now closed, but the waters can still be tasted in the former Pump Room, now the Tourist Information Centre, at the other end of the Crescent. The indoor garden of the Pavilion recalls more leisurely days. In Buxton, too, is an annual well-dressing festival and a blessing of the wells.

Eyam's festival is delayed until the end of August and combined with another, grimmer ceremony. A skull on a churchyard tombstone grins all too symbolically. In 1665 a box of clothes sent from London to a tailor living in Cooper's Cottage by the church brought plague germs with it. When the rector, William Mompesson, realized what had smitten his parish he appealed to the villagers not to leave and thereby

Above: *A death's head on one of the graves in Eyam churchyard. Many plague-stricken inhabitants lie elsewhere, with no marked tombs.* Left: *The thermal spring at Buxton produces a steady 250,000 gallons a day at a constant temperature of 28 degrees Centigrade throughout the year.*

risk spreading the disease to other communities. In this he had the support of his ousted predecessor, Thomas Stanley, a Puritan who had refused to acknowledge the Act of Uniformity. Guards were set about the village to ensure that nobody defected – though, to his shame, the rector later smuggled his own two children out – and the inhabitants paid for incoming supplies organized by the Earl of Devonshire by leaving money in water and vinegar at what is now remembered as Mompesson's Well. To avoid contagion within the church, the rector carried on his services in the open air from a rock in the hollow of Cucklet Dell. Eyam held out for just over a year, by the end of which only 90 of its original 350 inhabitants were left. The rector's wife is buried in the churchyard, but many others were hastily interred where they lay or carried out to be dug into the fields. On the Sunday after well-dressing, a modern procession makes its way to 'Cucklet Church' for an open-air commemoration service, during which many of the village women wear seventeenth-century costume.

Tunnels and caves

Villagers decorating their wells and implicitly genuflecting to deities on special feast days might from time to time have spared a thought for the results of some of their own day-to-day activities. The drying up of a number of sources and the rapid disappearance of rainwater has been partially attributed by some geologists to the lead-mining techniques of the Pennines and the Peak district. Extensive networks of fissures and man-made 'soughs' or drainage tunnels undoubtedly contributed to a marked lowering of the water table about the Derwent valley from the eighteenth century onwards. Yet one community's loss was another's gain: the efficient speeding of water out of the mine shafts provided pressure for the water-powered cotton-mills.

All down the Pennines on both sides, above Teesdale, Weardale and on the heights between Allendale and Allenheads, lead-mining has left its scars and monuments. The main veins, known as rakes, can be 10 or 20 feet across and several hundred feet deep, like vertical slices hammered down into the limestone. In fact they were formed not by being pressed down but by seething upwards: hot fluids bubbled up from within the earth long after the formation of the rocks, found their way into faults and crevices, cooled, and crystallized into mineral deposits. To extract the ore, shafts were driven at intervals along the course of the rake. These can still be identified by the little drystone shelters with which the miners capped them, and by their regularly spaced little sentinels of spoil, though attempts have been made to shield these by strips of woodland in striking contrast to the strips of drystone wall so commonplace over the rest of the fells. The trees have another purpose: they keep grazing animals off the old workings and so protect them from lead poisoning.

In the northern parts of the range one can visit the drainage adit entrance at Blackett Level, the great ore crushing wheel at Kilhope, Langley

Ores were brought from many neighbouring mines to be crushed and washed at the Odin Mine, which in the 1700s produced up to 800 tons of ore annually.

Drystone 'beehive' cairns cover old lead-mining shafts from which horizontals were driven out along 'flats' parallel to the enclosing limestone strata.

keep its fumes away from people and cattle – fumes which eventually made the surrounding area sterile, so that the only plant able to exist there is the appropriately named leadwort. Wakebridge mine buildings and storage pond can be found not far north of Crich quarry with its tramway museum. But perhaps the most complete picture can be studied at the Magpie Mine near Sheldon, whose buildings have been preserved as a Field Centre for the Peak District Mines Historical Society, including the orehouse, powder magazine, engine house and weigh house; and in the near neighbourhood are remains of a raised tramway and a horse-gin circle.

The Romans made use of Pennine and Peak ore, and some of their crude ingots surface from time to time. There are so-called Roman galleries at Matlock Bath. The Saxons were not so assiduous, but must have worked to some purpose around Wirksworth, which belonged to Repton abbey and whose mines had to supply a fixed rental in lead every year to Christ Church, Canterbury. When the Danes destroyed Repton in 874 they took over the mines, and it is thought that the Odin Mine near Castleton owes its name to their operations. In Norman times a number of mines were leased to William the Conqueror's illegitimate son Peveril – 'Peveril of the Peak' – but when he fell into disgrace they reverted to the Crown.

Late in the thirteenth century the miners thought it prudent to have their rights codified instead of relying on ancient traditions which might at any time be overruled by regal or local decree. At Ashbourne in 1288 an Inquisition was held by command of Edward I to set down laws which lasted until the end of the nineteenth century. They stipulated that, while any man might look for a vein and stake his claim to part of it by making pick marks in the rock, before setting to work he must 'free' it by applying to the Crown's Barman for registration. An initial royalty must then be paid against later profits, in what were known as 'freeing dishes'. In 1513 Henry VIII presented the Peak miners with a standard dish to measure ore

to Remayne in the Moote Hall at Wyrkysworth hanging by a cheyne so as the Merchantes or Mynours may have resorte to the same at all times to make the trew measure at the same.

And in Wirksworth Moot Hall it does remain.

Mill like a huge obelisk against the horizon, and Langley's flue interior, to which there are several entries on its downhill zig-zag route. Lead and coal mining gave new names to the region: Leadgate being a road down which lead was transported (*gate* deriving here, as in so many places, from the Danish *gade*, a street); Coalcleugh a coaly ravine. In Derbyshire, workings which can be visited with care include Red Rake sough, completed in 1851, the New Engine Mine's engine house at Eyam, Russet Well at Peak Cavern gorge near Castleton, and the Speedwell Mine. This latter has a waterway devised for boats carrying ore and waste, but the boats now carry tourists along the subterranean canal to a spacious natural cavern called the Bottomless Pit. Below Mam Tor lie remains of the Odin ore crushing circle and wheel – an iron track, an iron-tyred wheel, and a gritstone crusher. Stone Edge smelter chimney is reputed to be the oldest factory chimney in the world, set on lonely moorland outside Ashover to

For centuries lead-mining provided only part-time occupation for any man or his family. Most divided their labours between small-scale farming and part-time mining, according to the weather and the seasons; and housed the products of both in one barn.

Working of the mines was improved when the Industrial Revolution brought steam pumps for drainage, and machinery to bore tunnels. And the demands of a growing chemical industry for fluorine compounds was to bring profit to Eyam, which has one of the world's largest fluorspar mines. In Treak Cliff at Castleton is a translucent, coloured, striped variety which as 'Blue John' has been steadily extracted for the creation of vases and other ornaments since the seventeenth century, when old tunnels worked by the Romans were accidentally rediscovered.

With the new machinery came also the railways. John Ruskin looked down with disapproval on Monsal Dale, 'where you might expect to catch sight of Pan, Apollo and the Muses ... now desecrated in order than a Buxton fool may be able to find himself in Bakewell at the end of twelve minutes and vice versa'. Possibly he would be

Finders of new lead ore veins in the High Peak were granted two 'founder meers' of ground – 64 yards in length – after advance payment in 'freeing dishes', the standard being set by this Henry VIII measure.

mollified by the conversion of some abandoned lines into nature walks, including nearly 12 miles of the Tissington Trail along the old track between Ashbourne and Buxton.

Palaces of the Peak
At Kedleston Hall, north-west of Derby, there is an inlay of Blue John in the music room chimney-piece; and some fine specimens are kept at Chatsworth. But the great houses of Derbyshire are, in general, cosmopolitan rather than provincial. It is doubtful whether any other county can boast such a richness of stately homes.

Among the Peak territories granted by the bastard William I to his own bastard, Peveril, was the estate of Haddon Hall. In the following century it was acquired by the Vernon family, and since then has been in the hands of only two families. The ostentatious style of living in which Sir George Vernon indulged himself in Henry

Bess of Hardwick's re-creation, in her old age, of Hardwick Hall, topped with the initials ES to boast of her ultimate status as Countess of Shrewsbury.

VIII's time earned him the title of 'King of the Peak', and he was as dictatorial in all his doings as any monarch could have been. When his younger daughter Dorothy fell in love with Sir John Manners, son of the Earl of Rutland, Sir George disapproved and forbade the two to meet. Disguised as a forester, Manners defied the prohibition, made a number of secret assignations with Dorothy, and eloped with her on the night of her older sister's wedding. Her father must in due course have come round, since on his death the estate was left to Dorothy and her husband, from whom is descended the present Duke of Rutland, whose father beautifully restored the medieval house. In the stonework and elsewhere are many heraldic boars' heads and peacocks – the crests of the Manners and Vernon families.

Another Vernon possession was Sudbury Hall, begun in 1613 and completed half a century later by another Sir George, who with inspired good taste engaged two London plasterers and the painter Laguerre to produce some superb ceilings, and Grinling Gibbons for much of the woodwork. Queen Adelaide stayed here for a while after the death of her husband, King William IV.

But if the Tudor Sir George could be called King of the Peak, its virtual Queen in Elizabethan times was surely another Elizabeth – Bess of Hardwick.

The date of the girl's birth is uncertain, but was probably somewhere between 1518 and 1526; and even more probable that her birthplace was the family home of Hardwick Hall. She married when, according to surviving records, she was under 16; and within 18 months was widowed. In 1547 she married again, this time acquiring Sir William Cavendish, 22 years older than herself, and along with him a healthy amount of property and income from the Dissolution of the Monasteries. One of Cavendish's estates was that of Chatsworth, where Bess encouraged him to build a new house. But although he had managed to stay in royal favour and make a great deal of money through the reigns of Henry VIII, Edward VI and Mary, disgrace threatened when the Lord Treasurer unearthed evidence of bribery and embezzlement on a colossal scale. Before Sir William could present his defence, he died; and Bess was once more a widow. She married again; and again was widowed.

When she calculated her fourth marriage it was a most rewarding one. She had property to bring, but the sixth Earl of Shrewsbury contributed more. A widower whose first wife had been one of the Manners family and sister of the Earl of Rutland, he offered four sons, three daughters, great expanses of land in five counties, and eight major country houses – among them Welbeck and Worksop – as well as residences in London and Chelsea. With her passion for decorating and redecorating, furnishing and refurnishing, Bess had enough houses to play with. She played with such extravagance that she almost brought her preoccupied husband to ruin.

Queen Elizabeth appointed Shrewsbury custodian of that slyly booby-trapped time-bomb Mary, Queen of Scots. The duty left him little time to care for his own interests. Bess and the chaperoned queen seem to have struck up a genuine friendship, sharing as they did an interest in political gossip and fine embroidery; but the brunt of polite, prudent, protective duties fell on Shrewsbury's unhappy shoulders, which left Bess time to conceive unsupervised expansive and expensive building schemes, among them an ambitious reconstruction at Chatsworth, part of her dowry to the marital mélange. Little of her work now remains apart from Queen Mary's moated bower, where the unhappy Scottish schemer whiled away many dismal hours.

When Mary was at last executed and thereby relieved her guardian of his distasteful task, Shrewsbury found that his wife had been squandering vast sums on her architectural fantasies. For the rest of his life he engaged in bitter legal squabbles with her.

Bess's second son, inheritor of Chatsworth, was created first Earl of Devonshire. It was the fourth Earl, elevated as first Duke of Devonshire in return for his espousal of William III's cause, who contributed most to Chatsworth as we see it

today. Starting out with the modest idea of extending the original building, he was repeatedly captured by fresh notions and lashed out right, left and centre, so that one might say he had lost all sense of proportion ... if the final proportions were not so splendid. The impressive west front is probably one of his own concepts. He also had the taste to employ Capability Brown on the landscaping of the park and the diverting of the river. The sixth Duke who added further touches in the nineteenth century had as head gardener Joseph Paxton, who designed the conservatory and went on to design the Crystal Palace for the Great Exhibition of 1851 in London.

Widowed for the fourth time after Shrewsbury had exhausted himself in litigation, Bess turned her attention back to her own birthplace. The original family house was soon obscured and is now only a ruin in the shadow of a stylish mansion carrying the Countess of Shrewsbury's monogram, ES, in stone tracery, and such a wealth of spacious windows that an old tag refers to 'Hardwick Hall, more glass than wall'. In its long gallery is hung a collection of more than 100 Tudor and Elizabethan portraits, and there are many specimens of Bess's interest in needlework.

She founded almshouses in Derby, and quite some time before her death made sure that a monument was designed and built according to her own tastes for establishment above the Cavendish family vaults in what is now All Saints cathedral, Derby.

As well as brick, stone and glass she left a substantial human legacy to her country. Among the descendants of this small Derbyshire squire's daughter are the Dukes of Devonshire, of Newcastle, of Kingston, and of Portland; and there is even a connection with the Dukes of Norfolk.

Some authors daydream their way through colourful, melodramatic, romantic, historical novels. Bess of Hardwick lived just such a vivid story for herself. She was one of the greatest greediest English egocentric eccentrics. Reader, if you would seek her monuments, go to Derbyshire and look around.

BUSINESS IN GREAT WATERS

WITHIN THE MEDIEVAL COURTYARD of Dover castle stands a *pharos*, a Roman lighthouse, which was probably once complemented by another on the opposite headland. In a similarly commanding position above Newquay in Cornwall is a whitewashed 'huer's house', from which a lookout would in busier times have watched for the appearance of pilchard shoals.

The road running parallel with the Liverpool waterfront, once lined with warehouses and slave cellars, was called the Goree after an island off Senegal where slave-ships assembled to collect their cargoes. In Liverpool's great competitor in that and other maritime trades, Bristol, there are four bronze tables outside the Corn Exchange on whose round tops merchants put their cash to clinch deals: known as 'nails', these gave rise to the phrase, 'paying on the nail'. And in a Bristol dry dock – the very dock from which she was launched in 1843 – lies Brunel's pioneer screw-propelled steamship, the *Great Britain*, salvaged in 1970 from dereliction in the Falkland Islands and towed home on a pontoon for restoration, on her way passing under the Clifton Suspension Bridge completed to Brunel's plans by friends after his death.

At South Shields in the county of Tyne and Wear is preserved an 1833 lifeboat. And many miles inland, the rectory of the little village of Wetheringsett in Suffolk remembers its rector, Richard Hakluyt, whose *Principal Navigations, Voiages and Discoveries of the English Nation* combined patriotic history with scientific analysis of sixteenth-century seafaring problems. Well might Edmund Waller, in the following century, declare:

Above: *Bronze table outside Bristol Corn Exchange known as a 'nail' where merchants used to clinch deals.*
Left: *The 1833 South Shields lifeboat saved 1028 lives during its years of service.*

Others may use the ocean as their road,
Only the English make it their abode.

The fishermen
There can hardly have been a time when coastal dwellers did not find ways of gathering in the harvest of the sea. The spread of Christianity and

Cornish 'huer's' house on a clifftop above Newquay.

its insistence on days of abstinence from meat may have meant penance for some but certainly meant prosperity for fishermen and the owners of salt-pans. Monastic and manorial fishponds or rivers could not supply enough freshwater fish to meet the demand. Herring preserved in salt was carried to all parts of the land. So many royal concessions were made to the providers of this essential food, including freedom from official commandeering of their craft in time of emergency, that by the middle of the fourteenth century many labourers were deserting the fields and taking to the boats. Owners or lessees of salt-pans, needed for the preservation not merely of fish but of other flesh, both at home and in ships setting out on long voyages, made such profits that they could comfortably, if reluctantly, pay taxes to the royal treasury on their evaporating pans along the coasts and estuaries. Seasalter in Kent took its name from this occupation; and the pack-horse distribution routes are marked by places such as Saltergate, Salterford and Salters Bridge.

In Elizabethan times, when observance of the fast days was less rigorous than under a Catholic régime, the fishing trade was threatened with a slump; but Elizabeth, needing the seamen's goodwill and perhaps their services when a defence fleet might hurriedly have to be assembled, imposed special 'fish days' when it was a punishable offence for any of her subjects to eat meat.

Colchester smacks once went dredging all around the British Isles for oysters. Until comparatively recent times this was a staple food of the poor: during his spell of service as American Consul in Liverpool, Nathaniel Hawthorne wrote a description of a labourer on a Mersey ferry-boat taking one after another from his pocket, flipping the shell open with a pocket-knife, and tossing the empty shells overboard. Today the oyster has become a luxury, carefully cultivated in special beds. During the catastrophic east coast floods of 1953 the long-established oyster fisheries at Tollesbury and Mersea, where the beds had been cleaned by years of essential dredging, were inundated by a great tide of mud and silt which, when the tide ebbed, remained to suffocate hundreds of thousands of full-grown oysters. Of those remaining, the majority were too weak to breed. One night's devastation can damage an industry just as effectively as decades of erosion. The whole long process of building up a new hard, clean surface for the larvae to settle and form their spawn, the re-stocking and cultivation, all has to begin over again.

But how does one re-stock a whole ocean? In the West Country, pilchard fishing was once a staple occupation. Today the shoals rarely appear in these over-fished waters, and even the mackerel are threatening to disappear. Mevagissey, its name deriving from Saints Meva and Ida, has records of fishing as far back as 1410, and for centuries subsisted on its catches of cod, hake, and above all pilchard. From his vantage point on a clifftop the local 'huer' would guide the seine boats to the shoals by a complex tic-tac system. Once upon a time a season's catch could amount to 50,000 hogsheads. Today such riches are remembered only in the characteristic shape of the local courtyard house, around which were 'cellars' for pressing and pickling the fish. Clovelly and Lynmouth, now thought of as holiday centres rather than fishing communities, were noted for their herring.

The introduction of steam-driven drifters and trawlers made longer voyages possible, and larger catches could be carried back from Newfoundland or the Arctic to growing towns like Fleetwood in Lancashire and Grimsby on the Humber estuary. Grimsby owed a lot of this prosperity to the railway. In 1848 the place had fewer than a hundred houses, and only one fishing-boat. But in that year the Manchester, Sheffield and Lincolnshire Railway opened a line, constructed a special fish dock, and offered free tickets to merchants ready to open up business in inland towns which had never before known fresh fish. Guarantee of fast transport to these inland markets made Grimsby a perfect distribution centre, and fishermen from Hull, Scarborough, Manningtree and the Norfolk coast brought their families to settle here. Within just over 10 years there were more than 100 boats operating out of the harbour; by the end of the century, more than 800, now unhappily dwindling as international restrictions tighten to prevent further over-fishing.

Great Yarmouth had been busy in the herring trade from the thirteenth century onwards, and by 1900 was the leading herring port in the world. Every year during the season Yarmouth and Lowestoft to the south were crowded with Scottish girls gutting herring; but, as the herring itself threatens to do, they have ceased to come. Behind the tall black 'net shops' on Hastings beach in East Sussex is a fisherman's church and museum housing the last sailing lugger built for use off that beach. It may not be long before at Fleetwood, Grimsby or Lowestoft there is a museum containing the last diesel-powered trawler, while the towns themselves seek desperately – as the once mighty trading port of Liverpool has unsuccessfully sought – to rebuild around new light industries.

The men of war

'The royal navy of England hath ever been its greatest defence and armament; the floating bulwark of the island.' So wrote William Blackstone, the eighteenth-century jurist. The words have a splendid ring to them but are not strictly true. During many periods of our history the navy was at best a makeshift assembly of whatever vessels could be seized, hired or hastily built in time of need. Its officers frequently knew nothing of seamanship; its seamen were often pressed unwillingly into service, treated appallingly, and cast aside when the emergency was over. Even after distinguishing themselves in their country's cause, as during the repulsion of the Spanish Armada, sailors would find themselves on the streets with no money, no food, and no employment. Yet still, in time of crisis, a fleet was somehow assembled; and over the centuries it was indeed fashioned into an impressive bulwark.

Alfred the Great is generally regarded as the founder of the Navy. Faced with repeated Danish assaults, he saw the importance of meeting the invaders at sea rather than waiting for them to get a foothold on the land. For centuries ships carried soldiers as their fighting complement, to wage war on foreign beaches or to ward off foreign attacks. The sailors' duty was simply to sail the ships. It was not until the reign of Henry VII that the Royal Navy as we know it began to take shape; and then to grow in importance under Henry VIII, who used some of his pickings from the looted monasteries to build new men-of-war and crew them with mariners who were also fighting men.

When in July 1588 Philip of Spain sent his Armada against Henry's daughter, Elizabeth I, it was officered by aristocrats appointed because of their blood rather than their skill. This fleet had to face a tough professional force built up by the

Plymouth slaver and privateer, John Hawkins, who as Treasurer of the Navy changed the whole concept of warship-building from unwieldy sea-going fortresses to speedier galleons with continuous gun-decks and fewer top-heavy structures; and, running those ships, experienced and adventurous seamen such as Francis Drake and Martin Frobisher, under the command of Lord Howard of Effingham, who knew and trusted his most gifted men.

Drake's drum and other personal relics are kept in what used to be Buckland Abbey at Buckland Monachorum in his home county of Devon. After the Dissolution it had become the property of Sir Richard Grenville, grandfather of that Grenville who died aboard the *Revenge* in battle with the Spaniards off the Azores, and was bought in 1581 by Drake after his circumnavigation of the world. The drum is said to have been used by Sir Francis to beat his crew to quarters, and even to this day is supposed to give out a drumbeat whenever England is threatened by invasion from the sea.

On Plymouth Hoe a statue of Drake stands close to the green where he is supposed to have insisted on completing a game of bowls before turning his attention towards the approaching Armada. From the Barbican at Plymouth sailed many a warlike expedition and many a one of trade or exploration. Most of the Tudor warships were built along the Thames and Medway, where four royal dockyards were supplemented by the yards of over 150 independent shipwrights; but Portsmouth and Plymouth were later to take precedence, with a new complex on Plymouth Sound acquiring the name Devonport. A figure of King William IV, known to his subjects as the Sailor King or 'Sailor Billy', stands above the gateway to the Royal William Victualling Yard.

Dartmouth, also in Devon, supplied nine ships to the fleet which scattered the Armada. In the nineteenth century it became the anchorage for the *Britannia*, a training ship for naval cadets, to be superseded in 1905 by the Royal Naval College. In Bayard's Cove an incised stone recalls the departure of the *Mayflower* for America in 1620; and from these waters in June 1944 an American force of 500 ships headed for the Normandy beach-head.

Portsmouth and Chatham were in the forefront of shipbuilding for the Royal Navy, but there were other important subsidiaries, now half forgotten. Many of the ships fitted out at Portsmouth had in fact been built up the river Beaulieu at what is now the quiet little village and sailing centre of Buckler's Hard. There are still indications of the old importance there, however: a local hotel is the Master Builder's House, and the width of the main street is surprising until one realizes that it was laid out this way to allow space for stacking and weathering timbers, cut and sawn from New Forest oaks. Horatio Nelson's *Agamemnon* was built at Buckler's Hard; and it was the home port of Chichester's *Gipsy Moth IV*. In 1963 Earl Mountbatten opened a maritime museum in a converted inn.

Horatio Nelson was born in 1758 in the parsonage of Burnham Thorpe, Norfolk. This has since been demolished, but the site is marked by a roadside plaque, the local inn sign preserves the hero's name, and there are several souvenirs in the church where his father once officiated. The first-rate ship of the line in which he died at the battle of Trafalgar, the *Victory*, lies in dry dock at Portsmouth. And, of course, Trafalgar Square in London commemorates that naval victory not merely in its name but in the column rising from its centre. We are so accustomed to the sight of it that it is hard to believe there was once some doubt about its erection. Nelson died in 1805, but it was not until 1829 that Trafalgar Square was laid out by Sir Charles Barry, and not until 1840 that a committee was formed to discuss a possible monument. Some opponents thought the view of the National Gallery would be spoilt by too obtrusive a column. One suggested it should be set to one corner of the square in case the centre was needed in due course for some worthier national figure. But at last, in 1849, work was completed save for Landseer's lions, which were not added for another 20 years.

Nelson's native county had been less dilatory. Great Yarmouth laid the foundation stone of the first Nelson's Column in 1817. It was in this town that, presented with the freedom of the borough and asked to take the oath with his right hand, he had replied: 'That is at Tenerife.' The column's first caretaker, in charge of visitors wishing to climb the 217 steps inside, was a Yarmouth man who, press-ganged into the Navy, was on the *Victory* at Trafalgar and helped to carry the dying Nelson down to the cockpit. In the maritime museum further along the front is a piece of the funeral shroud which draped the coffin on its way to St Paul's Cathedral. This coffin was actually made from the mainmast of the enemy flagship,

The Victory, Nelson's flagship, in dry dock at Portsmouth.

L'Orient, filled with spirit to preserve the corpse on its journey back to England, and then set within a marble sarcophagus originally designed for Cardinal Wolsey.

When we consider that Trafalgar was won with massive sailing ships in 1805, and the war not finally settled until 1815, it is salutary also to realize that the first steam warship took to sea in 1814; the first ironclad in 1860. The first steamer actually built for British government service was a postal packet, the *Sovereign*, in 1821. In 1837 it was taken over by the Royal Navy and renamed *Monkey*, its original name being considered too regal for such a mundane vessel. The Navy then took over or built a fair number of paddle steamers for towing or general use; resisted the idea of screw propulsion for a long time; and until late in the nineteenth century still insisted that masts and sails should be retained in case of mechanical breakdown. In the interim period when fuel was conserved by unfurling sail and taking advantage of any suitable wind, a change back to the engines was announced by the order, 'Up funnel, down screw'.

The superiority of screw propulsion over paddles was shown when Isambard Kingdom Brunel arranged a tug-of-war between two sloops, the *Rattler* fitted with a screw and the paddler *Alecto*. At full steam the *Rattler* tugged her opponent away at a rate of nearly 3 knots.

In 1896 Charles Parsons introduced steam turbines into a little experimental vessel, the *Turbinia*, with three propeller shafts, which to the outrage of assembled dignitaries ran in and out of the great warships assembled for the Spithead Naval Review in the year of Queen Victoria's Diamond Jubilee, at such speed that nothing could catch her. She now rests in the Museum of Science and Engineering in Newcastle.

In 1971 H.M.S. *Belfast*, a cruiser named after the city in which she was built just before the Second World War, was paid off and steamed from Portsmouth dockyard to the Thames, where she lies by Tower Bridge as a floating museum.

The merchantmen

In spite of Elizabeth I's institution of 'fish days'

By Falmouth quay stands the King's Pipe, a brick chimney once used for destroying captured contraband tobacco, which now bears a plaque explaining its former purpose.

to safeguard their livelihoods, West-countrymen found, like others, that there was still a decline. Many of them turned to part-time piracy or joined explorations of the Americas which in their turn often became little more than piratical attacks on Spanish possessions. Geographical discovery was not an end in itself but a pathway to trade and, ideally, conquest.

In 1583 Humphrey Gilbert, who had earlier published a *Discourse on a North-West Passage to India*, founded the first British colony in North America and called it Newfoundland. On his return journey he was lost at sea, but English settlers were quite convinced of their right to take over this and any other parts of the coast on which they might chance to land. In 1584 Sir Walter Raleigh was charged for the benefit of trade and to compete on an equal footing with Spain's

developments in the Caribbean 'to discover, search for, finde out, and view, such remote, heathen and barbarous lands, countreys and territories not actually possessed by any Christian Princes, nor inhabited by Christian people'. He reached the Americas and laid claim to a territory which, in honour of the queen, was called Virginia. The following year he fitted out another expedition under the command of Sir Richard Grenville, part of whose task was to establish a military base which would support Francis Drake's projected expedition to the West Indies in 1585 and 1586. In fact the garrison fell foul of Indians, stores failed to arrive, and instead of backing up Drake, they had to be taken off by him on his return from privateering around Spanish Caribbean possessions. Not until after Elizabeth's death was the colony consolidated, with a capital at Jamestown named after King James I.

Many a great discovery was made by captains nominally on military duty but also expected to further trade and, alone or with expert advice, to provide scientific reports on whatever they encountered. As a jack of all trades – or should we acknowledge him as master of them? – James Cook of Marton-in-Cleveland would take some surpassing. Born in 1728, he received the smatterings of an education at 'dame school', worked as a haberdasher's assistant in the fishing village of Staithes, and then went to sea as an apprentice in a collier. He soon showed himself a talented navigator and was offered promotion, but decided to join the Royal Navy. It was his surveying of the St Lawrence river which enabled General Wolfe to make his decisive attack on Quebec and so open the way for the conquest of Canada, after which Cook was put in charge of the North American squadron and spent three seasons on further work in the St Lawrence and along the coast of Newfoundland.

At the invitation of the Royal Society he set out in the *Endeavour*, a collier converted according to his specifications, from Plymouth in August 1768. The Society's first choice had been Alexander Dalrymple, who had already made a mark with his theories about the great land mass known tentatively as Terra Australis Incognita; but the Admiralty would cooperate only if a naval officer were in charge, so Cook got the job. After completing a study of the transit of Venus, Cook sailed on to rediscover New Zealand, reported by Tasman in 1642 but thereafter neglected, and to explore the coastline of what he christened New

South Wales. On a later voyage he defined the positions of many Pacific islands and groups, including the Society Islands named in honour of the Royal Society, and the Sandwich Islands named after the Earl of Sandwich, First Lord of the Admiralty. His ship on this and a third expedition was the *Resolution*, which ultimately gave so much trouble with defective masts and spars that he had to put in to Hawaii for a refit, where he met his death in an unfortunate squabble with islanders in February 1779.

In 1834 Cook's cottage at Great Ayton, North Yorkshire, was dismantled and shipped for re-assembly in Melbourne, but his own county still retains many mementoes. At Marton, as well as a granite vase marking the site of the cottage where he was born, are the parish church in which he was christened, and a museum; in Great Ayton his schoolroom and, on the moor above, the Captain Cook monument; and at Whitby, where he signed on in the Merchant Navy, a Cook statue and a special wing in the town museum.

Old ports expanded to meet new demands, and new ports came into being. Bideford flourished between the sixteenth and seventeenth centuries, but was left behind in the era of industrialization. Morwellham on the river Tamar was busy handling ore from copper and manganese mines at the foot of an inclined plane whose waterwheel pit and sleeper blocks can still be detected above the abandoned harbour, its life ceasing only at the beginning of this century. Teignmouth has a plaque in New Quay Street commemorating the installation of that new quay to ship Dartmoor granite for the rebuilding of London Bridge. In 1790 Sir William Hamilton began to build the town of Milford Haven, and in 1801 he and his wife Emma, Lady Hamilton, showed Horatio Nelson proudly over it.

With ready access to and from the western ocean, Bristol and Liverpool had competed in the export of slaves to work the American and West Indian plantations and in the import of raw cotton. As the cotton industry around Manchester surged ahead, Liverpool also took the lead as a commercial port.

Dover, once a vulnerable target for enemies across the English Channel, now flourishes in the service of Channel passenger and freight ferries in spite of two ominous features which might be thought to symbolize a threat to its survival: the granite outline of an aeroplane in North Fall meadow where Louis Blériot landed in 1909 at the end of the first cross-Channel flight; and the trial borings further inland for the often mooted, often deplored, and repeatedly postponed Channel Tunnel. At nearby St Margaret's Bay is the favoured terminus for those who prefer yet another means of crossing this stretch of water – Channel swimmers.

Dover's rival in the European ferry trade is Harwich, associated in many people's minds with the mine-sweepers of two World Wars, and preserving other souvenirs of an unbroken maritime past: an old dockyard treadmill crane, within whose drum men used to trudge to turn it; in King's Head Street, the house where lived Christopher Jones, captain of the *Mayflower*; merchants' houses of the sixteenth, seventeenth and eighteenth centuries; and, directly across the estuary, the abandoned flagstaff and buildings of H.M.S. *Ganges*, the boys' naval training establishment at Shotley. Harwich's main moorings are now upriver, a situation which came about because of a dispute between the town and the old Great Eastern Railway, leading to the railway establishing its own terminus and naming it Parkeston Quay after the then head of the company.

On the other side of the country, Brunel sought in 1837 to win backing for continuing the proposed Great Western Railway through Bristol all the way to New York by means of a steamship. The *Great Western*, built in a Bristol shipyard, made its first crossing in 15 days and became the first steamship to operate a regular Transatlantic service. Knowing that Liverpool interests had hoped to pioneer a reliable steam service, Bristol was jubilant at having got away to such a start. But Brunel's later expensive failure, the *Great Eastern*, proved a hopeless proposition in all but laying ocean cables, and ended her days ignominiously lying off Liverpool as a floating fairground advertising Lewis's department stores. In the end it was Liverpool which took over the Atlantic passenger traffic, until the great liners grew so monstrous that Southampton, favoured with four instead of two high tides a day, an easier waterway than the Mersey, and a time-saving access to Cherbourg, stole the passengers; while in our own day Rotterdam and other Continental ports have stolen much of the freight. Liverpool's magnificent dockside warehouses stand empty above deserted basins, and floating landing-stages which once awaited the luxury liners are now rotting away.

Sailing barges, once actively plying their trade in coastal waters, spend most of their time at rest in harbour. These are by the hythe at Maldon in Essex.

Brunel's *Great Britain* found its way back to Bristol. No relic of later leviathans is preserved in our own country: the *Queen Elizabeth* burned out in Hong Kong harbour in 1972; the *Queen Mary* has become another funfair, this one at Long Beach, California; the *Queen Elizabeth II* is afloat at the time of writing, strictly for the rich on luxury cruises – but for how long?

Of the lesser merchantmen, few ply their trade in coastal waters now. Norfolk wherries serve more often as pleasure craft than as carriers of stone or other goods. Sailing barges emerge for occasional races, but spend most of their time demurely at rest at Pin Mill in Suffolk, by the hythe of Maldon in Essex, or in the care of the Dolphin Sailing Barge Museum at Sittingbourne in Kent.

For those in peril
The value to seamen lost in storm and darkness of a light warning them off treacherous rocks would seem too self-evident to warrant a mention. Yet one should never take for granted those who first tried to set up their primitive beacons in places which, almost by definition, were barely accessible. Establishing a firm base on jagged rocks and shipping necessary materials out to dangerous landings was an expensive and risky task, bravely undertaken.

Winstanley's first Eddystone lighthouse, a fantastically ornate wooden tower bearing uplifting slogans on some of its outer panels, was swept away in a storm in 1703. Its replacement displayed all too tragically another danger of such constructions: in the days before electricity, when illumination was provided by coal or wood braziers or glorified candelabra, it was all too easy to set fire to the whole thing – which happened with Rudyerd's Eddystone replacement. A major step forward came with the introduction of oil lights and parabolic reflectors, first used in the river Mersey in 1763.

Not all lighthouses were established in a spirit of benevolence. A Cornish tradition has it that Killigrew's first lighthouse at the Lizard early in the seventeenth century was put there to lure ships close in so that the inventor and his gang might board and rob them.

The Longstone lighthouse on the Farne Islands has gone down in history less for its own sake than for that of the daughter of one of its keepers. In September 1838 the merchant ship *Forfarshire* was wrecked on one of the ragged, rocky outcrops. The lighthouse keeper, William Darling, rowed out with the help of his daughter in their coble to save any lives they could. They managed to rescue nine people, and Grace Darling became not just a heroine but a symbol of what might be done and what still needed to be done for those in peril on the sea. The boat itself, together with some personal relics, can be found in the Grace Darling museum at Bamburgh. But it was not officially a life-saving craft from a recognized life-saving station: such ideas were not yet coordinated.

In 1798 so many horrified spectators had witnessed the *Adventure* being wrecked only a few hundred yards from the shore at South Shields – so close, yet beyond human aid – that a public meeting was called and a prize offered for the design of a rescue boat which might cope with such disasters. Henry Greathead, a local shipwright, won the award and put several sturdy oar-propelled boats into commission.

Another witness of such a tragedy close to the shore was Captain George Manby, Master of Yarmouth Barracks, who in 1803 was so appalled by a ship sinking without any rescue attempt being possible that he set about devising a mortar to fire a lifeline, and also experimented with a boat containing buoyancy chambers. By the middle of the nineteenth century there were 45 mortar stations in England. Manby also invented the breeches buoy. Models of his devices are displayed in the Great Yarmouth maritime museum. Later, John Dennet adapted the mortar principle for a rocket-fired line, and then Captain Boxer improved it with a double rocket system.

In 1824 Sir William Hillary in the Isle of Man founded the Royal National Institution for the Preservation of Life from Shipwreck, which in due course became the Royal National Life-boat Institution.

South Shields was hit by further tragedy when in 1849 its life-boat capsized at the mouth of the Tyne with a loss of 20 lives, whereupon there was another clamour for improvement. In 1851 the Duke of Northumberland appealed for funds and there was a new competition, this time for a self-righting vessel, won by James Beeching of Great Yarmouth. The first steam life-boat came into service in 1890; the first to be converted to motor propulsion was on station at Tynemouth in 1904.

Some sailing and rowing life-boats were in use well into this century, and even the most welcome advances in design have never done away with the freakish and perilous tricks of storm and tide.

In November 1928 the *Mary Stanford* put out from Rye Harbour in Sussex in response to a call from a ship from Riga. She was soon recalled but, turning homewards, capsized with the loss of all 17 hands: a staggering blow to the few families of the little harbour community. Within the church, its barrel roof so reminiscent of an upturned hull, is a memorial tablet of Manx stone from the birthplace of the R.N.L.I., and in the churchyard the men's grave with a sad but noble statue above.

Family traditions were strong in the life-boat service at Rye Harbour, and examples multiply elsewhere. For three generations there has been a Lethbridge at the wheel of St Mary's boat in the Isles of Scilly, of whom the most recent has been awarded the British Empire Medal and three silver R.N.L.I. medals.

But the most beribboned coxswain of all time was the man after whom one of Cromer's two life-boats is named. Henry Blogg served Cromer and its neighbouring coastline for nearly 40 years, including some heroic sorties during the Second World War, and for his incredible achievements was awarded the R.N.L.I. gold medal three times, the silver four times, plus the George Cross and the British Empire Medal.

Grace Darling, Henry Blogg, the men of Rye Harbour and men of other stricken crews are dead; but still there is never, anywhere around the shores of England, a lack of volunteers for this physically taxing, financially unrewarding task. It is all summed up best in the words of a witness at the inquiry into the loss of Caister's life-boat some years back. Asked if he thought the puzzling calamity had taken place when the boat, failing to reach its goal, had tried to turn back, he responded simply: 'Caister men never turn back.'

IMMIGRANTS AND EMIGRANTS

AT THORNEY ABBEY CHURCH in the Fens there is a French inscription to the memory of Ezekiel Danois of Compiègne, one of the Huguenots who fled to this country to escape religious persecution. Settling here, he ministered for 21 years at Thorney until his death in 1674. Many services continued to be held in French under Huguenot pastors until 1715. This was true also of the church at Wisborough Green in West Sussex, where the Huguenot community provided many of the most skilled workers in the glass-making industry which had spread from Chiddingfold.

England has welcomed many refugees during the course of her history. Yet there is another side to the coin: in Boston, Lincolnshire, there remain cells in which Puritans wishing to leave England to join a community in Holland and perhaps go on to America to worship in their own fashion were imprisoned.

There has always been not just a two-way traffic of incomers and outgoers, but a further sub-division into the willing and the unwilling. And in addition to mass or group movements there have been many individuals fancying a change of climate or a chance of profit, or finding themselves forced along by fancies not their own. Some have been assimilated, here or abroad, taking an old name with them or bringing a new one in. Some have left little trace; others live on in their contributions to societies into which they were not born.

Washington Old Hall in the modern county of Tyne and Wear was the home of the Hartburns, who changed their name to de Wessyngton on acquiring the manor, and who were direct ancestors of George Washington.

Exports

In the cloisters of Durham cathedral is a memorial to John Washington of Washington in the county of Durham, 1416–1446, 'whose family has won an everlasting fame in lands to him unknown'. The Old Hall at Washington is now cared for by the National Trust. Later the family moved to Sulgrave Manor near Northampton, where the coat of arms over the porch suggests there could be some truth in the claim that it provided the basis for the original Stars and Stripes. The modern Stars and Stripes fly above the manor. The greatest rebel commander against the English was undoubtedly of the very best English stock!

British settlement of the Americas lagged behind the Spanish acquisitions, in spite of the fact that an expedition had set off fairly promptly after news of Columbus's finds reached Henry VII's ears. Having been offered the chance of backing Columbus and turned it down, Henry was not going to let another opportunity slip. He granted a royal patent to a seaman who had been, as it were, an import from the east before being sent off further to the west. Giovanni Caboto had been, like Columbus, Genoese: he then became a naturalized Venetian and then a Bristol merchant under the name of John Cabot. While the Spaniards were committing themselves to Central and South America, Cabot and his sons discovered what Gilbert was later to call Newfoundland, and explored the coast from Labrador down to Virginia. Later came Elizabeth's captains, venturers and pirates.

The Virginia Company, once firmly established, was none too scrupulous in its methods of recruiting labour for the new colony, especially

A plaque above the Dart estuary records the arrival of the unseaworthy Speedwell *and the* Mayflower, *which on 6 September 1620 sailed for the New World alone.*

after John Rolfe's profitable discovery of the most effective way to cure tobacco. As well as adult settlers and indentured servants, child apprentices were needed to safeguard the future craft and labour force. When not enough were forthcoming voluntarily, paupers and orphans were summarily selected by the City of London 'out of their superfluous multitude'. The company's treasurer reported:

It falleth out that among those Children, sundry being ill-disposed and fitter for any remote place than for this Citie, declared their unwillingness to go to Virginia; of whom the Citie is especially desirous to be disburdened; and in Virgina under severe Masters they may be brought to goodnes.

Whether the children liked it or not, they were duly transported. Even the most pious and upright elders of the community rarely saw anything wrong in such treatment, perhaps seeing them-selves as the severe Masters who would bring their apprentices to that 'goodnes'; nor, later, did many of them see anything immoral in the development of black slavery.

In spite of hardships, westbound traffic on the Atlantic increased. Physical hardships were, to certain austere elements, preferable to spiritual antagonism in the old country. Early in the seventeenth century Puritans such as William Brewster and William Bradford seeking to leave the country in search of religious tolerance had been imprisoned in the Guildhall of St Mary in Boston, where their iron-gated cells can still be seen. Next door, Fydell House has become the Pilgrim College, with a room set aside for the use of American visitors.

Those who were at last successful in escaping formed a community of about 100 under the ministry of John Robinson in the Dutch town of Leyden. When they began to plan emigration to the New World they were offered a home in the Dutch colony there, but in spite of their disputes with their own countrymen they wished to remain English and for their descendants not to forget this inheritance. For a while they negotiated with the

One of the oldest buildings on Canvey Island, Essex, is a cottage which probably housed Dutch drainage engineers and is now a Thames shipping museum.

Virginia Company, but realized in time that they would be but exchanging 'one form of persecution for another'. Finally Thomas Weston, a merchant adventurer of Bristol, offered financial support; but was more interested in potential profit than religious freedom, and caused many early troubles with the local Indians.

In 1620, after much tribulation, the *Mayflower* carried the Pilgrim Fathers out from Plymouth in England to a landing by the granite rock thereafter named Plymouth Rock in New England. In 1621 a further shipload of emigrants sailed to swell their numbers.

By 1630 Charles I's intransigence was driving more to turn their gaze westwards. In April of that year 15 ships set out under the command of John Winthrop. The Winthrop family, highly successful in the East Anglian cloth trade, had acquired the manor of Groton in Suffolk at the Dissolution. John, born in 1588 in the neighbouring village of Edwardstone, married twice and outlived both wives: they, as well as his father and grandfather, are buried in Groton church, to which in 1875 his descendants donated the east window. Castling's Hall nearby is the once-moated house where he met and wooed his second wife.

John Winthrop studied law at Cambridge, found himself in sympathy with Puritan principles, and was convinced that God's wrath against the depravities of England was such as to necessitate founding a true city of God elsewhere. Reaching America with his flock of about 500, he established a new colony about Massachusetts Bay, and in defiance of what the faraway British government might think he decreed that it should be self-governing, with himself as first governor. A sincere but strict man, he enforced strict control over the religious and moral views of any would-be newcomers. Most of his followers were East Anglians, and the first three regions to be developed within Massachusetts were named Norfolk, Suffolk and Essex. Winthrop married a third time, died in 1649, and is buried in the city which he helped to found and named Boston after the rallying point of the original Pilgrim Fathers.

In the year after Winthrop's voyage, another emigré was John Eliot, who won fame as 'the apostle to the Indians'. He learned Indian tongues, became minister at Roxbury near Boston, and his translation of the Bible into Mohican was the first Bible to be printed in America. There is a copy of it in the library of his old college – Jesus College, Cambridge.

A further influx of dissenters came when, after the Restoration, harassed Quakers began to seek a refuge. In 1667 William Penn, whose ancestors came from the parish of Penn in Buckinghamshire, published a diatribe, *Sandy Foundation Shaken*, and was sent to prison. He was released on the intervention of his father, Admiral Sir William Penn, but continued teaching and preaching. When Sir William died, the younger William came into a fortune, much of it from the family ironworks near Hawkhurst in Kent. He acquired land in North America, although the Puritans already settled there had shown themselves just as hostile to Quakers as authority in the homeland had done, and in 1681 founded the colony of Pennsylvania.

Penn was not one of those leaders who stayed on to oversee the development of their new territories. Three years later he was back in England. Among the many places at which he preached, some of them since demolished, was a house called the Blue Idol at Coolham in Sussex. Its odd name has two possible explanations: one, that a figurehead from a ship of that name was incorporated in the original timbers; two, that parts of the building were once painted blue and that it was 'idle' through some years of disuse. Many of Penn's addresses were framed as he walked here across the fields from his house at Warminghurst. His daughter Letitia is buried by the Blue Idol, which is still a Friends' Meeting House, with an accompanying guest-house. Another place of assembly was Jordans Farm near Chalfont St Giles, now the Old Jordan Hostel, with a barn which is said to include timbers from the *Mayflower*. A red-brick Friends' Meeting House took its place in 1688, and Penn is buried nearby.

By the beginning of the eighteenth century each province had its own legislative assembly, usually under a governor appointed by the king, with the duty of ensuring that no locally made decisions conflicted with official British policy or British commercial interests. But restrictions imposed from faraway London grew more and more oppressive – a Stamp Act, monopoly of

A statue of the republican Tom Paine, presented by the Thomas Paine Foundation of America, defies the Royal Arms on the adjacent King's House in Thetford.

goods transport under Navigation Acts, taxes on tea, lead, glass and paper, coercive acts to close ports and cripple traders who showed any sign of protest – and, in the views of the American colonists, less and less easy to justify. British troops were at loggerheads with provincial militia. In April 1775 a British contingent was ordered towards Concord, the main militia supply depot in Massachusetts, where there had been murmurs of revolt. The soldiers were intercepted at Lexington by a provincial detachment; and somebody opened fire with 'the shot that was heard around the world'. In spite of misgivings among many colonists, including George Washington, the American War of Independence was on. It lasted until October 1781, when Washington, with the aid of French allies, forced the surrender of the British at Yorktown.

An Englishman much in and out of the country during these revolutionary years was Thomas Paine, son of a Norfolk farmer. Born in White Hart Street, Thetford, in 1737, he became an excise officer but spoke out too bluntly against certain abuses and was discharged. At the end of 1774 he sailed for America with a letter of introduction to Benjamin Franklin, and in Philadelphia founded a magazine to which he contributed outspoken articles about slavery and female emancipation. When war broke out he published a pamphlet, *Common Sense*, analyzing the causes of the conflict and urging the rebels to frame a Declaration of Independence. His share in this led to his being dubbed 'The Godfather of America'. Paine enlisted in the revolutionary army, and after victory worked for the new government until his return to England in 1787. In the first part of *The Rights of Man* he attacked Edmund Burke's views on the French Revolution; and the second part aroused such a storm that he had to flee to France in order to escape arrest. There he was elected to the Convention, spoke out against the execution of Louis XVI, and was lucky to find himself in prison until Robespierre's execution and not under the guillotine. On returning later to America he found much to disillusion him, and died in New York in 1809. In 1964 a gilded bronze statue of Tom Paine was erected before the King's House in Thetford.

Also in Norfolk is the village of Hingham, whose rector Robert Peck left with a group of parishioners in the early seventeenth century to found Hingham in Massachusetts. He was soon joined by another Hingham family, the Lincolns, one of whose descendants was Abraham Lincoln.

Canada remained loyal, though some of its people were lured south of the border; and the West Indies were proving a lucrative investment; but a new large slab of Empire was needed to make up for the loss of England's North American settlements and trading territories.

The first emigrants to Australia went in no mood of high adventure. Britain had for a time contemplated offering land there to loyalists driven out of the United States; but opted instead for establishing a penal colony. A contingent of convicts with troops and officials in charge – 1,000 in all – were transported to Botany Bay, in 1788. After seven years had passed, such felons were allowed to become 'free settlers' and have a personal stake in opening up the new continent. Progress was slow. The land around the first penal settlement was not as fertile as had been predicted, the officers in charge maltreated their prisoners, and went in for unscrupulous land speculation and trading. When William Bligh was appointed Governor of New South Wales in 1805 he tried to remedy some of these abuses, but did it with such harshness and lack of imagination that he found himself with a mutiny on his hands – the second in his career, after the famous mutiny on the *Bounty* – and spent two years in prison.

One reason for the slow development was the uncertainty on the high seas during the Napoleonic wars. The Royal Navy could spare few escorts for civilian voyagers with their stores and belongings. If the result of those battles had gone the other way, there is little doubt that the French would have possessed themselves of large tracts of Australasia. Even when the seas were clear, however, prospects in this new land still did not seem too promising. Free settlers were offered cheap convict labour as an inducement; but when released these slaves did not always make the best neighbours, especially to those who had ill-used them.

It took the crossing of the Blue Mountains to open up richer lands, and the expansion of sheep farming attracted more immigrants. In 1840 penal transportation to the mainland was stopped, though a prison colony lingered on in Van Diemen's Land until 1853, when the island was renamed Tasmania.

In 1829 Edward Gibbon Wakefield, serving a gaol sentence in Newgate for abducting his second wife, had applied himself to considering the whole question of colonial development. He published his views on the evils of transportation and the need for a freer spread of British interests, and in 1830 inspired the foundation of the Colonization Society. He urged that emigrants should represent a healthy cross-section of the English people and should be financed from an emigration fund which would offer land at realistic prices, encouraging men to work it for a wage while they acquired capital, and promising them eventual self-government.

The first Australian enterprise under his auspices did not fare too well until Sir George Grey arrived. After eight years in the army, Grey had explored north-western Australia on behalf of the Royal Geographical Society, and in 1841 was appointed Governor of South Australia. His influence was so beneficial that he was then sent to restore peace in the colony of New Zealand, annexed by Britain in 1840 but torn by troubles between Maori natives and get-rich-quick agents of the well-intentioned New Zealand Association in which Wakefield also had a part. Grey went on to become Governor of the Cape of Good Hope province to deal with lingering resentments from the Kaffir wars; and returned eventually in justifiable good spirits to become Premier of New Zealand in 1877.

Africa, India, Australasia ... the names of expatriates accumulate, and only with hindsight can we smugly persuade ourselves that many of their ambitious schemes were foredoomed to failure. Statues raised in imperial times have been torn down as one state after another has gained its independence. Yet the occasional trivial personal souvenir is often more evocative than, say, a King George collapsing from his New York plinth when his American subjects had rebelled against such subjection. In Christchurch Mansion, Ipswich, a sad little exhibit testifies to some of the rigours of the pioneering days. In 1797 Margaret Catchpole, a serving girl in the Cobbold brewing family, stole one of her employer's horses to ride to London in aid of her lover, a wild young smuggler. Arrested and put in Ipswich gaol, she escaped and tried to flee to Holland with her smuggler. Trapped, he was killed and she was sentenced to transportation to Australia, where she died in 1819. During her exile she sent home a stuffed lyrebird. Near it in Christchurch Mansion museum is a painting of Margaret by Richard Cobbold, clergyman son of the family, who wrote a best-selling novel about her when he was rector of Wortham in the mid-nineteenth century.

Imports
Explorers would as a matter of course bring back specimens of what they had found overseas. The earliest adventurers in the Indies and the Americas returned with natives for the edification or amusement of their friends. Occasionally one such would be a person of some distinction. Perhaps the most celebrated was the Red Indian princess, Pocahontas, who when still a little girl interceded in Virginia with her father, the powerful chieftain Powhatan, for the life of the captured Captain John Smith. Educated thereafter at a missionary school, she became the first Red Indian to adopt Christianity, and married John Rolfe from Heacham in Norfolk. In 1616 she accompanied him to England and was received at the court of King James I. Finding the British climate not to her taste, she begged to go home, but was already so ill that at Gravesend she had to be taken off the ship, dying, and was buried in St George's church. This has since become a Chapel of Unity for seafaring folk of all denominations who come ashore here. There are two windows to her memory, and in the former churchyard stands a statue presented by the people of Virginia. Pocahontas also lives on in the village sign of her husband's birthplace, Heacham.

Not only in the Americas but also close to home were England and Spain forever in conflict. In 1629 an envoy from the Spanish Netherlands – what is now Belgium – visited London as an envoy to negotiate a truce in a war for which neither side had much appetite. Charles I praised this envoy for his skill and tact, and in March 1630 knighted him; but it was as a painter that he most admired Peter Paul Rubens from Antwerp. Sir Peter was engaged to design a ceiling for Inigo Jones's rebuilt Banqueting House in Whitehall: he produced nine spacious canvases in his Antwerp studio, and despatched them to London in 1635. Three years later he received his fee and the gift of a gold chain.

But it was one of Rubens's pupils who was to bring a quite new vision to portraiture in this country. Anthony van Dyck, whose paintings of royalty and nobility so often featured the sharply pointed beards of contemporary fashion that they are still referred to as Vandyke beards, was first invited to visit England by the Earl of Arundel. James I gave him a pension and allowed him to travel so that he might continue his studies. Returning to England in 1632, Van Dyck was knighted by Charles I, who assured him a pension of £200 a year and a house at Blackfriars, and even chose a wife for him.

In the National Gallery is the famous study of King Charles on horseback. Van Dyck painted many pictures of his patron – one of them a fascinating montage of the king's head seen from three different angles – and of the queen, Henrietta Maria. Several are in the royal collections, but a few have flown: Oliver Cromwell sold off the contents of certain royal residences, and a particularly vivid study of Charles and Henrietta Maria now rests in the picture gallery of the bishop's palace in Kroměříž (Kremsier) in what used to be Moravia and is now part of Czechoslovakia.

Sir Anthony went on to paint a great sequence

The statue of Princess Pocahontas at Gravesend.

of revealing pictures of the English aristocracy, transforming all the hitherto accepted tenets of portraiture in this country. The stiffly formal approach gave way to a full-blooded, dashing modern style, not so much capturing the subject on canvas as dragging him or her right out of it into reality.

Van Dyck died in London in 1641. His memorial in the crypt of St Paul's cathedral is close to the graves of distinguished later artists: among them Lawrence, Millais, Reynolds and Turner.

When the Stuarts had finally been driven from the throne and in due course the house of Hanover took over, a German resident in London had reason for alarm. Georg Friedrich Handel had long overstayed his leave of absence from the Hanoverian court, preferring the patronage of Queen Anne; but when she died, his royal pension stopped, and the Elector of Hanover he had so much offended was now King George I of England. It is said that they were reconciled by the stirring performance of Handel's *Water Music* suite given by 50 instrumentalists alongside the royal barge at a concert on the river Thames. Most of the last 40 years of the composer's life were spent at 25 Brook Street, London, much altered since his day. He generously supported Thomas Coram's Foundling Hospital north of Holborn, in what is now Coram's Fields, and trained the choir there. In the present offices of the Thomas Coram Foundation are kept Roubillac's bust of Handel, his organ keyboard, and an original score of *Messiah*.

Roubillac also designed the monument to the composer in Westminster Abbey. Unlike that of Sir Christopher Wren in St Paul's Cathedral, Handel's tomb cannot boast, *Lector, si monumentum requiris, circumspice* – 'Reader, if you seek his monument, look around'. Musicians leave nothing tangible. Even the scores of their masterpieces are only marks on paper, meaningless until converted into sound. But is sound so ephemeral? Handel might reasonably demand of us not that we should look around but that we should listen: let us open our ears and hope that the echoes will be more enduring than mere stone.

Johann Christian Bach, son of Handel's great contemporary Johann Sebastian Bach, came to England in 1762 and was soon music master to the queen. His operas and cantatas were a great success; but even more popular were the songs and instrumental pieces which often had their premières in the bandstands and shaded walks of Vauxhall Gardens, the pleasure park in London ultimately closed by Victorian prudery. Another garden, on the site of St Pancras Old Church yard, is the burial site of 'the English Bach'.

We have also imported many a writer, especially from those once defiant American colonies. Some set foot warily on our soil. The novelist Henry James dealt in several early novels with the innocence of Americans abroad and the dangerous, age-old seductions of European society. But in 1876, at the age of 33, he settled in London and dined out avidly, greedy as much for snippets of gossip and possible stories as for food. Staying in Rye, Sussex, in 1896 he saw Lamb House and began renting it the following year; later he was to buy it. After that he spent most of his summers in Rye and gossipy winters in London, returning in more and more convoluted prose to his favourite theme of innocence and

corruption, American and European. He remained an American citizen until 1915 when, hating German military aggression, he became a naturalized British subject, justifying this to a friend by saying he had taken the step 'Chiefly because I wanted to be able to say *We* – with a capital – when I talked about an advance'. In January 1916 he received the Order of Merit, and died at the end of February.

The garden room at Lamb House in which he dictated much of his later work to a stenographer was demolished by a Second World War bomb from that country of which he had so much disapproved; but the house itself is cared for by the National Trust, and his substitute study is open to the public on Wednesday and Saturday afternoons from March to October. As if determined to extirpate all mention of this neutral who had once dared to espouse the cause of their enemies, the Germans managed to destroy another relic – the tablet in Chelsea Old Church which called him 'lover and interpreter of the fine amenities, of brave decisions and generous loyalties: a resident of this parish' – (mainly in winter, they should have added) – 'who renounced a cherished citizenship to give his allegiance to England in the first year of the Great War'.

Only close friends of the author of this book are allowed to inspect two other Henry James souvenirs: his inkstand, which is before me as I write this page, and his copy of Holloway's *History of the Town and Port of Rye*, on the adjoining bookshelf.

An even more alien writer set foot on English soil in June 1878. Jósef Korzeniowski, born in 1857 in a Polish Ukrainian province then under Russian rule, had gone to sea at the age of 17. In April 1878 he joined an English vessel in Marseilles, and reached England at Lowestoft, which he later referred to as his spiritual birthplace. He served on a Lowestoft trawler, made some coastal trips, and then went off to Australia in a wool clipper and returned by steamship. In 1886 he became a naturalized British subject under the name of Joseph Conrad, and studied the language intently enough to write a novel, *Almayer's Folly*, in 1889, based on his experiences in the Belgian Congo. After its publication he took the risk of surviving as a professional writer. For some time

Lamb House, Rye, whose steps were so often occupied by amateur painters that Henry James found he had to 'take flying leaps over industry and genius'.

he lived and worked at Pent Farm in Kent; took a house called Someries near Luton; and returned to Kent, living and in 1924 dying at Oswalds, Bishopsbourne, now the village rectory.

Conrad befriended the American novelist Stephen Crane, who arrived in London in 1896, after the success of *The Red Badge of Courage*. He set up house with Cora Taylor, a twice-married lady of unlikely virtue, and in 1899 took the fine medieval haunted house, Brede Place, in Sussex. Crane was already a tuberculosis sufferer, and the dampness of the old house did nothing to help his condition. Cora persuaded him to go with her to the Black Forest in the hope of a cure, but he died there the following year at the age of 29.

Katherine Mansfield came to England from New Zealand; Philip and Jack Lindsay from Australia; and both Indian and West Indian writers have been tempted to try their literary luck on these shores. And if we exported some Eliots to America long ago, we reclaimed one of their descendants in the same year that Henry James died.

Thomas Stearns Eliot was born in St Louis, Missouri, but came from a family which had settled in Boston in the seventeenth century. He edited the London literary journal, *Criterion*, and became a director of the distinguished publishing house of Faber & Faber, as well as being one of the authors on their list with his volumes of poetry. The title of one of his *Four Quartets* is taken from the village in Somerset, East Coker, from which his ancestors set out for America; and T.S. Eliot is buried there and commemorated in a stained glass window in the parish church.

Scientists immigrate or emigrate with the greatest of ease and often with the greatest profit. The Germans who once tried hard to destroy us now earn fortunes from the sale of their destructive talents to us and our allies. If they leave anything in their memory, it is all too likely to be a series of funereal chasms in the earth.

This book is not designed as a personal memoir, though any book must to a large extent be a personal expression of the author's predilections. But I think the story of a friend of mine who died in 1978 has some significance in this present context. He came to England with no scientific secrets or special technology to sell; he lived quietly, worked conscientiously, and it is unlikely that there will ever be a plaque on his house or a street named after him. His name was Arnold Bender. Foreseeing what Adolf Hitler

The Bridge Hotel, Newhaven, was a quiet refuge for
Louis Philippe and his queen after the 1848 revolution,
before the railways took over the harbour.

must mean, he came to this country some years before the Second World War, married an English girl, and tried to continue his career as a writer – a matter of some difficulty, since nothing he wrote in his own language would be accepted in his own country, and in spite of speaking English fluently he never quite managed to write it with ease. When Thomas Mann, with the cooperation of publishers in the United States, the United Kingdom and France, offered a prize for the best novel by a refugee from Nazi oppression, Arnold won it. The Nazis protested that there were no such refugees, since there was no such oppression; and the German ambassador to the United States persuaded the publisher there to back out of the agreement. The English publisher, William Collins, was more courageous and, in spite of a personal intervention by Ribbentrop, went ahead and published. So, I believe, did the French. But

when Arnold continued writing after the war he suffered the fate of many expatriates: in his own language, in the country of his birth, he was still not published; his English writing did not appeal to English editors, though he collaborated with some success on the translation of Annemarie Selinko's *Desirée*; and for some years it was only in France that he achieved publication of a novel. He and his wife made a living by running 'Simon the Pieman', a tea-shop in Rye, before retiring to Port Isaac in Cornwall. Late on in life he was invited to a number of literary meetings in Germany, and at last was commissioned to write a book for a German publisher: a book all about the English.

So no monuments, no relics, save in the memories of those of us who knew him. Is this irrelevant to our main theme? I don't think so.

Visitors

Mozart's first symphony was composed in 1764 when, at the age of eight, he was staying at 180 Ebury Street, Chelsea. And in the year before he flung himself into the composition of *Don Giovanni* there was a possibility of his following his favourite singer Nancy Storace and settling in London to work with her at Drury Lane and with her brother, the king's opera supervisor. It all fell through, and we can only speculate what might have resulted if Mozart had taken up permanent residence in England.

Many temporary residents have come here simply to sit out a storm. The romantic writer Chateaubriand left France during the Terror and lived for a while at Bungay in Suffolk, making a living from teaching French privately at home and at a school in Beccles. The tongues of the Waveney valley found his name a hard one to get round, and he was soon known throughout the neighbourhood as Monsieur Shatterbrain.

Another refugee from the revolution was Louis Philippe, son of the Duke of Orléans, who had declared himself a republican but with insufficient fervour, so that he had to flee. A plaque on Angel Hill in Bury St Edmunds recalls his stay in 1791 at the house known as St Edmund's Hotel. For a while he resided at Twickenham, then returned to France, left it again, but was invited to return as king after the revolution of 1830. After yet another revolution in 1848 he once more fled to England, and with his wife stayed for a time at the Bridge Hotel in Newhaven before settling at Claremont in Surrey, where he died two years later.

In that year of 1848 Karl Marx and Friedrich Engels published their *Communist Manifesto*. After his experiences in the 'year of revolutions', Louis Philippe would surely have disapproved of the marking of Marx's lodgings in Dean Street, Soho, with a commemorative plaque.

During the Second World War hospitality was offered to a number of governments and royal families in exile. Norway still shows gratitude for this by providing a tall Christmas tree for Trafalgar Square every year.

And as welcome visitors to this country came, in two wars, the descendants of those rebels who took over the United States for themselves. On a wall in The Swan Hotel, Lavenham, is a section of the wartime bar counter on which scores of American airmen carved their names. The military cemetery at Madingley outside Cambridge is the resting place of many who never returned.

One who went home was John T. Appleby, who loved his temporary surroundings so much that he wrote a delightful little book, *Suffolk Summer*, about his experiences, donating all the profits to the upkeep of the little rose garden behind St Edmundsbury cathedral.

Old comrades in arms come together again in the church of St Clement Dane's in the Strand, London. One of Christopher Wren's most beautiful churches, it was gutted during a 1941 bombing raid, but carefully restored after the war as the Royal Air Force church. There is a shrine in honour of the United States Air Force, and crests of Commonwealth air forces are inset in the floor. The altar and sanctuary in the crypt were given by the Royal Netherlands Air Force, a marble font by the Royal Norwegian Air Force. And a stone in the floor at the head of the staircase acknowledges a debt to Georgia, where many R.A.F. pilots trained during 1941 and 1942.

HOME COUNTIES

WHILE MANY OF THE GREAT landed families preferred, and still prefer, to stay on their estates far from the capital, there have always been those with a need or appetite for metropolitan life; and if they could combine this with the pleasures of an emparked mansion within easy reach of London, so much the better. A great many political and financial decisions have been framed in the near-suburban houses of statesmen and well-to-do hosts. Ambitious courtiers schemed in such settings. Others, more wary, kept as far away from the royal presence for as long as possible. During many periods of our history, and especially during Tudor times, it was a delicate decision for many a nobleman as to whether continued absence from Court would arouse more suspicion and disapproval than too assiduous a presence.

Stately homes and statesmen's homes

One who believed in keeping close to the throne, whoever might be sitting on it, was John Morton, a Lancastrian who switched allegiance to Edward IV when he thought it politic to do so, and was rewarded with the bishopric of Ely. Imprisoned by Richard III, he escaped to ally himself with the future Henry VIII, who made him archbishop of Canterbury in 1486 and Lord Chancellor the following year. To his royal master's delight Morton devised the tax system known as 'Morton's Fork': if merchants were richly attired and lived lavishly, he said they could obviously afford to pay heavy dues to the State; if shabbily, they were obviously mean and must have saved fortunes, part of which the Exchequer had a right

Old Palace Yard and the gateway of Richmond Palace.

to claim. He was made a cardinal in 1493, and in 1497 began to build himself a mansion at Hatfield in Hertfordshire.

Henry VIII took over the property at the Dissolution as a home for his children. When his older daughter Mary refused to admit the validity of her father's marriage to Anne Boleyn or the legitimacy of her half-sister Elizabeth, she was made as a punishment to wait on the younger girl at Hatfield. Their brother Edward shared lessons in the house with Elizabeth, and the two frequently went riding together in the neighbourhood. Then, after Edward's short reign, Mary became queen and turned the tables: Elizabeth lived in seclusion here and at Ashridge, keeping what is known today as a low profile. In spite of this she was for a while imprisoned in the Tower with no assurance that she would ever come out alive. But it was back at Hatfield that she learned of Mary's death and her own succession. There is an oak tree in the park under which she was sitting when the news arrived; and it was either under this same tree or in the hall of the house that she addressed her first Council.

Once Elizabeth had left Hatfield she never returned, perhaps because the later years of virtual imprisonment had soured earlier happy memories of the place. But it still holds some of her possessions, including garden gloves and a straw hat, and what may have been the first pair of silk stockings to reach England. There are also sombre mementoes of Mary, Queen of Scots: the only surviving specimen of the 'Casket Letters', pointing to her connivance in the murder of her husband Darnley; and her death warrant, reluctantly signed by Elizabeth and rushed off by her advisers for fulfilment before the hesitant queen could change her mind.

It was during the reign of Elizabeth's successor, son of the Queen of Scots, that the building began to take its present shape. James I disposed of the house to his Secretary of State, Robert Cecil, in exchange for Theobalds near Cheshunt, which had been built by Cecil's father, Lord Burghley. Created Earl of Salisbury, Cecil set about pulling down a large part of what is now called Morton's Old Palace, and in its place erected a Jacobean mansion in glowing red brick. To ensure greater privacy he extended the park and set three gardeners to work, including the elder John Tradescant, later to become Charles I's gardener. There is a story that in shutting himself away so arbitrarily he obliterated an old right of way, thereby incensing one of his neighbours so much that the man paid an annual visit solely in order to ride his horse in through the north doorway of the house and out on the far side.

The first creation of a Marquess of Salisbury was in 1789. In 1850 the second Marquess welcomed the arrival of the Great Northern Railway at Hatfield, laid down a new drive for better access to the station, and persuaded the company to add a private waiting-room to that station so that he could take his ease there while his own private coach was shunted into the adjacent bay.

The third Marquess was three times Prime Minister during Queen Victoria's reign, and the Cecil family has continued to play its part in politics and literature to this day.

Another politician and writer had his home not far north of Hatfield. In the seventeenth century Sir Robert Lytton built a house at Knebworth, three sides of which were pulled down in 1811 by General Earle Bulwer's widow. Her son, Edward Bulwer Lytton, was brought up at Knebworth under his mother's domineering influence. At the age of 24 he wanted to marry a girl called Rosina Wheeler, of whom his mother disapproved without ever having met her. When the young man insisted on the marriage, he was thrown out of Knebworth without a penny. In desperation he decided to try his hand at writing fiction in order to make some money. His first novel, *Falkland*, showed that he had chosen the right profession, and he went on to greater successes with *The Last Days of Pompeii* and *The Last of the Barons*. In 1831 he entered Parliament, and in 1866 was created first Baron Lytton. Although his mother proved to have been right, and Rosina was a plague to him for the rest of his life, he finally inherited Knebworth and began converting it into a flamboyant piece of Victorian Gothic. A few surviving Jacobean features are mixed with such oddities as a nineteenth-century papier-mâché staircase. Here Bulwer Lytton entertained political acquaintances and fellow writers such as Charles Dickens and Wilkie Collins.

However much Elizabeth I may have resented her own incarceration, she certainly did not hesitate to imprison others when it suited her. When she discovered that the Protestant favourite as her successor, Lady Catherine Grey – sister of the ill-fated Lady Jane Grey – had secretly married the Earl of Hertford without her permission, she rushed both Catherine and her husband to the Tower, where they had two children. Released in custody, Catherine was sent first to Chequers Court in Buckinghamshire for a couple of years, and then to Cockfield Hall at Yoxford in Suffolk, where she died. Chequers has other echoes, housing as it does the country's most extensive collection of Oliver Cromwell relics, unfortunately not open to inspection by the public: since 1922 it has been the country residence of the Prime Minister of the day, Lloyd George having been the first to take advantage of this privilege.

One of Cromwell's cousins lived not much more than a mile away. John Hampden of Hampden House represented Wendover in Charles I's first three parliaments, and became one of the king's most outspoken critics. Refusing to pay what he considered to be an illegal royal tax, Ship Money, he was found guilty by the Court of Exchequer but discharged. When Charles swooped on the Commons with the intention of arresting five members for treason, Hampden was one of this number; but they escaped, and when in the following year it was clear that a Civil War was no longer avoidable, Hampden assembled a contingent of Buckinghamshire militia to fight the Royalists. He fell in a skirmish at Chalgrove, died soon after at Thame, and was buried in Hampden church. Between Hampden and Prestwood stands a roadside monument to 'The Patriot'.

After the Restoration of Charles II there were many rumours of plot and counter-plot, some involving sly denunciations of his avowedly Catholic brother James, Duke of York. But one of many supposed assassination schemes included both Charles and James. Dissatisfied Whigs and ex-Cromwellians had for some time been evaluat-

ing the chances of a further revolution, though their activities resulted only in many of them being driven into exile. In 1683 some hotheads planned at Rye House, near Hoddesdon, to murder the brothers on their way back from Newmarket. The plot was uncovered in time, and a number of dissentients who had in fact done little more than voice discontent without ever truly contemplating regicide were arrested and executed. Nothing is left of Rye House now but its fifteenth-century castellated brick gate-house, restored by the Lea Valley park authority near a sanctuary of the Royal Society for the Protection of Birds.

In the eighteenth century a brick house in Buckinghamshire was refashioned in Palladian style by Sir Francis Dashwood, who with a group of dissolute friends had been a founder of the 'Hell Fire Club' at Medmenham abbey, where they dabbled in black magic rites. When Dashwood altered his house at West Wycombe, he also used money bequeathed to him by one of the Medmenham 'monks' to build a mausoleum. It was originally intended that this should be a repository for urns holding the heart of each

John Morton, Bishop of Ely and pioneer of Fenland drainage, built himself a palace at Hatfield of which only a wing survives the Cecils' rebuilding.

deceased member of the club, but there is no evidence of any having been deposited there, save for that of an aspiring poet for whom Dashwood arranged a profitable sinecure and whose heart in a casket was at one time immured in the mausoleum. Caves dug out under the church to provide material for a new road were used in place of the Medmenham meeting-place; and on the church itself Dashwood poised a large golden sphere, with seats inside for himself and eight of his cronies, one of whom used to refer to it as his favourite Globe Tavern.

Looking back, it seems remarkable that such a self-proclaimed dilettante and self-indulgent rake as Sir Francis should have not merely entered Parliament – that was a simple matter for the landed gentry of the time – but should in due course have been appointed Chancellor of the Exchequer. Or, looking at some recent holders of that post, does it? Even more splendidly absurd was his elevation as fifteenth Baron Le Despencer, making him premier baron of England. In our present century one of his more enlightened descendants, Sir John Dashwood, has presented West Wycombe House and the entire village, together with a stretch of parkland, to the National Trust.

Also in the keeping of the Trust is another Buckinghamshire home of a politico-literary figure. After Benjamin Disraeli, novelist and one of the two members of Parliament for Maidstone, had married his late colleague's widow, he was able to use her money to buy in 1847 an estate at Hughenden near Bradenham, where he had spent some youthful years and where his father Isaac was to die a year later. Full of enthusiasm not just for Queen Victoria but for all things Victorian, he decided in 1862, with financial aid from Conservative supporters who wanted their putative Prime Minister to have a worthy architectural setting, to gothicize the basically Georgian house with brick refacings and some extravagant interiors. His desk, pens, and some sheets of writing paper remain in the library where he wrote his last novel, *Endymion*, and there is some correspondence from Victoria. In spite of her own requests she was not allowed to visit him on his deathbed because, Disraeli confided, he was afraid she would want him to take some fulsome message to 'dear Albert', her deceased Prince Consort.

Hughenden church was extensively rebuilt according to Disraeli's wishes after his wife's death. The marble tablet to his memory has an inscription worded by the queen. Although she did not attend his funeral, a few days later she came quietly to place a wreath on the grave, and members of the Primrose League, a Conservative organization founded by his admirers in 1882, come annually to do the same.

Across the valley a tall red granite pillar between the trees is the statesman's own monument to his father Isaac, also buried in the family vault.

When raised to the peerage in 1876, Disraeli took the title of Earl of Beaconsfield – a local town where two other writers of consequence, Edmund Waller and Edmund Burke, are buried.

Of Jewish origin but baptized a Christian after his father's rejection of the synagogue, Disraeli had spoken out in support of his Whig rival Glad-

The preserved gateway of Rye House, where objectors to Charles II's flouting of Parliament and of local charters plotted his death.

Benjamin Disraeli's desk and other personal effects in his study at Hughenden Manor, Buckinghamshire, where he completed his last novel in 1880.

stone against Parliament's refusal, largely on the insistence of the House of Lords, to admit the properly elected Baron Lionel de Rothschild in 1847 as Liberal member for the City of London on the grounds that he could not take the required oath 'upon the true faith of a Christian'. Again and again Rothschild tried, was elected, and rejected; until, 11 years later, the Lords gave in with an ill grace and the stricture was ameliorated. The immigrant Rothschild family had long been friends of the convert's son, and although twitting him on his and his father's defection from the Jewish faith they appreciated his personal affection and ready wit. In November 1875 this mutual affection paid off in a big way for England. Disraeli, by now Prime Minister, was spending the evening at Lionel Rothschild's home at 148 Piccadilly when a message from Paris reported that the Khedive of Egypt had offered his shares in the French-built Suez Canal, opened six years earlier, to France, but was dubious about settling

on their proposed terms. Parliament was in recess; consultation was impossible; speed was essential. Disraeli assembled those of his ministers who could be reached in time, talked them into agreement, and with Rothschild's financial backing bought the 177,000 shares on offer, which, with other shares already held, gave Britain the controlling interest in the canal.

It seems appropriate that so many members of the Rothschild family should have settled, like Disraeli, in Buckinghamshire. Lionel and his relations bought up at one time and another Aston Clinton, Mentmore Towers, designed by Joseph Paxton of Crystal Palace fame – the sale of whose contents in 1978 aroused a storm of public concern and argument – and Halton House. Among their legacies to posterity, now in the care of the National Trust, are the Anthony de Rothschild collection of pictures and furniture at Ascott near Leighton Buzzard, and Ferdinand's pseudo-French château of Waddesdon Manor.

Though born to the Vienna branch of the family, Ferdinand Rothschild favoured the English way of life and, after naturalization, became M.P. for Aylesbury. He was sociable, gregarious, and generous, distributing braces of pheasants to London omnibus drivers at Christmas – they in turn, decked their whips with yellow and blue ribbons, the Rothschild racing colours. He was fired by many enthusiasms, amongst which the family business was not included. Having travelled widely and amassed works of art from every corner of Europe, he decided to create a worthy setting in which to display ·them. In 1874 he began work at Waddesdon by ordering that the top of a hill should be sliced off and levelled. Bath stone was carted on a specially constructed steam tramway from Quainton railway station, and teams of heavy Percherons were imported to drag materials up the slope. Panelling was specially shaped to accommodate individual paintings. The place was carpeted with Ferdinand's unique collection of Savonneries originally designed for the exclusive use of the Bourbons. Queen Victoria, racked with curiosity and doubtless mindful of her debt to Disraeli's friends, condescended to visit and was treated to a sight-seeing tour of the grounds in a pony-drawn Bath-chair.

The village was refashioned and the houses adorned with crests of a crown and five arrows, symbolic of the five founding Rothschild brothers in Frankfurt. At the gates of the manor can still be found the Five Arrows hotel.

The Five Arrows Inn at the gate of Waddesdon Manor displays on its façade and its sign the emblem of the five Rothschilds of Frankfurt.

Sweet Thames, flow softly . . .

The true story of the Thames has long been a source of dispute also, arousing local loyalties and passions. The main river is, strictly speaking, formed by the confluence· of two streams: the Churn, rising some four miles from Cheltenham at Seven Springs; and the Isis or Thames near Cirencester. But the Thames Conservators plumped for the latter, and at Thames Head erected a statue of a reclining Father Thames.

The river has been called 'liquid history', and even its leisurely, winding upper reaches have villages and houses each with a paragraph to add to the nation's story. On its route it is joined by the Coln, the Leach, the Windrush and, near Oxford, the Cherwell and the Thame.

Above the meeting-place of Thame and Thames stands a Bronze Age hill-fort, stark and less comfortable than the riverside homes with their lawns, boat-houses and moorings. At Goring Gap begin the Chiltern Hills, once so thickly wooded that they provided shelter for highwaymen and outlaws of all kinds. The neighbour-

hood became so dangerous that a Steward of the Chiltern Hundreds was appointed to round up the evildoers and restore order. His job nowadays is less arduous, being a purely nominal one taken by any Member of Parliament wishing to resign from the House. This strange custom came about through a combination of the old statute forbidding any member to vacate his seat once he had been duly elected with a later ruling that anyone holding an office under the Crown was disqualified from membership and *must* vacate that seat. This useful contradiction has made it possible for any politician wishing to relinquish his task to apply for the Chiltern Hundreds, technically an office of profit, of which he can hold the stewardship until another member wishes to apply. One other such appointment is that of Steward of the Manor of Northstead in Yorkshire.

On flows the river through Pangbourne, with memories of Kenneth Grahame's *The Wind in the Willows* and Jerome K. Jerome's *Three Men in a Boat*, through Reading and Henley, where the world's first river regatta was held in 1839. At Cookham we are near the home of the royal 'Keeper of the Swans in the Thames from the town of Graveshende to Cicester'; and of the late Stanley Spencer, who drew so much of his artistic inspiration from local scenes and faces. His painting of the annual swan-upping ceremony hangs in the Tate Gallery. This operation is carried out in July, when the keeper of the royal swans joins the swanherds of two privileged city livery companies, the Vintners and the Dyers, in rounding up new cygnets on the river and marking their beaks.

Past Cookham towards Boulter's Lock we are below the wooded height of Cliveden, a great house commanding magnificent views down the river. In the building which once stood on this site there lived from 1739 onwards Frederick, Prince of Wales, son of George II. Like all Hanoverian princes he had quarrelled with his father, fallen in with opposition politicians, and caused a great turmoil with demands for his own establishment – 'a monster and the greatest villain that ever was born', said King George. It was in the grounds here that Frederick attended the first performance of Arne's *Rule, Britannia*; and here that in 1751 he died – some say from a chill contracted while playing tennis, others from his having been hit in the chest by a cricket-ball – leaving his son to succeed in due course as King George III.

The house he knew was burnt out in 1795, rebuilt, and gutted again in 1849, after which it was rebuilt for the Duke of Sutherland by Sir Charles Barry, architect of Trafalgar Square and the Houses of Parliament. In 1893 the American millionaire William Waldorf Astor bought it and, after naturalization, became first Viscount Astor. Nancy Astor, wife of the second Viscount, succeeded her husband as M.P. for Plymouth and so became the first woman to sit in the House. As political hostess she gathered about her the clique known before the Second World War as the 'Cliveden Set', credited with favouring the appeasement of Adolf Hitler and misleading him into believing that Britain would not fight.

The grounds contain all kinds of fancies and follies: a three-tier fountain decorated with a swarm of tiny terrapins, a statue of Marlborough in the Blenheim Pavilion, a kilted statue of Victoria's Prince Consort – and, of course, the swimming pool in which a certain Christine Keeler

sparked off quite another kind of political scandal in the 1960s.

It is not far now before the outline of Windsor Castle rises above the river, enshrining memories of every king and every twist of royal fortune from William the Conqueror onwards.

Nothing remains of William's original fort other than the motte on which, probably, a wooden keep was built to command the Thames. Henry I chose to make his home here, after building a hall and chapel. It was Henry II who added the first stone defences and the beginnings of the Round Tower, and each subsequent monarch made contributions according to personal taste or defensive needs – though there were few protracted periods of use as a fortress save for a siege of King John by his barons and an attack by Roundheads during the Civil War which inflicted considerable damage. For a while it fell from royal favour, but George III used it again as a home, and his son, as we have noted earlier, gave the whole complex the character we see today.

In 1750 George III had ordered the construction of a military look-out post on the fringe of Windsor Great Park, for a while manned by a small garrison of Cumberland's troops who had defeated Bonnie Prince Charlie. During George IV's time Wyatville added a tower. In 1930 Edward, Prince of Wales, asked his father if he might have this Fort Belvedere as a private residence, and, in spite of fears that it would be used largely for disreputable weekend parties, George V gave permission. For a while Edward's younger brother George, Duke of Kent, shared the premises with him until marrying Princess Marina. It was here that the Prince of Wales brought his close intimates, well away from the public eye: among them, the Mrs Simpson he was determined to marry. Even after his father's death, when Queen Mary had formally relinquished Buckingham Palace to him, he continued to live at Fort Belvedere.

It was from Windsor that King Edward VIII made a final broadcast after his abdication to tell the nation that he could not remain on the throne without the companionship of the woman he loved, and it was as newly created Duke of Windsor that he left his country.

There are two other royal palaces as the river

The Blenheim pavilion in the gardens of Cliveden shelters a statue of the Duke of Marlborough, commemorating his victory in August 1704.

At Runnymede the sealing by King John in 1215 of Magna Carta is recalled by a memorial donated by the American Bar Association. Higher up the hill is a memorial to John F. Kennedy, and at the top the Air Forces Memorial in honour of airmen who died in the Second World War and have no known grave.

carries us closer to London: Hampton Court still in full splendour, Richmond no more than a ghost.

Hampton Court was created by one of the most powerful and arrogant men in England, Cardinal Wolsey, who, though by birth only the son of a humble Suffolk grazier, for many years lived and entertained on a more lavish scale than King Henry VIII himself. He chose the site in 1514, finding the landscape and climate congenial, and appreciating the closeness of Richmond Palace. Its red-brick west front, with turrets and curly chimneystacks, is still much as Wolsey planned it. In 1525, realizing that Henry was beginning to view with doubt and envy his lord chancellor's grandeur, he tactfully made over the lease to the king; but continued to lodge and entertain his own friends and foreign dignitaries with unashamed pomp.

Though anxious to keep on good terms with the Pope, Wolsey reluctantly helped Henry to divorce Catherine of Aragon and marry Anne Boleyn; but his failure to deal satisfactorily with all the subsequent complications led to his fall from royal favour and ultimately to his being accused of high treason. He died while on his way to answer this charge. Henry claimed all Wolsey's property, and found Hampton Court much to his taste. He enlarged the palace, and the second gatehouse became known as Anne Boleyn's gateway. Wolsey's original hall by Clock Court was replaced by a greater hall with a fine hammerbeam roof. Jane Seymour died here after presenting Henry with a son. Edward VI and both his sisters in turn held court here.

In 1604 the Hampton Court Conference under James I attempted to resolve Puritan objections to abuses within the Church of England and certain wordings in the Prayer Book. Instead of

When Queen Eleanor died in
Nottinghamshire in 1290 her grieving widower Edward I
travelled with her corpse back to Westminster, building a
cross at each of 13 resting places along the route. Only
three remain: at Geddington, Hardingstone, and (much
restored) here at Waltham Cross in Hertfordshire. The
final resting place in Trafalgar Square, London, is now
occupied by an equestrian statue of Charles I, but a
replica of the demolished cross stands in Charing Cross
railway station courtyard.

yielding, the king accused the critics of aiming at a Scottish style of presbytery which 'agreed as well with a monarchy as God and the Devil', and threatened to harry them out of the land – 'or worse'. There was, however, one rewarding sequel: James commissioned a new translation of the Bible which came to be accepted as the Authorized Version.

But Puritan protest continued until, in course of time, Oliver Cromwell became Lord Protector and, succumbing to the charm and luxury of Hampton Court, took up residence. His daughter was married here in the Chapel Royal.

The next major alterations were carried out to the specifications of William III and Mary who, as dual monarchs, asked for two separate sets of state apartments to be installed, one for each of them, in the eastern part of the palace. Sir Christopher Wren was the architect, and among his triumphs were the Fountain Court and the garden frontage.

After George III's day Hampton Court was abandoned as a royal home, and now has been split up into 'grace and favour' residences allocated by the Crown.

Of Richmond Palace only the gateway bearing Henry VII's arms, and the Wardrobe Court within, remain; and even the courtyard was damaged by a Second World War bomb. What was first known as Shene Palace was in existence by the time of Henry I, growing in importance when Richard II brought his wife there. After her death he demolished it, but Henry V restored it, and it became a favourite residence of the Tudors. Henry VII changed the name to Richmond in affection for his Yorkshire earldom. Here his granddaughter Elizabeth I died in March 1603 after a fortnight of increasing weariness and dejection, during which a mounted messenger waited at the gateway for the news which would start him on his way to carry the tidings to her successor, James VI of Scotland and I of England.

Remains of the palace were later incorporated in a range of private houses. And from here on into London there is now little but the spread of suburban building, detached and semi-detached and terraced. The rural Thames has become a city thoroughfare, passing through Chelsea and past the Houses of Parliament, over subterranean tunnels and under a bridge whose ancestor was set up by the Romans; on towards the docks, another royal palace at Greenwich, and at last the traffic of the sea.

LONDON

ON FISH STREET HILL above Billingsgate fish market is the Monument, topped by a representation of a blazing urn. The column is 202 feet high and stands 202 feet from the site in Pudding Lane where the Great Fire of London broke out in 1666. There was once a stone in Pudding Lane itself, set up in 1681 on that site where 'by ye Permission of Heaven, Hell broke loose' through the supposed arson of 'barbarous Papists'. Today the stone is displayed in the Museum of London on London Wall.

The present appearance of the city owes much to the great clearances and rebuildings resulting from another great fire, when German bombers set London alight. One of the most famous photographs of the Second World War shows St Paul's ringed by smoke and flame – but escaping, which the Old St Paul's failed to do.

And there was a much earlier fire, started by other enemies, its traces spasmodically revealed when archaeologists have time to investigate excavations before new office blocks go up. In A.D. 61 the Iceni rebels under Boudicca, having destroyed Colchester, advanced on London and burnt out the whole Roman settlement. (A twentieth-century bronze statue of the warrior queen and her chariot rears up at the west end of Westminster Bridge.) The extent of the town in her time can be accurately established from the layer of burnt clay which she left behind. Burnt pottery has also been found and, in the approaches

Porters' resting board in Piccadilly donated in 1861 by a Shrewsbury MP for the benefit of porters and others carrying heavy loads in the metropolitan area. There were fewer of these than horses' drinking troughs.

to London Bridge, a handful of coins fused together by the heat of the flames.

Londinium

There were settlements in this region long before the Romans came. When ground was being cleared for Heathrow airport, an enclosure with a bank and ditch was revealed and attributed to about 700–500 B.C., with remains of circular huts and a farmyard. Somewhere in the fourth century B.C. a hill-fort was built on Wimbledon Common, later to be misnamed Caesar's Camp. There is no evidence that Caesar or any other Romans took over, however briefly, this Iron Age earthwork; but in the City of London proper there are plenty of authentic remains.

Although there are no extensive ramparts left along which to walk, as one may walk along the walls of York, it is possible to trace the course of the London wall which the Romans set up soon after A.D. 200. Reinforced and built upon by later Londoners, for centuries it regulated the proportions of that core which we refer to simply as the City. It began by Blackfriars Bridge, near to which in 1952 were found remains of a barge still loaded with Kentish ragstone brought up the Medway and the Thames. We know, incidentally, that the craft was built after A.D. 88, as a coin of that date had been put under the mast for luck. Heading north across what would have been gateways at Ludgate and Newgate, the lower courses of the wall are exposed in the G.P.O. yard near St Martin's le Grand, with a medieval bastion set above them. Walking up Wood Street we follow what was probably the central path of a fort built as barracks for the garrison quite some time before the wall, which incorporated two of its sides in the perimeter. Foundations of the fort, together with a corner turret, can be seen in Noble Street; the west gate is in London Wall; and there is a further mixture of medieval bastion on Roman foundations just beside St Giles Cripplegate churchyard. Cripplegate was once the northern entrance to the fort. Its name has nothing to do with the lame or the wounded, but probably comes from the Old English *crepel-geat*, a covered way. Another corner of the fort, forming part of the city wall also, is preserved in a public garden which was once St Alphege churchyard.

The wall continued eastwards, with openings at Bishopsgate and Aldgate, and comes to light again with medieval topping in Cooper's Row near Tower Hill; at Wakefield Gardens, Trinity Place; and within the Tower of London itself.

When Saxon pirates and then more strongly coordinated groups of raiders began to harry the coast and rivers, the three-sided enclosure was sealed off along the water's edge by completing a fourth wall. Fragments which have come to light suggest that the authorities were in such a hurry that they did not wait to ship in all the stone best suited for their purpose but broke down Celtic and other pagan shrines, using reliefs, tomb slabs and commemorative stones – anything which came to hand – in the defences.

The place which the Celts called Llyn-Din, 'the hill by the pool', had not been the most important centre for Roman consolidation after the Claudian invasion. Colchester remained the capital of the province until after the rising of the Iceni. But near the pre-Roman trading post the conquerors found it useful to build a bridge linking their supply port of Richborough with Colchester, and the supply roads to the legions in the north. Adapting the name to Londinium, the Romans later changed it, when the place became the capital, to Augusta; but the natives continued to call it London.

In the wall of the Bank of China in Cannon Street is set the London Stone, believed to have been the miliary, or Roman milestone, from which distances outside the city were measured.

Below Aldwych, in Strand Lane, is a brick reservoir fed by a spring which continues to advertise itself as a Roman Bath; but it has been generally agreed that, although the lead pipe may have been Roman, the rest is more likely to be of Tudor origin.

One of the most remarkable windows on to the past opened in 1954, when excavations for the foundations of Bucklersbury House exposed a basilican temple of Mithras, rich in marble sculptures and other relics. The old stream of the Walbrook, on whose east bank the temple was built, may well have been regarded as sacred from pre-Roman times, for many pagan figurines and votive offerings have been found in the neighbourhood at one time and another. A marble relief of Mithras sacrificing a bull was discovered in 1889; and now in our own century has been supplemented by fine heads of Mithras, Minerva and Serapis, and a group with Bacchus and Silenus, all thought to have been hidden away from despoilers when Christianity became the official religion of the province. These finds are displayed in the Museum of London, but the building stones of the Mithraeum itself have been set in concrete in Temple Court, Queen Victoria Street, to show the original ground plan.

Saxons, Normans, and the Middle Ages

The church of All Hallows Barking-by-the-Tower provides a fascinating palimpsest. Working backwards from what we see today, we have a 1959 Dutch-style copper steeple added to a rebuilding of 1957 after serious bomb damage in 1940; back to its establishment in 1922 as headquarters church of Toc H, the interdenominational Christian fellowship founded in Belgium during the First World War; further back, Samuel Pepys watched the Great Fire from its tower – the only example of Cromwellian church building in London; and earlier survivals are the remains of an eleventh-century Saxon cross, and a seventh-century Saxon arch using Roman bricks lower in the tower; and, as far back as we can go, a section of Roman tessellated flooring.

Walking the same route along the Roman wall after the imperial defenders had gone, we would have found the defences and the once-proud residences neglected. The Romano-British clung to their old way of life as long as possible, but when the Saxons had taken over in force the city went through a period of stagnation. Many decades passed before the Saxons, with time and confidence to build up their own trade to and from their new possessions, acknowledged the

In Cooper's Row the upper section of medieval wall stands on its Roman predecessor and incorporates a great deal of material from it.

importance of London's situation. Many of their early settlements were outside the walls, but in due course moved in closer, until London became the capital of the East Saxon kingdom of Essex.

When Augustine arrived to restore Christianity to the country, it was the papal intention that the premier English bishopric should be established in London; and but for the recalcitrant paganism and quarrelsomeness of the inhabitants this might have come to pass. But by the time Christianity had spread throughout the land, Canterbury was too firmly established for its power to be transferred. So the Saxon cathedral dedicated to St Paul never acquired the archbishop its builder, King Ethelbert of Kent, had expected.

One or two mystical theories about the locating of St Paul's have been advanced over the years. A modern American professor who believes that many Christian buildings in England were knowingly constructed above ancient pagan sites and along ancient axes related to the stars has suggested that a line following the axis of St Paul's Cathedral on through Great St Helen's would at the time of its construction have pointed directly at Aldebaran, and that below the church was once a moon temple.

The Saxon edifice was of wood, and burnt down in 961. In that same century they built their own London Bridge, also in wood. This was several times attacked by Vikings under Olaf Trygvason, until by lashing a number of ships to the supports and rowing off on the tide he managed to bring it down. The famous Old London Bridge which took its place at the command of Henry II was built of stone, with a gateway at each end and a drawbridge at the Southwark bank. This, carrying rows of shops and houses, and with a chapel in the centre, remained the only roadway across the Thames until 1749, and was of such importance that four Guilds were specifically charged with its maintenance and repair. The tangle of buildings had to be pulled down in 1760, and in 1831 William IV opened a new bridge, lit by lamps whose posts had been cast from cannon captured during the Peninsular War. This served until the late 1960s, when it was dismantled on completion of a modern substitute and taken for reassembly in the United States.

If there had indeed been a moon temple below St Paul's, it was balanced in legend with a supposed Roman temple of Apollo under a new foundation dedicated to St Peter, some two miles west of the city. In many respects the new building was an example of Norman rather than truly Saxon architecture. Edward the Confessor had spent his happiest times in Normandy, and his English court was markedly Norman in speech and behaviour. When he ordered work to start on an abbey church for the Benedictine west monastery or West-minster, it was laid out in characteristically Norman cruciform design. Its founder lived only 10 days after the consecration in December 1065, having declared that he favoured William of Normandy as his successor.

After defeating Harold at Hastings, William asserted his legitimacy by being crowned on Christmas Day 1066 in his predecessor's Collegiate Church of St Peter. He then set about building sentinel fortifications along London's river. Two trusted barons were given command of Montfichet Castle and Baynard's Castle. Both these have now disappeared, but substantial foundations of Baynard's Castle underlie part of Blackfriars and the Mermaid Theatre. Although the royal palace was to remain nominally at Westminster until Henry VIII's time, and William II was to build Westminster Hall there as the first council chamber from which Parliament was eventually to develop, the Conqueror himself accorded greater importance to the fort which, after whitewashing in the thirteenth century, came to be known as the White Tower. This keep of Caen stone was set up in the corner of the old city boundary diagonally opposite the Roman fort; but with its moat and accumulation of battlements and subsidiary buildings it soon shouldered its way out to the east. A palace was created by Henry I and used by many of his successors, though in its early days it seems to have been none too salubrious. The stench could be such that Henry III, returning from a royal peregrination, once found it imperative to write to his constable:

Since the privy in the chamber of our wardrobe at London is situated in an undue and improper place, wherefore it smells badly, we command you on the faith and love by which you are bounden to us that you in no wise omit to cause another privy chamber to be made ... even though it should cost a hundred pounds.

It was traditional for a king to spend the night before his coronation in the Tower before proceeding to Westminster Abbey. Charles II was the last to do so; and in fact the palace itself had

The Wren arch of Temple Bar was taken down from the junction of the Strand and Fleet Street in 1878 and re-erected 10 years later at Theobalds Park.

by then been dismantled by Oliver Cromwell.

Throughout the Middle Ages the mercantile life of the inner city continued to develop within the old boundaries, as if businessmen instinctively felt the advantage of huddling together within a protective wall, away from prying eyes. Guilds were formed to maintain 'closed shops' for individual trades and professions, and in 1411 a rich new Guildhall was commenced. Successive mayors and aldermen won privileges for the square mile under royal charters which it was difficult for even the king to repudiate once they had been granted. To this day it is customary for the monarch to 'ask permission' at Temple Bar, and receive the sword of state in a token gesture from the Lord Mayor, before entering the confines of the City.

Trade was so much the concern of this compact district that it was allowed to leak not just into the precincts of the cathedral – noted for its congregation of book, ballad and print sellers – but into the building itself. There was a veritable market-place in the nave, including stalls to sell badges and souvenirs. All through the week a number of professional scribes set up their tables to write letters and prepare legal documents for the illiterate. Youngsters and adults alike played ball games, and horses and mules were led at will through this useful short-cut. All through the sixteenth century and on into the seventeenth a curious stroller would be led inevitably into 'Paul's Walk' along the nave, the fashionable promenade where all the latest gossip was exchanged and any number of business transactions were carried on.

There came more horses during the Civil War, when Cromwellians stabled their mounts in this same nave. But soon after the Restoration came the conflagration which was at last to destroy the old contours and make new ones necessary.

Tudors and Stuarts

During Tudor times the Tower of London, always a stern and forbidding place, became less and less a royal residence and more a prison and place of execution. It is still a matter for acrimonious dispute whether it was the first Tudor king, Henry VII, or his defeated predecessor, Richard III, who disposed of the two young princes, Edward V and his brother Richard, Duke of York. Certainly during repairs to the Bloody Tower long afterwards there were found two childish skeletons; and the place's reputation grew bloodier. Henry VIII sent two of his wives to the block on Tower Green; his daughter Mary had her rival claimant to the throne, Lady Jane Grey, despatched in similar fashion; and Elizabeth later had her favourite, the Earl of Essex, beheaded on this same spot, marked now by a brass plate.

Although Henry VIII used the Tower for various purposes, he found other residences more comfortable. His new palaces of Whitehall and St James's were outside the City confines. He did, however, erect a third one within, at Bridewell (St Bride's Well) near Ludgate Circus. Later this was to become a house of detention and correction – at one time a viewing gallery was supplied so that spectators might watch insubordinate apprentices and vagrants being flogged – and the name is still applied to many a police station, especially in the provinces. In March 1978, excavations for a new building project revealed some foundations of the original palace, about 15 feet down from the present street level. Work was held back for six weeks so that archaeologists, sifting every fleck of dirt and clearing surfaces with a vacuum cleaner, could photograph the remains, which proved very similar to the layout of Hampton Court.

The Palace of Westminster, though abandoned by Henry as a royal residence and never used as such again, retains its title as the home of Parliament, and is still officially a royal palace, administered by the hereditary Lord Great Chamberlain.

Buildings, no matter how proud their creators may once have been of their apparent solidity, are destructible. Names – such as that of the Bridewell – often live longer than the materials with which they were associated. South of the river, where Southwark developed about the approach roads to London Bridge, there is another prison memory: no 'clink' now stands in Clink Street, but the word is still in common use. Bear Lane recalls the old bear-pit, and Rose Street was the home in Shakespeare's time of the Rose Theatre. His immortal Globe Theatre has vanished, but there is a plaque to its memory in the wall of a brewery combine's bottling plant, and in Borough High Street there are sometimes performances of his plays in the galleried courtyard of the George Inn.

North of the river, the name of Covent Garden recalls not merely the site of an old convent but a new trend in urban building. James I and his son Charles I, anxious to beautify their capital, encouraged more graceful architectural development outside the increasingly congested inner city. A great contribution was made, as much by his influence as his personal designs, by the Italian-trained, Palladian-minded Inigo Jones after his appointment as Surveyor to the King. His Banqueting House in Whitehall and the Queen's House out at Greenwich brought a neoclassical dignity to a country hitherto cluttered with random building and random notions. The Earl of Bedford commissioned him, with the approval of the King, to use the space behind Bedford House in the Strand for the building of town houses whose leases would profit the estate. When completed, Covent Garden formed a broad piazza with terraces of arcaded houses on two sides, Bedford House garden on the third, and St Paul's church on the other. The dimensions of the great square can still be appreciated, though none of the original buildings remains, and even the church is a restoration.

But although great magnates might build fine houses for themselves along and behind the Strand, and on towards Westminster, while poverty and illnesses frequently reaching epidemic proportions checked much increase of poorer populations to the east and south, the greatest concentration of London life was still around Old St Paul's.

In 1665 plague came to the city, driving those who had the resources out into the country, and slaying those who could not flee. Some had been so used to recurrent outbreaks in the past that they regularly adjourned to out-of-town properties on high ground such as Highgate. Westminster School was accustomed to spells of tuition in a house at Chiswick. But to render such seasonal shifts unnecessary, and to cleanse the city for a safer future, one thing was essential: the insanitary, tangled rookeries of rickety wooden houses, shops and reeking courtyards would have to be swept away. It is doubtful if any idealistic

The garden of the Freemason's Arms, Hampstead Heath, is the only place where the old French game of paille-maille (whence pell-mell and Pall Mall), resembling croquet, is still played.

The intimate little courtyard of Pickering Place, behind a fine eighteenth-century wine shop frontage in St James's, still preserves its gas lamps.

town planner would ever have been granted permission to effect the necessary clearance. In 1666 the job was done with ruthless energy by the Great Fire. When it had ended, more than 13,000 houses had been burnt; the Royal Exchange was completely destroyed; the Guildhall had been badly damaged (as it was to be again in 1940); only 22 out of 100 churches remained whole; and Old St Paul's was beyond salvage.

At one point there had been a threat to the Inner Temple, one of the inns of court so called because of its derivation from the military order of Knights Templar and its nearness to the City, as opposed to the Middle Temple and the now non-existent Outer Temple. The King's brother James, Duke of York, was himself a bencher of the Inner Temple and took charge of a platoon of firefighters when flames threatened the precincts. To his amazement he was locked out by fellow

benchers who feared the blaze less than they feared looting and the damage which might be done if gunpowder were used to blow up parts of the buildings. In fact it was essential to make such fire-breaks with the use of gunpowder, and after a set-to the Duke of York got his way. As a result, only part of a roof was burnt, and the beautiful hall and chapel were saved; but this did not stop voluble anti-Papist factions from later accusing James of having visibly enjoyed himself at the sight of such destruction and of having probably been involved in the start of the fire.

The late seventeenth-century pedestrian trying to find old alleys, markets and courtyards after rebuilding would have been as bewildered as a late nineteenth-century city clerk would be if set down in the London refashioned after the Second World War. One of the commission immediately appointed by Charles II, and later Surveyor of Works, Christopher Wren advocated a long-term plan which annoyed householders and shop-keepers who, having already lost their property, saw that the new shape of things would rob them of sites on which to rebuild. Similar piecemeal objections after 1945 crippled any chance of the promises of a newly beautified London being fulfilled. But in spite of many objections and setbacks, Wren managed to push through many of his enlightened ideas. His name is associated so irrevocably with St Paul's and the many City churches he restored that his overall town plan-ning work is too often overlooked.

Yet it is, to be sure, those ecclesiastical build-ings which, in spite of later bombing, have survived rather than the conformation of his streets and open spaces. Within the symbolic shadow of the old wall it is impossible not to be still awed by the sheer stylishness of St Mary le Bow, Cheapside; by St Stephen Walbrook near the Mansion House; St Benet, Paul's Wharf; or the restored essence of the bombed St Laurence, Jewry, the Lord Mayor's official church, with its outer east wall based on the design for St Paul's cathedral. Wren's own monogram is to be found on a unique canopied pew in St Margaret Pattens, near the junction of Eastcheap and Great Tower Street. This church takes its odd name from the pattens or overshoes, with an iron oval raising the sole above the mud, which were once the main product of nearby Rood Lane. Two pairs are kept in a case on the south wall.

Many rebuilt streets preserved old names but not necessarily old functions: Pudding Lane,

The George at Southwark is the last London inn with a galleried courtyard, famous in coaching days and as a setting for Shakespearean performances.

Bread Streat and Milk Street were no longer so specialized in their wares.

At first assessment it was thought that Old St Paul's could be reinforced and restored; but Wren persuaded the make-do-and-mend elements that only a completely new edifice would make sense.

Those who had once exchanged tittle-tattle in 'Paul's Walk' were driven out of the magnificent new building and found different meeting-places in the City. Taverns, though never altogether out of favour, found themselves with strange rivals: the coffee houses. Many a plot was hatched therein, many a good stage play sketched out therein, many a great conversation carried on therein and thereafter forgotten – unless recorded by some scribbler or some acolyte of great pontificators such as Dr Samuel Johnson, who from his homes in Gough Square or Bolt Court would

sally forth to share his favours between Fleet Street inns and Russell Street coffee houses.

Coffee seems to have been introduced to London in 1652 by a London merchant back from his travels in the Near East, and soon became fashionable. He set up his Greek servant in St Michael's Alley in Cornhill, announcing that coffee would be made and sold there 'by Pasqua Rosee, at the signe of his own Head'. More houses opened, and a walk round the rebuilt City would take one past a score of them in a matter of minutes. Some had a literary tone, some were centres of gossip, some the forerunners of the gentlemen's clubs which were to dominate late Georgian times, some served as business meeting-places. There was a particularly busy cluster about the Royal Exchange: the Union, the New Union, Sam's, Jonathan's, Tom's and many another. So much political debate was fomented that Charles II issued an edict for their suppression, but aroused such a storm that he had hurriedly to back down. By the end of the century there were more than 2,000 coffee houses in London. None survives in its original form today, but at any rate one has lived on in name and function: Lloyd's Coffee House in Lombard Street started by advertising ships for sale, soon produced *Lloyd's List* of shipping news and exchange rates, went on to offer insurance, and in due course became the Lloyd's we know.

As the fashion changed, some houses were turned into hotels or restaurants. Gossip, conviviality and argument went back to the taverns, perhaps to the regret of some employers:

Whereas formerly Apprentices and clerks with others used to take their morning's draught in Ale, Beer, or Wine, which, by the dizziness they cause in the Brain, made many unfit for business, they use now to play the Good-fellows in this wakeful and civil drink . . .

Not that the inns had ever fallen entirely out of fashion. Early in the sixteenth century a survey showed more than 1,000 ale-houses and licensed eating-houses in the City, and about the same period it was officially estimated that the population of Southwark consisted 'chiefly of inn-keepers'.

Georgians
One might expect a pub in Wardour Street called The Intrepid Fox to show an animal racing across what were once fields hereabouts with huntsmen

hallooing 'Soho' in pursuit. But the name is misleading. The reference is to Charles James Fox, the statesman who fell foul of George III and was the companion of George's resentful son, the Prince of Wales, later to become Prince Regent. The landlord of the tavern at this time was Sam House, who hospitably kept open for the benefit of Whig supporters during the Westminster election of 1784 when Fox was one of the few Whigs of the old guard to keep his seat in the tussle for power with William Pitt's faction. When House was dying, Fox brought his own physician to the landlord's bedside.

The reigns of the four Georges spanned 116 years. At George I's accession the streets of London were ill lit and dangerous, the countryside which fed it had not yet been stirred by the so-called Agrarian Revolution, and the most advanced inventions were Jethro Tull's horse-hoe and corn drill. Food for the capital was brought in by cart from rural areas within a reasonable distance, by coastal sailing ship up the Thames, or in the form of herds of cattle, geese and turkeys trudging the roads from hundreds of miles away. By the time of George IV's death, Stephenson had built the *Rocket*, goods were being shipped in coaches, barges, and the first few steam-hauled trucks; Lloyd's of London listed 81 steam-propelled paddle steamers on its register, some in cross-Channel service; and 500 miles of gas main supplied light to the metropolis.

To lump all military and social events of that century and more together with its architectural progress under the one heading of 'Georgian' is to generalize absurdly. Yet no other acceptable term has yet been devised. Even if the word is too crudely blanketing, we know what we mean by it.

When in fact we come to look at London's expansion we find little happening during the reigns of the first two Hanoverians. Continental squabbles occupied both of them; the appearance of their new inheritance made little impression. No coherent urban planning was attempted, and few of the ideas of Jones, Wren, or their royal patrons were followed up; though to George II's wife Caroline we do at least owe the clearing up of Hyde Park, the amalgamation of a number of separate ponds into the Serpentine, and the layout of Kensington Gardens, once the private enclave of Kensington Palace.

As late as 1766 a friend of Dr Johnson's could write of the West End and its wealthy, complacent estate owners:

Why so wretched an use has been made of so valuable and desirable an opportunity of displaying taste and elegance in this part of the town is a question that very probably would puzzle the builders themselves to answer.

In 1774 a severe Building Act laid down new standards for building materials, visual harmony, and precautions against fire. Later critics, disapproving of the uniformity thus imposed on house, street, square and crescent, denounced it as 'The Black Act'; but whatever its simplications and limitations, it provided the blueprint of what we must continue to call Georgian London.

The Georgian stamp is most evident outside the city, wherein new building was restricted and standardization impossible. But within that by now ghostly wall we have inherited the Mansion House, built between 1739 and 1753 with a Corinthian portico from which the increasingly worshipful Lord Mayor could watch formal processions and ceremonies; Trinity House, headquarters of the Brethren of the Guild who administer lighthouses, lightships and pilotage throughout Great Britain; and Hawksmoor's inspired church of St Mary Woolnoth in Lombard Street, containing a tablet to Edward Lloyd, original proprietor of Lloyd's Coffee House in that same street. There is also Watermen's Hall at Billingsgate, where the Court of the Company of Watermen and Lightermen regularly hold examinations of apprentices seeking to qualify as Thames Watermen and so be granted the Freedom of the River Thames.

But it was during the years of the Regency that some of the most significant and, in one form and another, lasting features were added to the London scene.

In 1783 George, Prince of Wales, persuaded his grudging father that he was entitled to an establishment of his own; and at once put the architect Henry Holland to work on the conversion of Carlton House in Pall Mall into a palatial dwelling. In spite of George III's protests against mounting extravagance, and similar noises from Parliament and people, the Prince demanded a colonnade to shield his home from the street, a large Corinthian portico, and a great Gothic conservatory in which to hold the lavish receptions

The Mansion House, from which
each November the newly installed Lord Mayor of
London departs in his State coach to be received by the
Lord Chief Justice at the Law Courts.

which so greatly rejoiced his heart and head. Soon after his appointment as Prince Regent, when his father had been removed because of porphyriac insanity, he summoned John Nash to re-design a whole section of London's West End between Carlton House and the old royal hunting-ground of Marylebone Park. This chase was renamed Regent's Park; rows of classical terraces and a number of small, supposedly working-class, villas were built in one corner; and a grandiose 'royal mile' led down through Portland Place and on through what became Regent Street towards the frontage of Carlton House.

We think of Georgian building largely in terms of well-balanced, unfussy brickwork; but Nash's 'Regency' style revelled in stucco, giving rise to the tag:

Is not Nash also a great master,
For he found us all brick and he left us all
plaster.

Beyond Carlton House, Nash re-modelled St James's Park. When the Prince Regent became King George IV, he also tackled the problem of converting Buckingham House into a true palace; but a lot of it had to be pulled down almost as soon as it had been put up, and after his patron's death Nash was summarily taken off the job. Later generations maltreated his fine Regent Street crescent shamefully; the Regent's Park scheme was never fully realized, and the canal went round instead of through the park; Carlton House was pulled down to give way to the government departments and clubs of Carlton House Terrace; but that last attempt at a coherent plan for a nobly proportioned London has left us plenty to be grateful for.

Victorians and after

With swifter and more reliable means of transport, London began to reach further and further out. The Great Wen, as William Cobbett called it, spread its stain over old villages and hamlets, gobbling up little rural communities and transforming them into suburbs of bleak streets. With the great railway boom its influence reached out into the Home Counties and ever outwards into the provinces with grasping tentacles which any medieval king would have envied. The nation, having established its nucleus and ensured the feeding of that nucleus, became the centre of an empire: the docks expanded, Disraeli shrewdly

In St Botolph's old churchyard near Post Office headquarters is Postmen's Park, an arcade donated in 1880 by the painter G. F. Watts, with plaques recording everyday acts of heroism by ordinary folk.

won Queen Victoria's undying partisanship by creating her Empress of India, and in a spirit of high religious fervour linked with gratitude for commercial success the philanthropists and entrepreneurs 'restored' – i.e., vulgarized – innumerable churches and buildings of an earlier era. Wren, Inigo Jones, the Adams and Nash were forgotten or derided.

Yet already we grow nostalgic over the supposed joys of Victorian England. Sherlock Holmes forever goes off through the fog in a hansom cab to see that justice is done – from a Baker Street address which never existed. Contented families gather about the piano with its flickering candles in their brass holders, happy to make their own music rather than watch the dehydrated clichés of television. Every man and woman knows his or her place and is content with it, upstairs or downstairs.

One needs to read a few pages of Dickens, Mayhew, or Charles Booth to hear, even from this distance, the echoes of poverty, violence, cruelty and despair on the one hand, and self-righteous complacency on the other.

Nevertheless, even the most downtrodden could be fired to patriotic enthusiasm for his country's achievements. Everything that Victorian England believed in was enshrined in the Great Exhibition of 1851 in Hyde Park, the concept of Queen Victoria's beloved consort, Albert. The Crystal Palace which Paxton designed to house the technical marvels of the age was later removed to Sydenham and, regrettably, gutted by fire in 1936. But although there may be no direct physical survival of that great display of Arts and Manufactures, apart from some odd plaster prehistoric animals in the Crystal Palace Park, a whole segment of London would be poorer without its aftermath. The success of the venture was so much greater than even the fervent Prince Consort had anticipated that in its wake a Museum of Manufactures was opened in Marlborough House, largely based on material from the Exhibition. In 1857 Prince Albert organized the purchase with 1851 profits of a site for a great cultural complex in South Kensington. The Marlborough House collection was moved to the bottom of what became for obvious reasons Exhibition Road, where it was renamed South Kensington Museum. After Albert's death it continued to expand, and Queen Victoria's last major public engagement was the laying of the foundation stone for what was now to be the Victoria and Albert Museum.

Other museums and institutes grew up in or moved to the district, including the Natural History Museum, the Imperial College of Science and Technology, and the Royal College of Music. After the Prince Consort's death, his widow ensured that his name was added like a magic charm to any number of new buildings which are now an integral and irreplaceable feature of the London landscape: the Royal Albert Hall of Arts and Sciences, the much-derided but ultimately winning Albert Memorial within which the Prince sits holding a catalogue of his Great Exhibition, and the Albert Bridge – not to mention innumerable streets and mansion blocks, and of course the Albert Embankment cutting through the site of lost pleasures in what were once Vauxhall Gardens, a celebrated musical venue.

And what of the things which have been torn from their true places of residence yet escaped utter destruction? Carlton House has gone; but its columns were transplanted to form the portico of the National Gallery in Trafalgar Square. Grim old Newgate prison has given way to the by no means prepossessing Old Bailey, but one old door is still preserved, together with a mocked-up cell, in the Barbican's Museum of London. The old permanent gallows at Tyburn proved, happily, impermanent. It is remembered by a plaque in the island at the foot of Edgware Road, near the Marble Arch. And the Marble Arch itself is far from where it was meant to be: John Nash designed it as the entrance to Buckingham Palace, but it proved too narrow for the state coach to go through, and in the year of the Great Exhibition was shifted to this corner of Hyde Park.

The Victoria Embankment has acquired somebody else's property of great antiquity. In 1819 Mahommed Ali, in gratitude for the defeat of Napoleon at the battle of the Nile, presented Britain with an obelisk originally raised at Heliopolis about 1500 B.C., moved by Cleopatra to Alexandria, and not shipped to London until 1877. Enclosed in an iron cylinder, it was towed away but had to be cut adrift in the Bay of Biscay, to be taken in tow again and brought at last to the Thames. Beneath this Cleopatra's Needle are buried, for the benefit of future archaeologists, a Bible, some newspapers, a razor, a baby's feeding-bottle, and a packet of hairpins. What a picture of nineteenth-century London this will all conjure up for the excavator!

And, remembering how we started our trip along old London Wall, we come back to the symbolic boundary of Temple Bar – to find that it is now marked only by a late nineteenth-century memorial crowned by a dragon or bronze 'griffin' and flanked by statues of Queen Victoria and her son. The ancient barrier on whose spikes were stuck the heads of executed traitors or criminals went long ago. And the great ceremonial archway set up by Christopher Wren to straddle the street in 1672 has also gone, to decay in a tangle of ivy at the entrance to Theobalds Park, Cheshunt.

Will anybody ever wish to preserve and re-erect the crudities of the Admiralty Arch or Euston station anywhere? Or, heaven help us, Shell Centre?

Hearthstones and Homesteads

UNTIL THE IMPROVEMENT of transport in the nineteenth century made it easier to carry heavy loads of stone, slate and brick considerable distances by road, canal, and above all by the railways, the majority of houses other than those of wealthy magnates relied on local building materials. The early popularity of Purbeck and Portland stones had been enhanced by the situation of their quarries near the Channel coast, from which large consignments could be moved cheaply by water. But these blocks were rarely chosen for small-scale domestic use, being designed mainly for ambitious projects in places such as Whitehall, Hampton Court, Oxford colleges and Wren churches.

Local styles dictated by local resources produced a homogeneous landscape. Stone homes grew out of granite moorstones and slates, out of the gritstone heights, and all along the great limestone diagonal from Dorset across the Cotswolds and on through

Cornwall and Devon in the south-western peninsula of England vary between extremes of hard granite, to be seen in ancient tors and prehistoric sanctuaries, and in miners' cottages and farmhouses, and soft clay which is compacted with earth and straw, preferably strengthened with chalk, to form cob. This amalgam is then rendered and usually whitewashed. To keep them dry the walls are supplied with 'a good hat and a good pair of shoes' – an overhanging thatched roof and a solid footing of tarred stone. Above: *Plastered cob with stone chimney at Higher Ashton, Devon.* Left: *Carneggan Farm, near Polruan, Cornwall.*

Northamptonshire. Timber predominated in the Weald and the Midlands, and clayey soils produced plaster or the basis for bricks to fill in the panels. Roofs were of stone slabs in one region, of straw or reed thatch in another. If sentimentalists are wrong to claim too dogmatically that man 'knew his proper place' and lived in closer harmony with his natural environment before the

explosions of the Industrial Revolution, it is at any rate true that his homestead and place of work – often one and the same – derived more directly from the regional landscape and settled into it more comfortably than later fabrications and prefabrications.

If today we find the most picturesque surviving homesteads in rural areas, this is largely because the pace of agricultural life has been slower; and it has to be admitted that it was less profitable, so the tendency was for farm workers to seek fresh employment in burgeoning industrial centres, leaving their ramshackle cottages for a later generation to buy and 'do up' as a holiday home or place for retirement.

Villages and towns have their periods of prosperity and of decline, each leaving its traces. Impoverishment has sometimes been followed by expansion in a quite different direction. Victorian prosperity built much, overran and tore down much more. But the Victorians were not the first

Cruck framing was the simplest form of timber construction, making the walls of a building serve also as its roof. Pairs of large trunks or branches were driven into the ground some feet apart and bent towards each other until they met to form arches. A ridge pole along the top held them fast, and then thatch or turves would be laid upon a support of interwoven branches down the steep roof to the ground. Crossbeams might later be inserted not only to strengthen the end crucks but to carry flooring for an upper storey, and a shallower roof could be added, resting on inserted stone walls, to allow space for windows. The medieval cottage at Didbrook in Gloucestershire, shown left, has also acquired a perky little porch.

Greensand is an iron-bearing sandstone appearing in many different hues from the Isle of Wight to Yorkshire, and in the Weald of Kent and Sussex. The truly green variety, owing its colour to the presence of the mineral glauconite, is the main building material of Shaftesbury in Dorset (below).

to destroy historic beauties. Fashions have changed unceasingly over the centuries; finances change; regional priorities change.

No matter how many houses and terraces and streets have been changed to suit later tastes, buildings usually offer some clue to their original shape and function. Large windows in comparatively small houses of the South-East, East Anglia and the Cotswolds remind us of the wool trade's 'outworkers', a tradition carried on in the long upper-floor windows of Yorkshire farmhouses and even in terraces of the early Yorkshire wool towns. Dutch brick gables in the Isle of Thanet recall the arrival and settlement of Flemish weavers.

The hall-house of the Kentish yeoman, maybe occupied today by a commuting stockbroker, derives straight from the spacious Saxon hall with its lesser accompanying rooms, before 'hall' became a term describing merely a constricted entrance lobby. Hall-houses common throughout

Surrounded on three sides by chalk uplands, the Weald has its sandstones and clay, but from the days of its once mighty forest has built predominantly in timber, leavened in later times with brickwork. Cranbrook in Kent displays a fine range of weatherboarding (known in the United States as clapboarding), including that of its windmill. Overlapping boards, sometimes tongued and grooved but more often simply shaved along one edge to provide a close overlap, are laid horizontally and pegged to a lightweight timber frame. Oak and elm, once common for the purpose, could be left in their natural state; but growing use of pine and other softwoods necessitated protective coats of paint, usually white or, in coastal communities, of black tar.

East Anglia display a different technique: though their creators here, too, treated the hall as the major feature, their subsidiary rooms were accommodated under separate roofs at right angles to the main block, thus producing the many-gabled pattern characteristic of the region.

Yeomen's or 'statesmen's' houses in the Lake District were built as oblongs to incorporate barns and outbuildings under one long roof, with front door and windows tending to face the fell rather than look out over the vista of deep valleys and so suffer the full impact of wind and weather. The roughness of much of the stonework is due to its having been built up with untrimmed stones simply gathered up from the ground. Many such a house has a covered gallery along one side: in harsh Cumbrian conditions, scraping a living meant that while the men were out in the fields their womenfolk had to make the most of daylight by sitting out on the gallery spinning wool.

Massive chimney stacks set against the ends of houses and cottages in several regions, particularly in the West, are usually there because the complex web of timber framing in the roof would have been upset by the introduction of an internal chimneypiece. Dormer windows tell us of the conversion of cramped lofts into further living space. A door and porch, a stableyard entrance and a remarkable generosity in side and back doors on a wayside house often betray its origin as an inn. And who can mistake a converted country railway station, even after track and signal-box and crossing-gates have vanished?

Traces of Roman occupation survive. Little remains of Saxon woodwork, but reconstructions of an old settlement can be seen at West Stow in Suffolk. Lovingly preserved and re-erected buildings of many centuries form the open-air museum of Avoncroft, near Bromsgrove in Worcestershire, and the Weald and Downland museum at Singleton in Sussex. But the best open-air museum is the entire countryside.

Worcestershire and other Midland counties have their sandstone and limestone beds, but one visualizes them most readily as a landscape of wood-and-plaster chequerwork. Above: This farmhouse near Clifton-on-Teme shows the squared-up nature of box-framing, in which panels of lime-washed wattle and daub fill the gaps between tarred or black-painted sustaining beams. Within the roof of such constructions the usual load-bearer for the roof was a timber truss whose rafters distributed weight over the vertical walls instead of letting it rest on the peaked roof-cum-walls of triangular cruck construction. Right: The purely practical use of strong vertical and horizontal timbers was extended by many a prosperous yeoman farmer, merchant or hosteler into decorative splendours such as the great town houses and inns of Stratford-upon-Avon, Ledbury, Ludlow and Chester. Much Wenlock in Shropshire boasts a remarkable number of houses and cottages intricately patterned with crosspieces, diagonals and ornamental lozenges, some of them set on sandstone plinths to bear the weight. Raynald's mansion, shown here, is a galleried, gabled house from the late seventeenth century.

*In East Anglia the almost entire
lack of any viable stone other than recalcitrant flint led to
building styles based largely on colour washed plaster and
timber, with later developments in brick, which, though
often made locally, had no specifically local character.
Although many timber frames were similar in design to
those of the Midlands and South-East, they were rarely
so exuberantly displayed, and in fact were often
completely plastered and painted over. The plainness of
these surfaces, in various pastel shades of which the
commonest are buff and 'Suffolk pink', was frequently
enlivened by scouring the wet plaster with combs or
special tools, or moulding it into floral and symbolic
reliefs. Left: Incised pargeting at Saffron Walden in
Essex, with a dash of flint and freestone flushwork across
the street. Above: Extravagant seventeenth-century relief
pargeting on a fifteenth-century cottage beside Clare
churchyard, Suffolk.*

The sandy heaths of Breckland
along the Norfolk and Suffolk border produced little
timber until Forestry Commission planting of softwoods
in this century, and no building stone other than flints
from the underlying chalk. Trimmed ('knapped') or split
and used with the dark interior outermost, they are
packed in with rubble and mortar to produce the chill-
looking but weather-resistant flinty walls of Breckland
cottages such as this (above, left), with its brick quoins
and surrounds, at Eriswell – actually one of a terrace
built in 1852 by the New England Company 'for the
Propagation of the Gospel in Foreign Parts'.

Millstone grit, a carboniferous
sandstone, features in Pennine farmhouses and villages,
and in the weavers' and miners' terraces of the northern
coal-bearing counties to either side. Easily cut into large
segments, the stone's sombreness is often broken
(especially in Lancashire) by lavish painting or
whitewashing of mortar between individual blocks, and
by smoother or lighter stretches of wide lintel, sill and
mullion round the windows. The building shown (above,
right) is in the village of Cambo, Northumberland, where
Lancelot 'Capability' Brown, architect and landscape
gardener, went to school.

*Along the limestone system underlying
nine counties from Dorset to the Humber, villages shade
through the mellow tones of Castle Combe in Wiltshire
via the Cotswolds towards the severer yet gratifying
splendours around the great quarries of Colly Weston,
Ketton, Clipsham, Ancaster and Barnack. From
Weldon came the thirteenth-century Eleanor crosses at
Geddington and Hardingstone, still resistant to the
ravages of time and weather. Within the superb town of
Stamford, whose St Paul's Street is illustrated below, is
as subtle a blend as one could wish of misty grey and
golden-brown stone in walls, roof slates, doorways,
mullions, and church steeples. It is appropriate that the
Society of Men of the Stones should have been formed in
Stamford in 1947 for preservation work and the training
of craftsmen.*

1800
BREAD
3/4 PER GALL.

1801
BREAD
3/10 PER GALL.

1904
BREAD
10 PER GALL.

1920
BREAD
2/8 PER GALL.
AFTER
THE GREAT WAR

1946-48
BREAD
RATIONED
SUBSIDISED PRICE
2/1 PER GALL

1965
BREAD
5/4 PER GALL

1971
BREAD
8/- PER GALL
DECIMAL
CURRENCY
40P

HOME TOWN

IT IS EASIER TO WALK round a strange town with open and appreciative eyes than round one's own. On home ground the sights are too familiar, too much a part of everyday existence – perhaps assimilated from childhood – and neither a building nor the name of a street strikes questioning chords in the way it might do when, on unfamiliar territory, the senses are sharpened and taken provocatively by surprise. That may be one reason why we derive such pleasure from showing a visitor round our own village, town, or even city centre. Seeing through his eyes we see everything afresh. And it is disconcerting to realize how many questions cannot be answered on the spot: a brick-nogged hall we have passed twice a day for 20 years means nothing to us, we don't know why this back street is called Horn Lane or why the pub on the corner is the Engineer's Arms when there is no trace of a factory anywhere near, or why the niche above the door of a grocer's shop holds a stone pestle and mortar. And what would one guess to be the origin of Unthank Road or the Dingle?

Stand in the centre of your own marketplace (provided it has a sheltering market cross and you are in no immediate danger of being annihilated by a car or delivery van) and look about you. The sign at each corner declares that this is Market Square, and from one of those corners a slope down to Ballygate proclaims itself Market Hill. Obviously the square was once of some importance: its dimensions are impressive for such a

Stones in the east wall of Great Wishford churchyard, Wiltshire, record the changing price of bread. One hardly dare contemplate probable successors.

small town, and the Town Hall with its Doric columns and white-railed balcony still dominates one side of it, though hemmed in now by tea-shoppes and chain stores. Yet there is no sign of a market.

Downhill we make our way to Ballygate, which curves off down a gentler slope between a supermarket and a bank where once stood the bailey-gate on the edge of the original walled settlement. On the level below is the track of the railway line which reached here in 1845. Beside the station were laid out pens for animals waiting until sheep and cattle trucks could take them away after sale. It was not long before the market itself was moved conveniently closer, spreading over the site behind the pens. And when the town's market day dwindled in importance, and farmers and their wives went by train or bus to the larger town five miles away, the space by the station became a bus terminus. The railway station itself, when the line narrowly escaped truncation under Beeching's axe, has become a private dwelling, though the platform still serves as a pay-train halt; and the Victorian market hall with its corrugated iron roof has been taken over by a small local pottery.

Perhaps the market cross in the old, abandoned square, now protected as an Ancient Monument, was once a shelter for specialized stall-holders. At Dunster in Somerset the octagonal Yarn Market recalls an old local trade; Shepton Mallet's is close to the medieval Shambles, where butchers slaughtered and sold their meat from long open sheds; many towns speak of their Butter Cross, often in a square or street still called the Butter Market; and additional cruel entertainment was

*The octagonal market cross at Somerton in Somerset,
rebuilt in 1673.*

offered market dealers in Bungay, Suffolk, where a cage was kept within the market cross rotunda for exposing malefactors to jeers and a bombardment of over-ripe market produce.

In 1866 the philanthropic Baroness Burdett-Coutts sponsored the building of Columbia Market in east London's Bethnal Green, to bring under one roof (a flamboyantly ecclesiastic Gothic roof) tradesmen who, in such dignified surroundings and under close surveillance, might cheat their customers less than they were wont to do in the shabbier back-street kerb markets.

Again taking care of approaching traffic, it is worth stepping back to study the upper storeys of your modern shopping street. They can give a picture of the town as it was before the arrival of plate glass and conflicting lettering along the ground floor frontages. At the end of the Georgian era and during William IV's and the early part of Victoria's reign, there began what we might describe as custom-built shops for customers. The casual stallholder lost much of his trade to

the permanently established retailer. Some were communally housed in covered promenades such as the Royal Arcade in Norwich, the Corridor in Bath, and of course the Burlington Arcade in Piccadilly, London. The grandiose emporium with a wide range of commodities in one extensive building did not really come into its own until the end of the nineteenth century, though many a shopkeeper in a small community found it necessary to be a general rather than particular commodity dealer: an eighteenth-century tradesman of East Hoathly in Sussex, for example, was the local grocer, haberdasher, draper, druggist, ironmonger and undertaker, as well as handling grain and hops.

With the growth of towns, particularly those where industry flourished, most retail outlets were adapted from the ground floor rooms of existing houses. The family lived over the shop, and if the proprietor were a producer in his own right he might have a workshop at the back. A few guild or craft signs survived, practical or ornamental, to identify commodities on sale: the tailor's shears, an ear or sheaf of corn over a bakery, and of course the pawnbroker's three brass balls. The more prosperous and impersonal a business became, the more damage it could inflict on a Tudor, Jacobean, Queen Anne or Georgian façade. Victorian and modern lettering, and recently neon signs, accord ill with a first floor of old timber and plaster, or possibly two upper pilastered storeys of brick and stucco. Only occasionally do we find frontages of the last century and a half of such style and vigour that we readily succumb to them. There is a splendidly gleaming tiled butcher's shop in Newmarket; a chemist in Bury St Edmunds displaying the Royal Arms because in Edwardian times the King came shooting in the neighbourhood and warded off colds with a special preparation from this establishment which the staff referred to as 'King Teddy's Mixture'; and another chemist, this one in Hexham, Northumberland, founded in the reign of William IV by J. Philip Gibson and still testifying on its glossy black and gold frontage to his pride in being a Freeman of the City of London.

Occasionally in the yard of an old coaching inn we find, lovingly preserved, the old boards listing coach arrival and departure times.

The very names of old inns can tell a local or national story. Many a White Hart is so called because of regional associations with the cause of Richard II, whose bodyguard of Cheshire men wore his livery of the White Hart and whose supporters before and after his downfall adopted it as their secret emblem, believing even after his murder in Pontefract castle that he was somehow, somewhere, still alive and would return to them. The legend lingered on with many mystical overtones – almost as eerie as the mysterious fertility figure of the Green Man found all over the country. Any cluster of Danish names such as Copenhagen or the Prince of Denmark will usually be found to date from the building of streets or whole suburbs at the time of Queen Anne's marriage to Prince George of Denmark; though there are a few scattered later testimonies to the Danish princess, Alexandra, who became Edward VII's queen. The Ordinance at Enfield has a clear connection with the Small Arms Factory there, to which powder, iron and coal were brought along the canal. At Newton in Cambridgeshire the Woadman's Arms is all that remains to remind us of the woad-making trade which came to an end at Parson Drove earlier this century. There are many Cricketers and many a Bat and Ball: though no matter how proud you

Cricket, first played on Broadhalfpenny Down near Hambledon, Hampshire, in 1774, is commemorated in the inn sign and a stone monument opposite.

may be of your local eleven you cannot identify quite so securely with the sign as do the villagers of Hambledon in Hampshire, where the game was invented in 1774. Still we may each have our own speciality. If on the corner of your street there is a Skinner's Arms, and to reinforce it a Tanner's Close round the corner, it should not be difficult to trace records of leather working in the vicinity in the not too distant past.

The actual words used for a street or lane vary from one part of the country to another. The little lanes of Brighton are known locally as twittens. Steep passages from Lowestoft's upper town to the remains of the old fishing quarter below are scores. In Chester-le-Street the side roads are called chares, and many north Yorkshire and Northumbrian towns share with Scotland the word 'wynd'. The alley or back entry known colloquially in Liverpool as a jigger is, in Northumbria, a back lonnen.

Pub and church stand companionably close in

many an English town and village. Within only a few miles of my own home I know of two places where the brewers' dray has to drive into the churchyard in order to reach the cellar flap of the inn.

Openings to publicans' cellars are not the only extraneous objects to be found in English grave-yards. The shed in which the sexton keeps his tools may once have been a 'watcher's hut', when the snatching of bodies to sell for medical dissection was such a common pastime that bereaved relatives tried, when they could afford it, to bury their loved ones in lead coffins under great slabs too heavy to move; and the parish found it necessary to build little shelters from which nightly guard could be kept for some while after a new interment. There are two such in one church-yard at Warblington, Hampshire.

Church and punishment, too, seem often to have gone hand in hand. In the vicinity of a church or in the churchyard itself we find relics of old torments: a pillory and whipping-post on Church Hill at Coleshill, Warwickshire; the stock bay forming part of the lychgate at Isleham in Cambridgeshire, though the stocks themselves have gone; a decidedly unpleasant finger pillory in Ashby-de-la-Zouch church; and, in a church-yard shelter at Colne in Lancashire, stocks form-ing an integral part of a cart which could be wheeled to any part of the town or dragged slowly through streets where every passer-by might, if he or she chose, take pot-shots at the wretches therein. Another set of movable stocks occupies Bilton village green in Northamptonshire. There are ducking stools at Canterbury and Fordwich in Kent, designed to quench the tirades of over-voluble harridans; and at Oswestry an even greater favourite of downtrodden male chauvinists – a scold's bridle.

Nodding to your local incorruptible policeman on the corner of Bridewell Alley, and catching a reflection from the polished brass plate of the firm of solicitors who have appropriated the most dignified house in Chapel Street above the Uni-tarian chapel, you may well be thankful that the law is administered less arbitrarily in our day and age. No matter how you may have transgressed, while awaiting trial you will be housed more comfortably in a modern police cell than in the old parish lock-up. Examples worthy of rueful inspection can be found at Alfreton in Derbyshire, Steanor Ashton in Wiltshire, and, most impres-sive of all, the so-called 'Clock Tower' of Fen-

Above: *Stocks on the village green at Great Tew, Oxfordshire, date from the early seventeenth century.* Left: *During the Great Plague of 1665 many villages and towns isolated victims in pest houses such as this one in Odiham churchyard, Hampshire, which was later used for French prisoners captured during the Napoleonic wars.*

stanton in Cambridgeshire.

Clocks do have a habit of straying. Great Canfield church in Essex acquired for its little wooden tower the stable clock from a nearby mansion which was once the rectory; and the original clock from Horse Guards Parade in London was removed by Sir William Blackstone, the eminent jurist, for insertion in the tower of St Peter's, Wallingford.

Do you know who set the clock face on your church tower, or in whose honour it got there? Rye church acquired its clock, still working, in Queen Elizabeth's time; but the same town's even older Landgate only got one in 1863 in memory of the Prince Consort. At Stratford-sub-Castle in Wiltshire, the single-handed church clock incor-porates signs of the Zodiac and inside the church

is a much older type of time-keeper, a seventeenth-century hour-glass.

From the church and its tower and its stocks and pillory we circumnavigate the market-place once more and, this time, choose an exit to the levels where successive new suburbs have begun. Between an old pub and a new housing estate stands, perhaps, a cottage not much favoured by modern young married couples: the cramped toll-gate house. To one side of the road is a terrace of Victorian houses which, in spite of the timbering and lovely pantiles of the older town, are roofed in cheap and depressing Welsh slate. Cross the road, and we are in an estate of semi-detached houses built just after the First World War; and, beyond them, an estate designed for young men returning from the Second World War, with streets called Churchill Avenue or Fiddler Close – Fiddler being a get-rich-quick builder who also happened to be on the Council. There's a recent comprehensive school, not far from the rubbish tip known as Stinkbottle. The name seems to be a contemporary derisive epithet . . . until one checks on old maps and records, to find that the site once belonged to the local

Above: *One gets the impression that some unruly prisoner was impatient to get away from the old lock-up or 'House of Correction' at Alfreton, Derbyshire.* Right: *Until banned in 1849 cock-fighting had for centuries been 'the royal diversion' and a popular sport in rural cockpits such as this at Lydbury North in Shropshire.*

monastic foundation of St Thomas the Apostle.

The bridge over the stream is called Monks' Bridge. And in the pastures behind what is now a small grouping of light industry, the polluted little ponds were once monastic fishponds or 'stews'. The Waggoner's Wells near Hindhead in Surrey were never, as one might suppose, water troughs for passing horses, but a series of fish-ponds called after the Wakener who dug them.

Who was your town eccentric? The man who was known in the eighteenth century to have a pioneer flying machine tucked away in his attic, now unfortunately lost? The benefactor who donated a park to the community but was so unwilling to let his name come forward that the space itself is still known as 'The Mystery'? Around Dallington and Brightling in Sussex we

Outside churches, inns and private dwellings the mounting-block was a familiar sight when horses were the commonest means of transport. This 1900 example at Blackwell, Bowness, must be one of the last ever built.

The Kempe family who contributed so much to the welfare of Finchingfield in Essex also contributed a star turn to the gallery of English eccentrics. In the seventeenth century William Kempe of Spains Hall unjustly accused his wife of infidelity and then, convinced that he was wrong, vowed as a penance not to utter another word and 'did by a voluntary constancy hold his peace for seven years' – at the end of which he was coaxed out of his silence by a new vicar whom he himself had appointed. During those seven years he built in the grounds of Spains Hall seven ponds, one for each twelvemonth, which are still to be seen.

At Histon in Cambridgeshire, Moses Carter's Stone harks back to a genial local giant who, doting on children and invigorated by a steady diet of boiled beef and dumplings, showed off by carrying the boulder from what was known as the Ballast Hole to the Boot pub. And another authentic giant was the 9-foot 'Child of Hale' in Lancashire, buried in the churchyard there and remembered in the local inn sign.

Ask questions about your own name. I started this book on a personal note, and am close to finishing on it. Before some wag grows too scathing about my own surname, let him be informed that the first appearance of the name Burke in the British Isles was not, as he may suppose, in Ireland, but in East Anglia – where I now reside. If you are a Mr Smith you may run a greengrocer's or work as a clerk (not a Clarke); but your ancestors must have been blacksmiths, silversmiths, or maybe goldsmiths. Nasmyth was a knife-smith. Draper, Dyer and Cooper are obvious enough; but who remembers that Billiter was a bell-founder or that Winn and Wynne come from an old word meaning a friend?

Parish registers and county record offices will tell you all you need to know about the background, once you know just what you are looking for. But the three-dimensional immediacy of places, their colours and breath and echoes, must come before rather than after the documentation: they pulse more truly and evocatively, even if sometimes too enchantingly misleading, than all the parchment and paper in all the record offices of the kingdom.

Although I have spent a great deal of time writing the foregoing pages, I have never for one moment supposed that England could ever be reduced to words on paper. England lived, lives, and shall live.

find a squire so extreme that he came to be known – affectionately, one feels – as Mad Jack Fuller. Mad? One of the last to make a tidy fortune out of the declining Wealden iron industry, plus some income from Jamaican sugar estates, he put some of his money into politics, became quarrelsome M.P. for Lewes, and when offered a peerage said roundly, 'I was born Jack Fuller, and Jack Fuller I'll die'. He helped the young painter Turner, saved Bodiam castle from utter ruin, and in time of depression subsidized local workers by commissioning a new wall all round his estate. Within that estate he set up a domed observatory, erected the obelisk of Brightling Needle, and at Wood's Corner conceived the most delightfully ludicrous 'folly' of them all: having bet a friend that a certain church spire was visible from his house, only to find that this was not so, he set up a replica known to this day as the 'Sugar Loaf'.

INDEX

ACKNOWLEDGMENTS

All the photographs, with the exception of those mentioned
below, were taken by Ian Pleeth. We are grateful to the
following for permission to reproduce their work on the pages
listed here:
John Bethell 89, 94; Leonard and Marjorie Gayton 88, 204,
205; A. F. Kersting 90, 91, 93, 94, 95, 96, 97, 99, 100, 101,
152, 202, 203, 207, 209; Jorge Lewinski jacket; The National
Trust 210; Edwin Smith 92, 206, 208, 210, 211.